D1314555

TAMPA TREASURES

Another classic cookbook from
The Junior League of Tampa, Inc.
Creators of *The Gasparilla Cookbook* and *A Taste of Tampa*

The Junior League of Tampa, Inc. is an organization of women committed to improving the community through the effective action and leadership of trained volunteers. Its purpose is exclusively educational and charitable.

All proceeds realized from the sale of *Tampa Treasures* will be returned to the community through the projects of The Junior League of Tampa, Inc.

Published by The Junior League of Tampa, Inc.
Printed in the United States of America by Arcata Graphics, Nashville, Tennessee

First Printing • 40,000 Copies • August 1992

Library of Congress Catalog Card Number 92-070191

ISBN 09609556-2-3 .

Copies of *Tampa Treasures* may be obtained from your favorite retailer or The Junior League of Tampa, Inc., P.O. Box 10184, Tampa, Florida 33679-0184. Phone orders may be placed by calling (813) 251-3443.

The cover photograph was underwritten by The Ferman Family.

Major Contributors

For their generosity and support of *Tampa Treasures,* we thank...

The Tampa Tribune

Tampa Bay Center

Dykema Gossett

WFLA Television
Channel 8

U-Save Supermarkets

Smith and Associates
Investment Co. Realtors, Inc.

SunBank of Tampa Bay

For their professional guidance and services we recognize...

Cover Photography and
Treasure Photography
 Ty B. Heston
with the exception of:

Fireworks Over Downtown
 Tampa/Hillsborough
 Convention and Visitors
 Association, Inc.
 Douglas Johns

The Gasparilla Invasion
 Gandy Photography

Sports at Tampa Stadium
 Brenda Harris-Nixon

Food Photography
 Douglas and Kathleen
 Johns
 assisted by:
 Dilip Chauhan

Food Styling
 Nice Minor
 assisted by:
 Ellen Stern
 Patricia Forrestal

Graphic Design
 Donna Craig
 Coyote Design

Tampa Treasures Committee

Development Committee

Chairman
Carol Ann Colbert

Treasurer, Assistant Chairman
Anne Comer

Design and Photography,
Assistant Chairman
Lesley Lee

Sustainer Representative,
Underwriting, Special Events
Pat Daley

Recipe Writing
Frances Kruse

Public Relations
Deborah Lester

Testing, Section Development
Kim Reed

Marketing, Future Planning
Barbara Ryals

Secretary, Recipe Collection
Leslie Ann Smith

Assistants
Kim Brannan
Terri Huerta
Maria Johnson
Janet Mendez
Kathy Nolen
Ashley Thomas
Michelle Williams

Section Captains
Debbie Anderson
Hedy Bever
Sue DePaoli
Mary Anne Ingram
Margaret Parker
Lynn Townsend

Marketing
Rebecca Aylward
Hedy Bever
Terri Huerta
Leslie Jennewein
Cindy Martin
Lynette McKown
Sue Rohrlack
Leslie Ann Smith
Mary Bruce Taaffe

Special Events Chairmen
Lisa Byrd
Janet Mendez
Laurie Roddy
Rebecca Walter

TABLE OF CONTENTS

The pirate ship symbol indicates a classic Tampa recipe from The Gasparilla Cookbook.

Dear Reader:

Tampa Treasures ... the name denotes gold doubloons and treasure chests left by pirates many years ago on Florida's West Coast. Today, when we think of treasures in Tampa, many wonderful and exciting places and events come to mind: sporting events, the arts, amusement and one of our greatest treasures, our Florida sunshine.

Three years ago, the Junior League of Tampa decided to create a new cookbook. What could be more fitting than to focus on another Tampa treasure, the fabulous food that is a major part of our celebration of events? With these thoughts in mind, we embarked on the journey that ended in the treasures within this book.

Treasures like these do not come easily. Each recipe selected for this book has been triple-tested for perfection. The photographs have been painstakingly taken. The story lines have been written to capture the true essence of life in the Tampa Bay area. For all of this, we are indebted to our league members and those in the community who gave tirelessly of their time and energy. A special thanks to the *Tampa Treasures* Committee and their "labor of love" in making this book a reality.

Finally, a thank you to you, our readers, without whom all of this time and effort would have been in vain. It is you who will allow us to continue to meet the needs of our community with the proceeds from this book. We invite you to enjoy the recipes and a taste of our heritage. We hope that you, too, will find gold in our *Tampa Treasures.*

> *Cindy Coney 1992*
> *Hilary Davis 1991*
> *Julianne McKeel 1990*
> *Robin DeLaVergne 1989*
> *Carolyn Chunn 1988*
> Presidents
> The Junior League of Tampa, Inc.

Introduction

Two hundred years ago, the bays and inlets around Tampa were havens for pirates who buried their treasures on our sandy shores. While the pirates are only a dusty memory, modern Tampa is still rich in treasures. No longer must we dig to find them, for they are all around us.

In 1961 the Junior League of Tampa published *The Gasparilla Cookbook*, named for the ship commanded by our most infamous pirate, Jose Gaspar. This book featured old family recipes, richly representative of Tampa's Southern heritage and diverse ethnic backgrounds. As lifestyles changed and faster and less complex recipes became the order of the day, a second cookbook, *A Taste of Tampa*, was published in 1978.

Although cooking styles continue to evolve, the foods we enjoy remain much the same. In Tampa we have always made full use of the bountiful fresh fruits and vegetables grown year-round and of the many species of fish and shellfish harvested from our waters. *Tampa Treasures* offers an exciting contemporary cuisine that has been enhanced by its journey from past to present. These recipes are an intriguing blend of the rich and sumptuous and the light and wonderful. Also included are truly classic Tampa recipes selected from *The Gasparilla Cookbook* .

Throughout this book, we will introduce you to events, places and pastimes that make life in Tampa a never-ending banquet. We invite you to come and experience our lifestyle, through our recipes for elegant dining, casual cuisine and outdoor entertaining.

The cover photograph and each page of this book feature the neo-classic balustrade, the ornamental railing that wraps six uninterrupted miles of Tampa's historic Bayshore Boulevard. We invite you to walk with us along Bayshore's sidewalks enjoying the lush green lawns, swaying palms and the gentle lapping of the waves. The balustrade, beloved by Tampans for many decades, is the perfect place to start your hunt for Tampa's treasures.

APPETIZERS & BEVERAGES

Fireworks Over Downtown

New Year's Eve finds us under a clear night sky enjoying spectacular fireworks over Tampa's downtown waterfront, the first stop on the treasure hunt. We join the crowds along Bayshore to watch as the dazzling fireworks, framed by a shimmering skyline, explode above the city and reflect in the waters of Garrison Channel.

Tampa's early growth centered around its importance as a seaport. Today the Port of Tampa continues to make a major economic impact as vessels navigate from the warm waters of the Gulf of Mexico to our port. As you wander along the waterfront, you can see palatial yachts, an occasional gondola or even a pirate ship.

Downtown Tampa, our primary business, financial and governmental center, is also our cultural center. Restaurants and cafes, serving thousands of daytime workers and tourists, continue to nourish theater, ballet and symphony lovers well into the night.

The state-of-the-art Tampa Convention Center, with its many trade shows, exhibitions and charity functions, is a popular downtown waterfront destination. Neighboring Harbour Island features festive shops, restaurants and night spots which stay busy long after the last sparkles have fallen from the fireworks.

In this section we feature appetizers and beverages to tantalize the palates of the most discerning guests. Star ingredients include Florida's fresh seafood lavishly piled on crusty bread, as in the Curried Lobster and Shrimp Croutons recipe, shown in the photograph. Savor the Greek flavor of Tarpon Springs' Stuffed Mushrooms and sample the Lemon Pepper Boursin, which is quick, simple and elegant.

Unique beverages add the finishing touches to any occasion. Toast the New Year with K.I. McKay's Champagne Punch, brimming with Florida citrus and "pirates" island rum. Let the wonderful scent of Holiday Spiced Tea welcome your guests.

**The Fireworks photograph was underwritten by
The 1991-92 Junior League of Tampa Provisional Class**

APPETIZERS & BEVERAGES

New Year's Eve Buffet

Grilled Tenderloin Tapas

Curried Lobster and Shrimp Croutons

Fresh Dill Salmon Mousse

Chutney Cheese Spread

Tarpon Springs Stuffed Mushrooms

K.I. McKay's Champagne Punch

**The menu photograph was underwritten by Christine Curry
and Tom, Leslie Ann, Mac, Emily Ann and Charlie Smith**

Grilled Tenderloin Tapas

1 (3 to 4 pound) whole beef tenderloin or London broil
1 cup A-1 sauce
¼ cup Worcestershire sauce
¼ cup fresh lemon juice
2 tablespoons salad oil
3 cloves garlic, minced
Salt and pepper to taste

Night before, or several hours ahead: Remove fat and skin from tenderloin. Combine remaining ingredients in large bowl. Add meat to marinade; turn to coat. Marinate several hours or overnight.

When ready to cook: For rare meat, broil in oven or grill over hot coals until outside becomes crusty (15 to 25 minutes). Serve with Cuban or French bread. *12 to 16 servings.*

Preparation Time: 10 Minutes   Cooking Time: 15 to 25 Minutes

Curried Lobster and Shrimp Croutons

1 loaf party-size French bread,
   unsliced
6 to 8 tablespoons olive oil
1 cup mayonnaise
¼ cup mango chutney, chopped
1 teaspoon curry powder
12 large shrimp, cooked, peeled,
   deveined and cut in half
6 ounces fresh Florida lobster
   meat, cooked and chopped
Cayenne pepper
Kumquat branches, watercress or
   parsley (garnish)

Make croutons: Preheat oven to 350° F. Cut bread into 24 slices ¼ to ½-inch thick. (Save extra bread for another use.) Brush both sides of bread slices with olive oil; place on baking sheet. Bake on center shelf of oven until crisp, about 10 minutes, turning after 5 minutes. Remove from oven; cool; cover until used.

When ready to serve: Combine mayonnaise, chutney and curry powder, mixing well. Spread generous ½ tablespoon of mayonnaise mixture on each crouton; top with shrimp or lobster meat. Sprinkle lightly with cayenne. Arrange on serving tray; garnish. Serve immediately. *Makes 24.*

Preparation Time: 15 Minutes   Cooking Time: 10 Minutes

Fresh Dill Salmon Mousse

2 (¼-ounce) envelopes unflavored
    gelatin
½ cup mayonnaise
1 tablespoon fresh lemon juice
1 tablespoon onion, finely grated
Dash Tabasco
¼ teaspoon sweet paprika
1 teaspoon salt
2 tablespoons fresh dill, finely
    chopped
2 cups poached fresh salmon or
    canned, finely flaked
1 cup heavy cream

At least 5 hours before serving: In large mixing bowl, soften gelatin in ¼ cup cold water. Stir in ½ cup boiling water; whisk slowly until gelatin dissolves. Cool to room temperature. Whisk in mayonnaise, lemon juice, onion, Tabasco, paprika, salt and dill. Stir to blend completely; refrigerate until mixture begins to thicken slightly, about 20 minutes.

Remove skin and bones from salmon; fold salmon into mayonnaise mixture. Whip cream until fluffy and peaks form; fold gently into salmon mixture. Transfer to a 6 to 8 cup bowl or fish mold. Cover; chill at least 4 hours.

When ready to serve: Unmold onto serving tray; surround with crackers or small slices of dark bread. If desired, garnish with paper-thin slices of cucumber.   ***12 to 16 servings.***

Preparation Time: 45 Minutes

Treasure Tip: To poach fish, simmer 6 to 8 minutes per pound, never letting the stock boil. Use just enough water to barely cover fish or, if desired, use a combination of water and wine. Aromatic vegetables and herbs can be added to make fish more flavorful.

Chutney Cheese Spread

8 ounces cream cheese, softened
4½ oz Major Grey's chutney, finely
    chopped
1 to 2 teaspoons curry powder
½ teaspoon ground ginger
½ cup pecans, chopped
½ cup flaked coconut

Mix all ingredients except coconut; form into log; roll in coconut. Chill thoroughly. Serve with crackers.   ***6 to 8 servings.***

Preparation Time: 10 Minutes

Treasure Tip: To determine how many appetizers to serve at a cocktail party, plan on 10 pieces per person. For a large reception, with no dinner following, serve 10 to 15 pieces per person.

Tarpon Springs Stuffed Mushrooms

1 (10-ounce) package frozen
   chopped spinach
½ cup Parmesan cheese, freshly
   grated
4 ounces feta cheese, rinsed and
   crumbled
½ cup whole green onion, finely
   chopped
½ cup parsley, finely chopped (or 2
   tablespoons dried parsley)
Salt to taste
24 large fresh mushrooms, cleaned
   and stemmed

Preheat oven to 350° F. Thaw spinach in colander. Squeeze all moisture from spinach. In mixing bowl combine all ingredients except mushroom caps; mix well. Fill mushroom caps; bake 20 minutes. Serve warm. **Makes 24.**

Preparation Time: 20 Minutes   **Cooking Time: 20 Minutes**

K.I. McKay's Champagne Punch

Famous in Tampa for 30 years!

8 cups cold tea
8 cups freshly squeezed orange
   juice
4 cups sweetened pineapple juice
½ cup fresh lemon juice
Sugar to taste
4 cups rum
2 cups gin
2 cups brandy
4 cups ginger ale
4 cups champagne
Ice ring

Early in day: Combine tea with orange, pineapple and lemon juices; add sugar to taste. Add rum, gin and brandy; stir well; chill.

Just before serving: Add ginger ale. Place ice ring or large ice block in punch bowl; fill with mixture. Add champagne; serve.
Makes 2 gallons (80 punch-cup servings).

Preparation Time: 20 Minutes

Treasure Tip: *To make a clear ice ring, pour distilled or boiled water into a metal or freezer-safe plastic ring mold. Do not use a glass mold as it could crack. If desired, freeze edible fresh flowers, pieces of fresh fruit or fresh mint leaves inside the ring mold.*

Pickin' Pork

Pork leg, roast, shank or fresh ham
Garlic, minced
Vinegar
Worcestershire sauce
Bay leaves
Salt and pepper
Lemon juice
Maury Calvert's Barbecue Sauce
　(see recipe below)

Have butcher trim pork of all fat. Season pork lavishly with garlic, vinegar, Worcestershire, bay leaves, salt, pepper and lemon juice. Place pork on large sheet of heavy-duty aluminum foil. Cover with lots of sauce; wrap tightly in foil; place in deep roasting pan to protect oven from spills. Bake at 200° F. for 10 to 15 hours. (Pork will be so tender it will fall apart.) Pick pork apart with two forks. Serve in chafing dish with small Parker House or round dinner rolls to make mini-sandwiches. Accompany with bowl of additional barbecue sauce.
　　A 17-pound fresh ham serves 80 to 100 at a cocktail party.

Preparation Time: 30 Minutes　　Cooking Time: 10 to 15 Hours

Maury Calvert's Barbecue Sauce

1 pound butter or margarine
1 (10-ounce) bottle Worcestershire
　sauce
2 tablespoons Tabasco
1 cup prepared mustard
1 pint vinegar
3 lemons (include juice and grated
　rind)
Salt, black pepper and cayenne or
　red pepper to taste

Melt butter; add remaining ingredients; blend thoroughly. Keep warm on grill while using to baste chicken, pork, ribs, steaks — anything you want to barbecue. Keeps indefinitely in refrigerator.

Preparation Time: 15 Minutes

This much-requested recipe was a closely guarded secret until Eleanor Crowder stepped down as president of the Junior League of Miami, Inc. As a parting gift to the League, she allowed its magazine, Tropical Topics, to publish her father's treasured Tennessee barbecue recipe. One of our members obtained it from a relative and serves it to rave reviews at parties.

Roasted Herb Pork Tenderloin

4 teaspoons fresh (or 1 teaspoon
    dried) rosemary, crushed
1 teaspoon dried thyme
1 large clove garlic, minced
2 (1½ to 2 pound) pork tenderloins
Garlic salt
Seasoned pepper
½ stick butter or margarine,
    melted
Peach or mango chutney

Preheat oven to 375° F. Combine rosemary, thyme and garlic; set aside. Sprinkle tenderloins with garlic salt and seasoned pepper. Brush with butter; roll in herb mixture, coating evenly. Place, fat side up, on rack in shallow roasting pan; bake 45 minutes to 1 hour. Slice thin; serve with party-size French bread slices and chutney. **10 to 12 servings.**

Preparation Time: 10 Minutes   ***Cooking Time: 1 Hour***

Sweet and Spicy Sausage-Stuffed Mushrooms

5 to 6 ounces sweet Italian sausage
Pinch of red pepper flakes
    (optional)
¼ cup yellow onion, finely minced
1 garlic clove, minced
Olive oil
¼ cup parsley, chopped
¼ cup black olives, chopped
⅓ cup mayonnaise
Salt and freshly ground black
    pepper to taste
12 large white mushrooms,
    stemmed and cleaned
Freshly grated Parmesan cheese, to
    taste

Preheat oven to 450° F. Remove sausage meat from casings; crumble into small skillet. Sauté gently, stirring often, until meat is thoroughly done. Season with red pepper flakes. With slotted spoon, remove sausage to a bowl, leaving drippings in skillet. Sauté onion and garlic in drippings, adding a little olive oil if necessary, until tender and golden, about 5 minutes. Stir in parsley; add to sausage in bowl. Add olives and mayonnaise; combine thoroughly. Season with salt and pepper to taste.

Sprinkle mushroom caps lightly with salt and pepper. Fill each cap generously with stuffing; arrange in lightly oiled square baking dish. Sprinkle caps with Parmesan. Bake until bubbling and well browned, about 15 minutes. Let stand 5 minutes before serving. **Makes 12.**

Preparation Time: 20 Minutes   ***Cooking Time: 15 Minutes***

Chutney Chicken Pâté

2 cups cooked chicken, cubed
¼ cup onion, minced
1 large sweet pickle, minced
½ cup fresh parsley, minced
1 teaspoon dried oregano
1 teaspoon dried thyme
3 tablespoons almonds, chopped
½ teaspoon salt
Pinch ground pepper
½ cup mango chutney, chopped
 (or more to taste)
¾ cup mayonnaise

Night before serving: In food processor with steel blade, mince chicken finely by pulsing motor several times. Transfer to bowl; stir in remaining ingredients. Pack pâté in crock; smooth top. Chill, covered, overnight. Serve with thinly sliced, crusty bread. ***Makes 4 cups.***

Preparation Time: 10 minutes

Treasure Tip: When cooking chicken to use in other recipes, dissolve a chicken bouillon cube in the cooking water. Simmer until chicken is tender; save the flavorful broth.

Layered Sweet and Sour Oriental Delight

Topping
¾ cup cooked chicken, chopped
½ cup carrots, shredded
¼ cup unsalted peanuts, chopped
3 tablespoons whole green onions,
 sliced
1 tablespoon fresh parsley, chopped
2 tablespoons soy sauce
1 teaspoon fresh ginger root,
 grated
1 garlic clove, minced
1 teaspoon dark sesame oil

Sweet and Sour Sauce
¼ cup dark brown sugar, firmly
 packed
2 teaspoons cornstarch
¼ cup catsup
2 tablespoons vinegar
1 tablespoon Worcestershire sauce
3 drops Tabasco

Base
8 ounces cream cheese, softened
1 tablespoon milk

Early in day, make topping: In medium bowl combine all topping ingredients; mix well. Cover; refrigerate several hours to blend flavors.

Make Sweet and Sour Sauce: In small saucepan combine brown sugar and cornstarch; mix well. Gradually stir in 1 cup water and remaining ingredients. Cook over medium heat, stirring frequently, until mixture thickens slightly, about 5 minutes. Cool; cover; refrigerate. Makes 1½ cups.

When ready to serve, make base: In small bowl combine cream cheese and milk; beat until smooth and fluffy.

To assemble: Spread cream cheese mixture evenly over bottom of 10-inch round serving dish. Spoon topping mixture evenly over cream cheese; drizzle with ½ cup Sweet and Sour Sauce. Serve with assorted crackers. ***8 to 10 servings.***

Preparation Time: 30 Minutes   *Cooking Time: 5 Minutes*

Pesto-Cheese Mushroom Caps

2 cups fresh basil leaves, packed
2 large garlic cloves
⅓ cup pine nuts
½ cup freshly grated Parmesan or
   Romano cheese, divided
⅓ cup olive oil, plus a little more
12 large, firm white mushrooms,
   stemmed and cleaned
1 small lemon, halved

Make pesto: In food processor with steel blade, combine basil and garlic. Blend to fine paste, scraping down sides of bowl as necessary. Add pine nuts and ¼ cup cheese; process until smooth. With machine running, pour ⅓ cup olive oil through feed tube in slow, steady stream; mix until smooth and creamy. (If pesto is too thick, gradually pour up to ¼ cup warm water through feed tube with machine running.) Transfer pesto to jar. Cover surface of pesto with film of olive oil about ⅛ inch thick. Seal with tight-fitting lid. Refrigerate, or freeze up to 3 months. Before using, stir olive oil film into pesto. Makes 1⅔ cups.

Up to several hours before serving: Preheat oven to 375° F. Brush bottom of square baking dish with olive oil. Rub mushroom caps with lemon; brush with olive oil. Arrange, rounded side down, in single layer in baking dish. Fill mushrooms with pesto; sprinkle tops with a little more than 2 tablespoons cheese. Drizzle small amount of olive oil over each.

Bake 8 to 12 minutes, until filling bubbles. Sprinkle with remaining cheese; serve hot. (Mushrooms can be prepared several hours before baking. Cover tightly with plastic wrap; refrigerate until ready to serve.)   ***Makes 12.***

Preparation Time: 10 Minutes   ***Cooking Time: 8 to 12 Minutes***

Treasure Tip: *To store fresh herbs, wrap in a moist paper towel and place in a plastic bag in your refrigerator's vegetable crisper. They should keep for about 5 days. Parsley, basil, mint and other leafy herbs can be placed in a jar of water in the refrigerator. Check herbs regularly; discard discolored leaves; change water often.*

Crème de Cassis Liver Pâté

1½ sticks butter, divided
1 cup onion, chopped
1 clove garlic, minced
1 pound chicken livers
1 tablespoon flour
1 teaspoon salt
1 teaspoon white pepper
1 bay leaf
⅛ teaspoon oregano
3 tablespoons crème de cassis or
    brandy

Night before, or early in day: Melt 1 stick butter in medium skillet; sauté onion and garlic until onion is soft and transparent. Melt remaining butter in another pan; sauté livers until tender. Add flour, salt, pepper, bay leaf and oregano to onion mixture. Cover; simmer 2 minutes; remove bay leaf. Combine mixtures; add crème de cassis; purée in blender. Mold; refrigerate until thoroughly chilled. Serve with crackers or party-size French bread slices. *15 to 20 servings.*

Preparation Time: 15 Minutes   *Cooking Time: 10 Minutes*

Treasure Tip: Do not throw out sprouting heads of garlic. Separate the cloves and plant them close together in potting soil. The young shoots that appear make a great fresh herb with a faint garlic taste.

Smoked Mozzarella and Salmon Rounds

8 slices homemade-type white
    bread
1 (8-ounce) bar mozzarella cheese
¼ cup clarified butter
3 ounces smoked salmon, sliced
    thin

Cut crusts from bread. Using knife or pastry cutter, cut two 1¾-inch rounds from each slice of bread. Cut mozzarella into 16 slices; trim to size of bread rounds. In skillet over moderately high heat, melt butter. Sauté bread rounds, turning once, 1 to 2 minutes or until golden. With slotted spatula, transfer to baking sheet; top with salmon and mozzarella. Preheat broiler; broil about 4 inches from heat until cheese melts 1 to 2 minutes. *Makes 16.*

Preparation Time: 15 Minutes   *Cooking Time: 6 Minutes*

Chilled Horseradish Crabmeat Mold

½ of a (10¾-ounce) can undiluted
   tomato soup
8 ounces cream cheese
1 tablespoon unflavored gelatin
8-ounces crabmeat
1 tablespoon prepared horseradish
Dash Tabasco
Dash Worcestershire sauce
½ cup celery, finely chopped
1 tablespoon whole green onion,
   chopped
Salt and pepper to taste
1 green olive, cut in half for
   garnish

Day before serving: In top of double boiler heat soup; add cream cheese; stir to melt. Soften gelatin in ½ cup water. Pick through crab carefully to remove any shell; add crab and remaining ingredients to soup mixture. Pour into oiled 4-cup fish mold; refrigerate. **When ready to serve:** Turn out on platter; use olive half for eye. Serve with crackers.   *Makes 4 cups.*

Preparation Time: 15 Minutes   *Cooking Time: 5 Minutes*

Treasure Tip: Decorated fish molds make attractive additions to cocktail buffet tables. For an elegant presentation, make tomato paste ripples for scales; use half a green olive for the eye and a lemon wedge for the mouth. Use fresh parsley for the fins.

Crabmeat Evander

2 pounds crabmeat, water pressed
   out, finely chopped
4 bunches whole green onions,
   chopped
1 tablespoon fresh ginger root,
   chopped
1 tablespoon garlic, minced
1 tablespoon salt
1 tablespoon white pepper
1 tablespoon curry powder
36 ounces cream cheese, softened
100 (4 inch-square) egg roll
   wrappers
1 egg yolk, beaten
Peanut oil for deep frying
Orange marmalade and Chinese
   plum sauce

Several hours before serving: Mix crabmeat, green onions, ginger, garlic, salt, pepper and curry powder into cream cheese. Lay out egg roll wrappers; place 2 heaping teaspoonfuls crab mixture in center of each wrapper. Pull corners up to form point at top; crimp with fingers. Seal with egg yolk; freeze for later use.

When ready to serve: Heat peanut oil in deep fryer or deep heavy saucepan to approximately 300° F.; fry egg rolls until golden brown, about 3 minutes per batch. Serve with dipping sauce made by mixing a little orange marmalade with plum sauce. Note: This recipe was created by Evander Preston, internationally known jewelry designer and fabled party-giver who lives on Pass-a-Grille Beach.   *Makes 100.*

Preparation Time: 2 hours   *Cooking Time: 1 Hour*

Treasure Tip: Store fresh ginger root in a jar in your freezer; use as needed.

Baked Crab Quesadillas

⅓ cup unsalted butter
¼ cup safflower oil
1 clove garlic, minced
½ cup onion, chopped
1 poblano chile, roasted, peeled and
    diced (or 2 fresh jalapeño
    peppers, stemmed, seeded and
    finely diced)
1 pound lump crabmeat
¼ cup mayonnaise
1 teaspoon salt
1 tablespoon fresh cilantro leaves,
    chopped
⅓ cup Monterey Jack cheese with
    jalapeño peppers, grated
16 flour tortillas

Preheat oven to 475° F. In medium saucepan melt butter and oil. Pour all except 2 tablespoons in small cup; reserve. In remaining butter and oil, sauté garlic and onion over medium heat. Remove from heat. Stir in chile or jalapeños, crab, mayonnaise, salt and cilantro; mix well.

Heat baking sheet. Lay tortillas on baking sheet; brush liberally with reserved butter-oil mixture. Turn tortillas over; spread half of each tortilla with crab mixture; top with a spoonful of cheese; fold over. Bake until tops are golden and filling is hot, 2 to 4 minutes. Cut into quarters; serve. **Makes about 48.**

Preparation Time: 30 Minutes   *Cooking Time: 2 to 4 Minutes*

Treasure Tip: Cilantro is also known as Chinese parsley or fresh coriander leaves. It is lighter in color than parsley, and is used often in Latin American cuisine. Coriander, the seed of the plant, has a different flavor and cannot be substituted for fresh leaves.

Tampa Bay Smoked Mullet Spread

1 cup smoked mullet (about 4
    ounces)
½ cup onion, finely diced
½ teaspoon prepared horseradish
1 tablespoon Worcestershire sauce
1 to 2 dashes Tabasco
½ teaspoon dill weed
2 tablespoons spicy mustard
½ teaspoon fresh lemon juice
¾ to 1 cup mayonnaise

Several hours before serving: Flake mullet. In medium bowl combine mullet with all other ingredients; chill. Serve with assorted mild crackers. **Makes 2 cups.**

Preparation Time: 20 Minutes

Treasure Tip: To smoke fish, soak 1 pound hickory chips overnight in 2 quarts water. Remove the fish head just below the collarbone; cut along backbone almost to tail, making the fish lie flat in one piece. Clean and wash fish, leaving skin on. Add 1 cup salt to 1 gallon water; stir until dissolved. Pour over fish; refrigerate 30 minutes. Drain, rinse and dry.

Place one-third of the wet chips on low-burning coals. Place fish, skin-side down, 4 to 6 inches from coals on well-greased grill. Baste fish with vegetable oil; cover grill; baste frequently during cooking. Cook 1½ hours or until flesh flakes easily with fork, adding remaining chips as needed to keep the fire smoking.

Tarragon Marinated Shrimp

5 pounds large shrimp, cooked,
  shelled and deveined
4 medium onions, thinly sliced
2 to 3 bay leaves
1 cup tarragon vinegar
2 cups light vegetable oil
1 (10-ounce) jar Durkee's
  Sandwich and Salad Sauce
1 tablespoon sugar
1 teaspoon salt

Day before serving: In large bowl layer shrimp, onions and bay leaves. Combine remaining ingredients; pour over shrimp. Cover; refrigerate 24 hours before serving.   **20 to 25 servings.**

Preparation Time: 15 Minutes

Treasure Tip: *Be careful when cooking shrimp; they are very easy to overcook. As a general rule, place shrimp in rapidly boiling water; cook until shrimp just turn pink, 1 to 3 minutes.*

Caviar Pie

32 ounces cream cheese, softened
Chopped onion to taste
Enough cream to moisten cheese
Lemon juice to taste
4 (3½-ounce) jars domestic black
  caviar
12 hard-boiled eggs
8-inch round piece of cardboard
12-inch round piece of cardboard
  (available at bakeries)

Early in day: In large bowl mix cream cheese and onion; add enough cream to mold mixture by hand. Cover 8-inch cardboard with aluminum foil. Place cheese mixture on cardboard; mold about 2 inches high to edge of board. Refrigerate.

When ready to serve: Add lemon juice, drain caviar; frost cheese mold with caviar. Place mold on foil-covered 12-inch cardboard. Grate egg yolks and whites separately. Place egg yolks around cheese mold; place egg whites around outer edge. Serve on large platter with water biscuits or wheat meal crackers. Note: Do not serve this on a silver tray, because egg whites will discolor silver.   **50 servings.**

Preparation Time: 25 Minutes

Orange-Curry Shrimp

1 pound large fresh shrimp, shelled
  and deveined
3 tablespoons catsup
3 tablespoons orange juice
1½ tablespoons soy sauce
½ teaspoon orange peel, grated
1 tablespoon fresh lemon juice
2 teaspoons sugar
1 teaspoon curry powder
¾ teaspoon sesame oil
1 tablespoon vegetable oil

Up to 6 hours before cooking: Rinse and drain shrimp; pat dry. In medium bowl combine all remaining ingredients; stir in shrimp. Refrigerate, stirring occasionally, up to 6 hours.

When ready to cook: Preheat broiler. Line baking sheet or broiler pan with heavy-duty aluminum foil. Arrange shrimp on foil in single layer. Broil as close to heat as possible until shrimp are opaque throughout and just beginning to brown on top, 2 to 3 minutes. If you want to try them "blackened," leave them in an extra 30 to 60 seconds. *Makes about 28.*

Preparation Time: 15 Minutes   *Cooking Time: 3 Minutes*

Gulf Coast Shrimp Spread

½ small onion, chopped
2 tablespoons fresh lemon juice
1 teaspoon Worcestershire sauce
1 teaspoon Tabasco
½ cup chili sauce (or more to taste)
1 (6-ounce) can shrimp, drained
8 ounces cream cheese, softened
Garlic salt to taste

At least 2 hours before serving: Combine all ingredients in medium bowl. Cover; refrigerate 2 hours. Serve with crackers.

Note: Canned shrimp must be used in this recipe, because they will shred and become distributed throughout the mixture. *Makes 2 cups.*

Preparation Time: 5 Minutes

Tampa Tapenade

1 (6-ounce) can pitted black olives,
  drained
1 (7-ounce) can albacore tuna,
  drained
¼ cup capers, rinsed and drained
¼ cup fresh lemon juice
1 tablespoon dark rum (or to taste)
1 large garlic clove
½ cup olive oil
Freshly ground pepper

Early in day: In food processor with steel blade combine all ingredients except oil and pepper; process until smooth. Slowly add olive oil, blending thoroughly. Season to taste with pepper. Cover; refrigerate until well chilled. Serve with crisp vegetables. *4 to 6 servings.*

Preparation Time: 15 Minutes

Treasure Tip: Tapenade, a condiment from Provence, France, can be used as a sauce for hard-boiled eggs, to flavor mayonnaise or to accompany grilled fish.

Bacon-Ginger Scallop Kabobs

32 (5 to 6 inch) bamboo skewers
12 strips thinly sliced bacon
16 large Gulf scallops, halved
    horizontally
16 small water chestnuts, halved
    horizontally
1/3 cup soy sauce
2 tablespoons rice wine vinegar
1½ tablespoons sugar
1 tablespoon Chinese rice wine or
    dry sherry
1 garlic clove, minced
1 teaspoon fresh ginger, minced

2 to 3 hours before cooking: Soak skewers in water 15 minutes to prevent burning on grill. Partially cook bacon until light brown; cut into pieces the same size as scallop halves.

On skewers alternate bacon, scallops and water chestnuts; arrange in shallow dish. In small bowl combine remaining ingredients; mix well. Pour over kabobs; cover; refrigerate 2 to 3 hours.

When ready to cook: Drain kabobs; pat dry. Grill about 4 inches above moderate coals, about 6 minutes per side, or cook under broiler 4 minutes per side, until scallops are barely firm. Serve immediately. *32 servings.*

Preparation Time: 30 Minutes   *Cooking Time: 8 to 12 Minutes*

Cranberry-Glazed Brie

3 cups fresh cranberries
¾ cup light brown sugar
1/3 cup dried currants
1/8 teaspoon dry mustard
1/8 teaspoon ground allspice
1/8 teaspoon ground cardamom
1/8 teaspoon ground ginger
1 (2.2 pound, 8-inch diameter)
    Brie cheese wheel
Apples and pears, garnish

Up to 3 days in advance, make marmalade: In heavy, non-aluminum saucepan combine 1/3 cup water and all ingredients except Brie and apples. Cook over medium-high heat, stirring frequently, until most of the berries pop. Cool to room temperature; cover; refrigerate.

Up to 6 hours before serving: Using sharp knife cut into top rind of Brie, leaving ½-inch border of rind. Place cheese in baking dish lined with aluminum foil. Cover with marmalade; refrigerate.

When ready to serve: Bring cheese and marmalade to room temperature. Preheat oven to 300 ° F.; warm cheese until soft, at least 15 minutes. With spatula, carefully transfer cheese to platter; surround alternately with apple and pear slices. *24 servings.*

Preparation Time: 15 Minutes   *Cooking Time: 15 Minutes*

Broccoli Soufflé Squares

2 (8-ounce) cans crescent rolls
2 (10½-ounce size) packages frozen
    chopped broccoli
2 eggs, beaten
1 cup mayonnaise
1 (10½-ounce) can cream of
    mushroom soup
1 medium onion, diced
8 ounces sharp cheddar cheese,
    grated, divided
Dash Tabasco

Preheat oven to 375° F. Spread crescent rolls out on cookie sheet or jelly roll pan; pinch seams together. Cook broccoli according to package directions; drain very thoroughly. In large bowl combine broccoli, eggs, mayonnaise, soup, onion, 5 ounces cheese, Tabasco and salt; mix well. Pour over crescent rolls; spread evenly; top with remaining cheese.

Bake until golden brown 20 to 30 minutes; cool slightly; refrigerate. When cold, cut in bite-size squares. At this point cover with plastic wrap and foil; refrigerate to serve later, or freeze. Reheat, covered with foil, 20 minutes at 375° F.

Makes 56 1-inch squares.

Preparation Time: 30 Minutes   *Cooking Time: 40 to 50 Minutes*

Golden Baked Colby Spread

1 cup Hellmann's mayonnaise
1 cup colby cheese, grated
1 cup onion, chopped (red onion
    makes it prettier)
2 dashes Tabasco (optional)

Preheat oven to 350° F. Mix all ingredients in pie pan or shallow baking dish. Bake until golden tan on top about 30 minutes. Serve with crackers. Note: A 10-inch quiche dish holds two recipes. **10 to 12 servings.**

Preparation Time: 10 Minutes   *Cooking Time: 30 Minutes*

Lemon Pepper Boursin

8 ounces cream cheese, softened
1 clove garlic, crushed
1 teaspoon caraway seed
1 teaspoon dried basil
1 teaspoon dill weed
1 teaspoon dehydrated chopped
    chives
Lemon pepper seasoning

A few days before serving: In small bowl blend cream cheese with garlic, caraway seed, basil, dill weed and chives. Place mixture on wax paper; pat into flat, round shape. Roll generously on all sides in lemon pepper. Cover, refrigerate to serve later. Serve with assorted crackers. **6 to 8 servings.**

Preparation Time: 10 Minutes

Festive Strawberry Cheddar Ball

8 ounces cream cheese, softened
4 ounces sharp cheddar cheese, grated
½ green bell pepper, finely diced
½ red bell pepper, finely diced
3 whole green onions, finely diced
12 ounces strawberry preserves

Day before serving: In medium bowl mix all ingredients except preserves; shape into ball. Refrigerate, covered, overnight. **When ready to serve:** Place cheese ball on plate. Shape into "doughnut" with deep center hole. Spoon preserves into hole; serve with onion or wheat crackers.

12 to 15 servings.

Preparation Time: 5 Minutes

Baked Brandied Cheese with Apples

7 ounces Gouda or Edam cheese, grated
1 cup sour cream
8 ounces cream cheese, softened
3 tablespoons brandy
Yellow and red apples, unpeeled, sliced

Preheat oven to 350° F. In medium bowl mix cheese, sour cream, cream cheese and brandy. Place in shallow baking dish; bake until mixture is golden brown and soupy, about 30 minutes. Let sit 10 minutes, it will become firmer. Serve warm with apple slices.

Makes 2 cups.

Preparation Time: 5 Minutes   *Cooking Time: 30 Minutes*

Chutney-Cheese Pâté

6 ounces cream cheese, softened
1 cup sharp cheddar cheese, shredded
3 tablespoons cocktail sherry or port
½ teaspoon curry powder
¾ cup mango chutney, finely chopped*
3 to 4 whole green onions, sliced

*You may make your own from recipe on Page 274

Several hours before serving: In small bowl of electric mixer thoroughly blend cream cheese, cheddar, sherry and curry powder. Spread mixture, about ½-inch thick on serving platter. Chill until firm. **When ready to serve;** cover cheese mixture with chutney; sprinkle with green onions. Serve with crackers.

10 to 12 servings.

Preparation Time: 10 Minutes

Torta di Pesto

¼ cup pine nuts
3 cloves garlic
2 cups fresh basil, tightly packed
½ cup best-quality olive oil
½ cup Romano cheese, freshly
   grated
16 ounces cream cheese, softened
2 sticks (or less) unsalted butter,
   softened
Cheesecloth
3 ounces sun-dried tomatoes (dried
   or packed in oil and drained),
   chopped

Early in day, or up to 5 days ahead: Preheat oven to 325 ° F. Roast pine nuts on cookie sheet 10 minutes (watch carefully to prevent burning). In food processor with steel blade, purée pine nuts, garlic and basil. Slowly add olive oil; blend. Add Romano cheese; pulse briefly; do not overblend.

In medium bowl combine cream cheese and butter; beat to blend smoothly. Cut an 18-inch square of cheesecloth. Moisten with water; wring dry. Smoothly line 6-cup plain or charlotte mold with cheesecloth, draping excess over rim of mold. Using rubber spatula, make an even layer with one-sixth of cream cheese mixture in the bottom of the mold. Cover with one-fifth of pesto, extending evenly to sides of mold. Arrange chopped tomatoes on top.

Repeat layers until mold is filled, ending with cheese. (If mold is wide, use fewer layers.) Fold ends of cheesecloth over torta; press lightly to compact. Chill several hours or overnight; or remove cheesecloth; wrap tightly with plastic wrap to refrigerate up to 5 days.

When ready to serve: Invert torta into serving dish. Gently pull out of mold; remove cheesecloth. Serve with crackers.

Makes 6 cups.

Preparation Time: 25 to 30 Minutes   Cooking Time: 10 Minutes

Herb Parmesan Triangles

½ cup mayonnaise
⅔ cup grated Parmesan cheese
¼ teaspoon garlic powder
¼ teaspoon dried basil
¼ teaspoon oregano
3 whole green onions, chopped
1 (8-ounce) can refrigerated
   crescent rolls

Preheat oven to 350° F. In small bowl combine mayonnaise, Parmesan, garlic powder, basil, oregano and green onions until evenly mixed. Separate crescent rolls; lay flat on cookie sheet. Spread mayonnaise mixture evenly over each piece. Bake until golden-brown 13 to 18 minutes; let cool a few minutes. Cut into triangles approximately 2-inch pieces. Serve immediately.

Makes 40.

Preparation Time: 15 Minutes   Cooking Time: 13 to 18 Minutes

Dill-Sour Cream Potatoes

1 pound (10 to 12) whole tiny new
   potatoes
2 tablespoons plain non-fat yogurt
3 tablespoons light sour cream
2 tablespoons whole green onion,
   finely chopped
2 tablespoons freshly grated
   Parmesan cheese
1¼ teaspoons snipped fresh dill,
   chopped (or ¼ teaspoon dried
   dill weed)
Dash pepper
Fresh dill sprigs (optional)

Preheat oven to 350° F. Scrub potatoes with vegetable brush. Place on cookie sheet; bake until tender 30 to 40 minutes, depending on size. Remove from oven; cool until you can handle them.

Combine yogurt and sour cream in small bowl. Cut potatoes in half; with small melon-ball scoop, remove a scoop of meat from each potato. Reserve centers for another use. Place 2 teaspoons yogurt mixture in each potato; sprinkle with green onion, cheese, dill and pepper. Garnish, if desired, with fresh dill.

For an elegant presentation, omit cheese, dill weed and pepper and sprinkle yogurt-filled potatoes with green onions and caviar.

Makes 20 to 24.

Preparation Time: 20 Minutes   *Cooking Time: 30 to 40 Minutes*

Filled Phyllo Triangles

Phyllo
1 pound phyllo pastry
2 sticks unsalted butter, melted

Crème Fraîche
¼ cup heavy cream
¼ cup sour cream

Spinach and Feta Filling
2 (10-ounce) packages frozen
chopped spinach
⅓ cup olive oil
1 bunch whole green onions,
chopped
Pepper to taste
Dash nutmeg
1 bunch fresh parsley, chopped
½ bunch fresh dill, chopped fine
½ pound feta cheese, drained and
crumbled
3 eggs, slightly beaten

Wild Mushroom Filling
5 tablespoons unsalted butter
1½ pounds chanterelle or shitaki
mushrooms, coarsely chopped
½ cup crème fraîche
¾ cup fresh parsley, chopped
Salt, pepper and freshly ground
nutmeg to taste

Night before, or up to 2 weeks before, make crème fraîche: In small bowl whisk cream and sour cream together. Cover loosely with plastic wrap; let stand in kitchen or other warm spot overnight or until thickened. Cover; refrigerate at least 4 hours (mixture will be quite thick). Tart flavor will continue to develop as mixture sits in refrigerator, up to 2 weeks. Makes ½ cup.

Night before: Thaw phyllo overnight in refrigerator.

Next afternoon, make spinach filling: Defrost spinach in colander; squeeze out all moisture. Heat oil in skillet; sauté green onions until tender, about 15 minutes. Add spinach and cook over low heat, stirring constantly, until mixture is dry, 10 to 15 minutes. Season with pepper and nutmeg. Cool to room temperature; stir in parsley, dill, cheese and eggs.

Make mushroom filling: Melt butter in large skillet over high heat. Add mushrooms; sauté 2 to 3 minutes. Remove from heat; cool slightly; drain well. Add crème fraîche and parsley; season to taste with salt, pepper and nutmeg. Cool completely before filling phyllo.

When ready to assemble triangles: Place one sheet phyllo on flat surface; brush very lightly with butter. Top with two more sheets, buttering each lightly. (Keep remaining pastry covered with a slightly damp towel.) With pizza cutter or sharp knife, cut buttered phyllo sheets into six or seven strips the short way. Spoon heaping teaspoonful of filling onto the end of each strip. Form triangle by folding one corner across the filling. Continue to fold (like folding a flag), until the strip is all folded. Do not wrap too tightly, as filling will expand as it cooks. Tuck any excess under. Continue cutting, filling and folding until all phyllo is used.

Preheat oven to 400° F. Place triangles on buttered baking sheet. Brush tops lightly with melted butter; bake until golden, about 10 minutes; serve.

Filled triangles can be refrigerated unbaked for 2 days or frozen immediately for future use. To bake frozen triangles: do not defrost. Place on buttered baking sheet; brush tops with butter; bake at 350° F. 30 to 40 minutes, until brown. *Makes 50 to 60.*

Preparation Time: 2 hours plus   *Cooking Time: 10 Minutes*

Crudité Dip

1 cup sour cream
½ cup mayonnaise
2 teaspoons prepared horseradish
2 tablespoons fresh parsley, chopped
½ teaspoon Worcestershire sauce
½ teaspoon fresh lemon juice
¼ teaspoon Accent (optional)
¼ teaspoon salt
½ teaspoon onion, grated
Tender Belgian endive leaves (optional)
Cherry tomatoes (optional)
Fresh snow peas (optional)

Several hours before serving: In medium bowl combine all ingredients; chill. Use as dip with fresh vegetables; spread a dollop on Belgian endive leaves, or fill cherry tomatoes or snow peas with mixture.   *Makes 1½ cups.*

Preparation Time: 5 Minutes

Treasure Tip: Try serving this dip with an array of fresh vegetables arranged like a garden. Prepare ¼ pound of dipping vegetables per person. Serve the dip in hollowed-out vegetables like bell peppers, squash or cabbage.

Cocktail Cheese Biscuits

1 stick butter (no substitute)
1 cup New York sharp cheddar cheese, grated
1 teaspoon salt
½ teaspoon cayenne pepper (or more to taste)
1 cup flour
Pecan halves

Preheat oven to 350° F. In large bowl cream butter. Blend in cheese; add salt, pepper and flour; mix thoroughly. Roll dough into small balls; press half a pecan on each ball to flatten. Place on ungreased cookie sheet; bake 15 minutes. Serve or store in airtight container.   *Makes 40 to 45.*

Preparation Time: 30 Minutes   *Cooking Time: 15 Minutes*

Almond-Bacon Dates

1 pound pitted dates
1 (4-ounce) package blanched whole almonds
1 pound sliced lean bacon

Preheat oven to 400° F. Stuff each date with one whole almond. Cut bacon slices into thirds; wrap a piece around each date. Secure with toothpick. Place on foil-lined baking sheet; bake until bacon is crisp 12 to 15 minutes. Drain; serve.
Note: Prepared dates can be frozen. Bake frozen dates at 400° F. until crisp.   *Makes about 48.*

Preparation Time: 10 Minutes   Cooking Time: 12 to 15 Minutes

Teriyaki Cocktail Nuts

2 tablespoons butter (no
  substitute)
1 teaspoon fresh lemon juice
1 tablespoon soy sauce
1/4 teaspoon garlic salt
1/2 teaspoon ground ginger
2 cups (12-ounce can) mixed nuts

Preheat oven to 325° F. In small saucepan over medium heat, melt together all ingredients except nuts. Spread nuts on jelly roll pan or cookie sheet; roast until lightly browned 7 to 10 minutes. Brush with butter mixture; roast 5 more minutes, until golden brown. Drain on paper towels; serve warm, or store in airtight can or jar.

16 servings.

Preparation Time: 5 Minutes   *Cooking Time: 12 to 15 Minutes*

Assorted Quick Hors D'Oeuvres

Chèvre and Sun-dried Tomato

Slice party-size French bread thin; toast lightly. Cover each slice with a slice of chèvre (cut a little smaller than bread), a dollop of sun-dried tomato and a piece of fresh basil.

Tapenade-Chèvre

Slice party-size French bread thin; toast lightly (or use Melba toast). Place a spoonful of tapenade (see recipe on page 19), a slice of chèvre and a tiny fresh basil leaf on each piece of toast.

Green Tomato-Cheddar

Slice cheddar cheese to fit Ritz crackers. Place a slice of cheese and a spoonful of green tomato pickle (see recipe on page 272) on each cracker.

Green Tomato-Cheese Canapés

Place a bowl of homemade green tomato pickles, a wedge of sharp cheddar cheese, a wedge of Saga blue cheese, rye and caraway bagel chips and a small bowl of mustard on a tray. Let guests fix their own canapés.

Grilled Italian Sausage

Place 2 to 3 pounds mild or hot Italian sausage in a bowl or zippered plastic bag; pour a 12-ounce bottle Mojo Criollo* over sausage; marinate overnight. Grill over medium-high coals 10 to 15 minutes. Cut in bite-size pieces; place in enough marinade to keep moist. Serve warm, with toothpicks.

*Spanish barbecue sauce, available at specialty markets and some supermarkets

Creamy Salmon Roe and Caviar

For each appetizer, spoon or pipe a tiny bit of sour cream into the bottom of a barquette (small canoe-shaped pastry shell). Add ½ teaspoon each salmon roe and black and golden caviar. Garnish with fresh chopped chives.

Smoked Scottish Salmon and Dill

Cut crusts off party pumpernickel bread; spread, if desired, with unsalted butter. Thinly slice smoked Scottish salmon; cut to fit bread slices. Place a slice of salmon on each piece of bread; garnish with a sprig of fresh dill.

Sizzling Chèvre and Black Olive

Brush both sides of party-size French bread slices with olive oil; lightly toast each side under broiler. Top toast with a slice of chèvre, half a black olive and a sprinkling of finely chopped fresh thyme. Dust lightly with very fine bread crumbs. Broil until cheese begins to soften and brown; serve hot.

Smoked Chicken and Cranberry

Mix 2 tablespoons of softened butter with 1 teaspoon minced fresh tarragon and a grinding of black pepper. Lightly butter one side of thinly sliced party-size French bread; toast lightly. Place small piece of thinly sliced smoked chicken on each piece of toast; top with a dollop of cranberry relish.

Sour Cream-Chutney Sausage

Cook 1½ pounds small sausages (Smokies) as package directs; drain. In saucepan mix 1 tablespoon brown sugar, ⅔ cup Major Grey's chutney and ¾ cup sour cream; add sausages. Simmer over low heat 10 minutes; serve warm.

Cream Cheese and Guava Paste

Put a block of cream cheese and a bar of guava paste (or a bowl of guava jelly) on a serving platter; surround with crackers. Let guests spread crackers with cheese, then guava paste. This is a typical Tampa dessert, but it is wonderful on a buffet table!

Asparagus Roll-ups

Cut crusts from a loaf of very fresh sliced white bread. Flavor 1 to 1½ cups mayonnaise to taste with Tabasco; spread on bread. Place 1 large canned asparagus spear in center of each bread slice; roll up; cut into thirds. Combine 2 finely chopped hard-boiled egg yolks and 2 teaspoons finely minced fresh parsley. Spread additional mayonnaise mixture on the seam of each roll; spread yolk-parsley mixture on mayonnaise. These have been served at Tampa parties for many years!

Sparkling White Sangria

1 small lemon
1 small orange
1 bottle (750 ml) dry white wine
½ cup canned pineapple chunks,
  drained
1 fresh peach, sliced, or ½ cup
  canned sliced peaches, drained
½ cup cognac
¼ cup sugar
7 ounces club soda
Small ice cubes or ice ring

At least 1 hour before serving: Cut lemon and orange in half. Squeeze half of each into a pitcher; thinly slice the other halves. Add fruit slices, wine, pineapple, peaches, Cognac and sugar to pitcher. Stir gently to dissolve sugar. Cover pitcher; refrigerate 1 hour.

When ready to serve: Add club soda and ice. Serve very cold, with pieces of fruit in each glass. Note: More fruit can be added, such as strawberries, seedless red grapes or unpeeled red apple slices. *6 generous servings.*

Preparation Time: 10 Minutes

Frosted Alexander

1 quart coffee ice cream, softened
2 ounces brandy
1½ ounces Tia Maria or other
  coffee-flavored liqueur
Whipped cream and chocolate
  shavings (optional)

Early in day, or weeks in advance: In small bowl of electric mixer, on low speed, blend ice cream, brandy and Tia Maria for a few seconds (do not let ice cream melt). Refreeze in ice cream container. Serve, frozen, in chilled, tulip-shaped champagne glasses. Garnish, if desired, with whipped cream and chocolate shavings. *3 to 4 servings.*

Preparation Time: 5 Minutes

Apricot Brandy Slush

2 cups hot tea
1½ cups sugar
1 (12-ounce) can orange juice
  concentrate, undiluted
1 (12-ounce) can lemonade
  concentrate, undiluted
12 ounces apricot brandy
Ginger ale, or lemon-lime soda

1 day or several weeks ahead: Prepare tea. While tea is hot add sugar, then 7 cups boiling water. Add orange juice, lemonade and brandy. Place in freezer-safe container; freeze.

When ready to serve: Remove from freezer; stir to make slushy. Place in glasses; add ginger ale or lemon-lime soda to desired strength. *Makes 14 cups.*

Preparation Time: 20 Minutes

Bellinis à la Venezia

Sugar Syrup
1½ cups sugar
¾ cups water

Bellinis
8 ripe peaches, peeled and pitted
½ cup fresh lemon juice
1 bottle (750 ml) Brut champagne,
   cold

Up to a week before serving, make sugar syrup: Place sugar and water in heavy saucepan; bring to boil. Reduce heat; simmer 5 minutes. Refrigerate in capped jar.

When ready to serve: Purée peaches in blender; stir in ½ cup sugar syrup and lemon juice. Divide mixture evenly among eight chilled crystal glasses. Top with ice-cold champagne; stir gently, just to blend. Note: If fresh peaches are not in season, an equivalent amount of frozen peaches can be used.   *8 servings.*

Preparation Time: 25 Minutes   *Cooking Time: 5 Minutes*

Treasure Tip: The sugar syrup in this recipe makes an excellent sweetener for lemonade and many other summer drinks

Spiced Wine Punch

9 cups pineapple juice
9 cups cranberry juice
4½ cups burgundy or red wine
1 cup brown sugar
4 sticks cinnamon
8 to 10 whole cloves

Place pineapple juice, cranberry juice and burgundy in a 30-cup coffee percolator. Place sugar, cinnamon and cloves in basket portion of percolator; perk for one cycle. If liquid has not settled at end of cycle, stir until basket is free of liquid. Serve hot or as a cold punch for parties.   *22 servings.*

Preparation Time: 5 Minutes   *Cooking Time: 15 Minutes*

Buccaneer Bloody Marys

4 cups V-8 juice
1½ cups vodka
¼ cup Worcestershire sauce
1½ teaspoons celery salt
¼ cup fresh lemon or lime juice
1 teaspoon Tabasco (or more to
   taste)
½ teaspoon prepared horseradish

Mix all ingredients in large pitcher. Stir well; serve over ice. Garnish as desired, with lemon or lime wedges, celery sticks or whole dilled green beans.   *6 to 8 servings.*

Preparation Time: 10 Minutes

Holiday Spiced Tea

½ teaspoon whole cloves
1 (1-inch) stick of cinnamon
Cheesecloth
4 teaspoons loose tea, or 4 tea bags
Juice of 2 oranges
Juice of 1 lemon
⅓ cup sugar

Tie cloves and cinnamon stick loosely in cheesecloth bag; add to 6 cups water; heat to boiling. Add tea, tied loosely in cheesecloth bag (or tie tea bags together); steep about 5 minutes. Remove tea. Heat orange and lemon juices and sugar, but do not boil; add to tea.   **8 to 10 servings.**

Preparation Time: 5 Minutes   Cooking Time: 10 to 15 Minutes

Apple Apricot Cooler

2 cups apple juice
1 (12-ounce) can apricot nectar
¼ cup fresh lemon juice
¼ teaspoon bitters
2 (6½-ounce) bottles club soda,
   chilled

In a pitcher combine apple juice, apricot nectar, lemon juice and bitters; chill. Just before serving, stir in club soda.
                                      6 to 8 servings.

Preparation Time: 5 Minutes

Treasure Tip: *This recipe can be doubled or tripled easily for parties. When serving in a punch bowl, make an ice ring by freezing apple juice, apricot nectar, lemon juice and bitters in ring mold with fresh mint leaves and apricot slices. As the ice ring melts, it won't dilute the punch.*

Café Brûlot

10 to 12 whole cloves
2 oranges, peeled (peel removed in
   one spiral piece, if possible)
1 (4-inch) cinnamon stick
2 lemons, peeled (peel removed in
   one spiral piece, if .possible)
2 tablespoons sugar
1 cup brandy
¼ cup Cointreau or Curaçao
2 cups brewed hot, strong coffee

Push cloves into orange peels; place cinnamon stick, orange and lemon peels and sugar in chafing dish over low heat. Mix brandy and Cointreau together; add to clove mixture, stirring until sugar dissolves. Turn heat up a little and light mixture with a match. Gradually add coffee. Using a long-handled ladle, slowly and gently mix until flame dies down. Serve in café brûlot or demitasse cups.   **4 servings.**

Preparation Time: 10 Minutes

Treasure Tip: *Nothing welcomes guests better than delicious smells coming from the kitchen. In winter, keep a small pan filled with apple juice, cinnamon sticks or cloves simmering on the stove. If a fire is burning in the fireplace, toss orange or lemon peels, cloves, or cinnamon sticks on top of the logs.*

EGGS & CHEESE

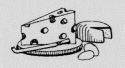

The Gasparilla Invasion

Our treasure trail brings us to the first Saturday in February, when the world's only fully-rigged pirate ship, with cannons booming and flags waving, sails into Tampa Bay to "invade" the city of Tampa. We join a throng of merrymakers to watch the Gasparilla ship enter the harbor accompanied by a flotilla of hundreds of pleasure boats.

The ship is manned by local business leaders disguised as pirates, who disembark to lead a colorful parade along Bayshore Boulevard into downtown Tampa. Bands play, horses prance and revelers smile atop fanciful floats as the pirates and members of all the krewes salute the city and open a month of gala Gasparilla events.

In the following weeks numerous activities, both large and small, cater to those in a festive mood. While many parts of the country are still blanketed by snow, we are enjoying magnificent weather at the Florida State Fair, at Fiesta Day in Ybor City and at the Gasparilla Sidewalk Art Festival.

The State Fair features live country music, a variety of agricultural exhibits and one of the country's largest midways. A unique attraction is Cracker County, a village of historic buildings where artisans demonstrate the crafts and trades of pioneer Florida. While at Fiesta Day's concerts and arts and crafts exhibits, participants sample free Spanish Bean Soup, Cuban coffee and Cuban bread. These are true Ybor City basics. For the serious art collector and the causal enthusiast the Gasparilla Sidewalk Art Festival is one of the largest juried shows in the Southeast.

Gasparilla is a time for parties on our streets and in our homes. Many of us collect treasure chests and other pirate memorabilia to use as party decorations. This section features recipes perfect for a brunch, including many favorites that can be made the night before, such as Spanish Chorizo and Eggs, Baked Cheese Grits and Florida Oranges in Red Wine Sauce.

**The Gasparilla Invasion photograph was sponsored by
Kim Bever Reed**

EGGS & CHEESE

A Pirates Brunch

Herb Tomato Quiche

Baked Cheese Grits

Plant City Strawberry Omelet

Florida Oranges in Red Wine

Buttermilk-Corn Muffins

Spicy Rum Brunch Punch

**The menu photograph was underwritten by
Laura and Lee Bentley
Shirley and Mickler Bentley**

Herb Tomato Quiche

3 tablespoons butter
2 cups onions, thinly sliced
1 tablespoon flour
2 eggs
1 cup milk
1 teaspoon salt
⅛ teaspoon pepper
2 tablespoons fresh parsley, chopped
1 tablespoon chives, chopped
½ teaspoon tarragon
½ teaspoon basil
1 cup cheddar cheese, grated
1 deep-dish pie shell, unbaked
6 slices fresh tomato

Preheat oven to 425° F. Melt butter in skillet; sauté onions until tender. Stir in flour and set aside. Beat eggs and milk together; add salt, pepper, parsley, chives, tarragon and basil. Place sautéed onions and cheese in pie shell; add milk and egg mixture. Bake 15 minutes. Reduce heat to 350° F.; bake 15 minutes more. Arrange tomato slices on top of pie; bake until tomatoes start to brown, about 10 minutes more.

To freeze: Bake as directed 30 minutes without tomatoes; cool; refrigerate until thoroughly chilled. Wrap tightly in foil or freezer wrap; date; freeze no more than 1 month. To serve, remove wrapping; place frozen quiche in preheated 350° F. oven. Bake until warmed through, 45 to 50 minutes. Arrange tomato slices on top; bake about 10 minutes more, until tomatoes start to brown. *4 to 6 servings.*

Preparation Time: 15 Minutes   *Cooking Time: 40 Minutes*

Baked Cheese Grits

2 teaspoons salt
1 cup regular grits
2 cups milk, divided
4 eggs, beaten
1 cup extra sharp cheddar cheese, grated, divided
1 stick butter or margarine
1 teaspoon Worcestershire sauce
Black pepper to taste

In medium saucepan bring 4 cups water to boil; add salt and grits. Cook until thick, beating often. Add 1 cup milk; stir well; cook until thickened. Preheat oven to 350° F. Add eggs, most of the cheese, butter, Worcestershire, pepper and remaining milk. Stir to blend thoroughly; pour into buttered 2-quart baking dish. Sprinkle with remaining cheese; bake 1 hour. *8 servings.*

Preparation Time: 30 Minutes   *Cooking Time: 1 Hour*

Plant City Strawberry Omelet

2 eggs
1¼ teaspoons powdered sugar,
    divided
1 drop vanilla extract
1 teaspoon margarine
2 tablespoons sour cream
Sliced fresh strawberries
Pinch of grated lemon or orange
    peel
Powdered sugar for garnish

In small bowl of electric mixer, beat eggs until very light and fluffy. Stir in 1 teaspoon powdered sugar and vanilla extract. In omelet pan or small skillet, melt margarine over medium-low heat. Pour egg mixture in pan; cover. Cook about 4 minutes (top will be a little soft). Combine sour cream, ¼ teaspoon powdered sugar and grated peel. Spread sour cream filling on omelet; remove to plate; fold in half. Add strawberries; sprinkle with powdered sugar.

1 serving.

Preparation Time: 5 Minutes   *Cooking Time: 5 Minutes*

Florida Oranges in Red Wine

¾ cup sugar
1 cup red wine
2 whole cloves
1 vanilla bean
1 cinnamon stick
4 lemon slices
6 Florida oranges, peeled, seeded
    and sliced horizontally

Place sugar and 1 cup water in medium saucepan; bring to boil. Add all remaining ingredients except oranges; boil 15 minutes. Strain sauce; pour over oranges. Serve hot, in chafing dish, or at room temperature.

4 to 6 servings.

Preparation Time: 5 Minutes   *Cooking Time: 20 Minutes*

Treasure Tip: This tasty, elegant side dish is fabulous to serve during the holidays. Its aroma will greet your guests at the door and get them in the mood for a festive evening.

Buttermilk-Corn Muffins

½ cup yellow cornmeal
½ cup regular oats
1 cup buttermilk
1 egg
½ cup brown sugar, packed
1 cup flour
¾ teaspoon salt
1 teaspoon baking powder
½ teaspoon baking soda
¼ cup vegetable oil

At least 1 hour before baking: Place cornmeal and oats in large bowl; slowly pour in buttermilk; let stand at least 1 hour.

When ready to bake: Preheat oven to 400° F. Add egg and brown sugar to oat mixture, mixing well. Add remaining ingredients; stir until well blended. Spoon batter into greased muffin pan or individual fancy-shaped pans; bake 20 minutes for large muffins, 12 to 15 minutes for small muffins.

Makes 12 to 24.

Preparation Time: 15 Minutes   *Cooking Time: 12 to 20 Minutes*

Treasure Tip: When making these muffins, do not pour the buttermilk in all at once. Cornmeal absorbs liquid slowly. If you pour the liquid in too fast, your muffins could have a gritty texture.

Spicy Rum Brunch Punch

3 pieces sliced fresh ginger
1 large cinnamon stick
8 whole cloves
4 cardamom seeds
Fine cheesecloth bag
1 gallon apple cider
1 quart pineapple juice
6 lemons, peeled and sliced thin
6 small oranges, peeled and sliced
  thin
1½ cup rum (add to taste)
Cinnamon sticks (garnish)
Orange peel (garnish)

Combine ginger, cinnamon stick, cloves and cardamom in cheesecloth bag; tie. Pour cider and pineapple juice into large pot; add spice bag and lemon and orange slices. Bring to low, simmering boil; simmer, stirring, 15 minutes. Remove spice bag. Add as much rum as you choose; serve warm. If desired, serve in mugs; garnish with orange peel wrapped around cinnamon sticks. **40 to 50 servings.**

Preparation Time: 10 Minutes   **Cooking Time: 15 Minutes**

Treasure Tip: *For clear liquids, use whole, not powdered, spices in beverages and for pickling. Powdered spices dissolve through the liquid and make it cloudy.*

Spanish Chorizo and Eggs

1 large potato, peeled and cut in
  small pieces
1 small onion, chopped
1 small green bell pepper, chopped
2 medium tomatoes, seeded and
  chopped
3 chorizos, (Spanish sausage)
  sliced thin
6 eggs, scrambled
Toasted, buttered Cuban bread, or
  10 flour tortillas

Place potatoes, onions, peppers and tomatoes in large greased skillet; cook until potatoes are done. Add chorizos; cook until mixture is blended and chorizos are hot. Scramble eggs; stir into chorizo mixture. Serve with Cuban bread or wrapped in warm tortillas.
10 servings.

Preparation Time: 20 Minutes   ***Cooking Time: 15 Minutes***

Spicy Mexican Brunch Eggs

1 pound bulk sausage, crumbled
¼ pound fresh mushrooms,
  chopped
1 medium onion, diced
Salt to taste
Freshly ground pepper to taste
8 eggs
3 tablespoons sour cream
6 tablespoons hot or mild Mexican
  tomato salsa
8 ounces Velveeta cheese, diced
8 ounces mozzarella cheese, grated
8 ounces cheddar cheese, grated

Night before, or 35 minutes before serving: Preheat oven to 400° F. In large skillet, over medium-high heat, combine sausage, mushrooms and onion. Sauté until sausage is cooked completely. Drain well; season to taste with salt and pepper. Combine eggs and sour cream in blender or food processor; whip 1 minute. Pour into greased 9 x 13-inch baking dish. Bake until eggs are softly set, 4 to 7 minutes. Spoon salsa evenly over top of eggs; add sausage mixture. Top first with Velveeta, then with mozzarella and cheddar.

To serve immediately, turn oven to broil; broil until cheeses melt. To serve the next day, refrigerate overnight. Bake at 325° F. about 30 minutes, until cheeses melt. Cut and serve with flat spatula.
8 to 12 servings.

Preparation Time: 25 Minutes   ***Cooking Time: 10 Minutes***

Treasure Tip: *To determine whether an egg is fresh, place it in a glass of water. If it sinks to the bottom, it's fresh; if it floats, throw it away.*

Tampa Bay Brunch Soufflé

A delicious make-ahead soufflé

1½ pounds bulk pork sausage
8 slices bacon, chopped
9 eggs
3 cups milk
6 slices fresh or dry bread
1½ teaspoons dry mustard
1½ cups cheddar cheese, grated
Black pepper to taste
½ teaspoon salt
½ teaspoon Worcestershire sauce
Dash cayenne pepper
1 whole green onion, finely minced
1 rounded tablespoon brown sugar

Night before: In large skillet over medium heat, cook sausage and bacon until sausage is cooked through and bacon is crisp 10 to 15 minutes; drain well. Beat eggs and milk together. Break bread into small pieces. Stir sausage-bacon mixture into egg mixture; add bread and remaining ingredients. Pour into greased 13 x 9-inch baking pan. Cover; refrigerate overnight.

Next morning: Preheat oven to 350° F. Bake, uncovered, 50 minutes to 1 hour.   *12 to 16 servings.*

Preparation Time: 25 Minutes   *Cooking Time: 1 Hour*

Create-Your-Own Omelet

4 eggs, separated
⅛ teaspoon salt
⅛ teaspoon pepper
2 tablespoons butter or margarine

Preheat oven to 350° F. In small bowl of electric mixer beat egg yolks until thick and lemon-colored. Add ¼ cup water, salt and pepper, mixing well. Beat egg whites until stiff but not dry; fold into yolk mixture. Heat oven proof 10-inch omelet pan or heavy skillet over medium heat until a drop of water in the pan sizzles. Add butter, rotating pan to coat bottom and sides. Pour in egg mixture; gently smooth surface. Reduce heat to low. Cook 5 minutes or until puffy and lightly browned on bottom.

Add your choice of fillings-diced cooked ham, crumbled cooked bacon, diced onion, diced green pepper, shredded cheese, etc. Bake, uncovered, 7 minutes or until knife inserted in center comes out clean. Remove from oven; gently fold omelet in half. Cut into serving-sized pieces; serve on warm plates.

2 servings.

Preparation Time: 10 Minutes   *Cooking Time: 12 Minutes*

Omelet with Fresh Herbs

6 eggs, lightly beaten
1/4 cup, plus 2 tablespoons, milk
1 tablespoon butter or margarine
1/2 teaspoon salt
1 teaspoon fresh parsley, chopped
1 teaspoon fresh chives, chopped
1 teaspoon fresh marjoram,
  chopped
1 teaspoon fresh rosemary, chopped

In small bowl combine eggs and milk; mix just until blended. In 10-inch omelet pan or heavy skillet, over medium heat, melt butter. Pour egg mixture into skillet all at once. As mixture starts to cook, gently lift edges of omelet with spatula; tilt pan to allow uncooked portion to flow underneath. Cook until set but not dry. Combine parsley, chives, marjoram and rosemary. Sprinkle all except 1 teaspoon herb mixture over half the omelet. Fold opposite side of omelet over herbs; transfer to warmed serving platter. Garnish with reserved herbs; serve immediately. *3 to 4 servings.*

Preparation Time: 5 Minutes   *Cooking Time: 5 to 10 Minutes*

Creamy Corn Omelet

4 ears fresh corn
1/2 cup half-and-half
1/2 teaspoon salt
Dash black pepper
4 eggs, separated
2 tablespoons butter or margarine

Cut corn from cob, scraping cob to remove pulp. In large bowl combine corn, half-and-half, salt and pepper. Beat egg yolks until thick and lemon-colored; stir into corn mixture. Beat egg whites until stiff peaks form; fold into corn mixture.

Preheat oven to 350° F. In large oven proof skillet, over low heat, melt butter. Add corn mixture; cook 15 minutes. Transfer omelet pan to oven; bake 15 minutes or until set. Remove from oven; carefully fold in half, or cut into serving-sized pieces. Slide onto warmed serving plates; serve immediately. *2 to 4 servings.*

Preparation Time: 20 Minutes   *Cooking Time: 30 Minutes*

Bread-Cheese Soufflé

8 slices day-old bread
1 1/2 pounds sharp cheddar cheese,
  grated
6 eggs, beaten
2 1/2 cups milk
1 rounded tablespoon brown sugar
Paprika to taste
1 whole green onion, finely minced
Pepper
1/2 teaspoon dry mustard
1/2 teaspoon salt
1/2 teaspoon Worcestershire sauce
Dash cayenne pepper

24 hours before cooking: Remove crusts from bread; cut bread into small cubes. In large bowl mix all ingredients except bread. In buttered baking dish, alternate cheese mixture and bread cubes in layers. Refrigerate 24 hours.

When ready to cook: Preheat oven to 300° F.; bake 1 hour.
8 to 10 servings.

Preparation Time: 15 Minutes   *Cooking Time: 1 Hour*

Treasure Tip: This is a perfect recipe for a light supper or brunch. Serve with salad, a light white wine and fruit for dessert.

Chiles Rellenos Bake

1 cup half-and-half
4 eggs
1/3 cup flour
3 (4-ounce) cans whole green
  chilies
8 ounces Monterey Jack cheese,
  shredded
8 ounces cheddar cheese, shredded
1 (8-ounce) jar mild picante sauce
Freshly grated Parmesan cheese
  (optional)

Preheat oven to 375° F. In medium bowl beat half-and-half with eggs; add flour; blend until smooth. Split chilies; remove seeds; drain on paper towels. In baking dish alternate layers of chilies, egg mixture and cheese; pour picante sauce over top. Sprinkle with Parmesan, if desired. Bake 30 minutes.   *4 to 6 servings.*

Preparation Time: 15 Minutes   *Cooking Time: 30 Minutes*

Treasure Tip: To make fluffier scrambled eggs, do not add milk. Beat in a small amount of water instead.

Shrimp and Swiss Cheese Bake

6 slices firm white bread
1/2 stick butter, melted
1 cup Swiss cheese, grated, divided
2 whole green onions, chopped,
  divided
2 tablespoons fresh parsley,
  chopped and divided
3/4 pound small fresh shrimp,
  slightly cooked, divided
3 eggs
1/2 teaspoon salt
1/2 teaspoon dry mustard
1 1/2 cups milk
1/2 cup sour cream

Night before: Remove crusts from bread. Cut slices in half diagonally; dip in melted butter. Arrange six pieces of bread in 8 x 8-inch baking dish. Sprinkle with half of cheese, half of onions, half of parsley and half of shrimp. Repeat layers. In large bowl of electric mixer beat together eggs and remaining ingredients; pour over mixture in casserole. Refrigerate overnight.

Next morning: Preheat oven to 350° F. Bake until puffed and golden, 40 to 50 minutes. Let stand 10 minutes. Cut into squares; serve.   *6 servings.*

Preparation Time: 30 Minutes   Cooking Time: 40 to 50 Minutes

Cinnamon-Apple Pancake Puff

2 large Granny Smith or other
    green apples
1 stick butter
¼ cup sugar
2 teaspoons cinnamon
4 eggs
1 cup flour
1 cup, plus 2 tablespoons, milk
1 teaspoon vanilla extract
Powdered sugar

Preheat oven to 425° F. Peel, core and thinly slice apples. Melt butter in large, shallow, oven-proof skillet, over medium-high heat. Stir in sugar and cinnamon; add apples. Cook, stirring, until apples are translucent, about 5 minutes. Place pan in oven while you prepare batter. In large bowl of electric mixer beat eggs. Add flour, milk and vanilla; beat until smooth. Pour batter evenly over apples in pan. Bake, uncovered, until pancake is puffy and golden, about 15 minutes. Sift powdered sugar over pancake. Cut into wedges; serve immediately. **6 to 8 servings.**

Preparation Time: 35 Minutes   *Cooking Time: 15 Minutes*

Cheese Lover's Casserole

1 large loaf day-old Cuban, French
    or Italian bread
¾ stick unsalted butter, melted
¾ pound domestic Swiss cheese,
    shredded
½ pound Monterey Jack cheese,
    shredded
9 thin slices Genoa salami,
    coarsely chopped
16 eggs
3¼ cups milk
½ cup dry white wine
4 large whole green onions, minced
1 tablespoon spicy mustard
¼ teaspoon freshly ground black
    pepper
⅛ teaspoon ground red pepper
1½ cups sour cream
⅔ to 1 cup Parmesan, freshly
    grated (or Asiago cheese,
    shredded)

Night before: Butter two shallow 9 x 13-inch baking dishes. Break bread into small pieces; spread over bottoms of baking dishes. Drizzle bread with melted butter. Sprinkle with Swiss and Monterey Jack cheeses and salami. In large bowl of electric mixer beat eggs, milk, wine, green onions, mustard and peppers until foamy. Pour mixture over cheese. Cover dishes with foil, crimping edges; refrigerate overnight.

Next morning: Remove from refrigerator about 30 minutes before baking. Preheat oven to 325 ° F. Bake, covered, until mixture is set, about 1 hour. Spread mixture with sour cream; sprinkle with Parmesan. Bake, uncovered, until crusty and lightly browned, about 10 minutes. **12 servings.**

Preparation Time: 15 Minutes   *Cooking Time: 1 Hour*
10 Minutes

Treasure Tip: For best results when poaching eggs, always start with the freshest eggs. If you do not have an egg poacher, fill a saucepan with 2 to 3 inches of water; bring to simmer. Break eggs into water and let cook 3 minutes for soft yolks, 5 minutes for firmer yolks. Some cooks add 1 or 2 teaspoons of vinegar to water to help eggs retain their shape.

Cheddar Florentine Soufflé

1 loaf Pepperidge Farm Original
    white bread
Softened butter
1 (10-ounce) package frozen
    chopped spinach
Salt and pepper to taste
1 tablespoon butter
1/4 pound fresh mushrooms, sliced
4 whole green onions, chopped
8 ounces cheddar cheese, grated
6 eggs
2 cups milk
1/2 cup buttermilk
Dash garlic salt
Dash cayenne pepper
Dash seasoned pepper
Dash Tabasco

Remove crusts from bread; spread with softened butter. Place in greased 2½ to 3-cup casserole. Cook spinach as package directs; squeeze out moisture. Season spinach with salt and pepper; place on top of bread slices. In small skillet melt 1 tablespoon butter; add mushrooms and green onions; sauté until tender. Pour over spinach; sprinkle cheese on top.

Preheat oven to 300° F. In large bowl of electric mixer, beat eggs with milk and buttermilk; add seasonings. Pour mixture over cheese in casserole; bake 1 hour. **8 servings.**

Preparation Time: 45 Minutes   *Cooking Time: 1 Hour*

Treasure Tip: For a successful soufflé, eggs should be at room temperature. The right casserole dish will ensure proper rising, the best is a porcelain dish with straight sides.

Baked Cinnamon French Toast

Half a loaf of French bread, cut
    into 1-inch slices
6 large eggs
1½ cups milk
1 cup light cream or half-and-half
1 teaspoon vanilla extract
1/4 teaspoon cinnamon
1/4 teaspoon nutmeg
1/2 stick butter or margarine,
    softened
1/2 cup firmly packed brown sugar
1/2 cup nuts, chopped
1 tablespoon light corn syrup

Night before: Butter 9 x 13-inch baking dish. Arrange bread slices, overlapping, in single layer to fill bottom of dish. In medium bowl combine eggs, milk, cream, vanilla, cinnamon and nutmeg; mix well. Pour over bread slices. Cover; refrigerate overnight.

Next morning: Preheat oven to 350° F. In small bowl combine butter, brown sugar, nuts and corn syrup; spread over bread. Bake 40 minutes. Serve warm, topped with maple syrup.
6 to 8 servings.

Preparation Time: 15 Minutes   *Cooking Time: 40 Minutes*

Treasure Tip: To fold beaten egg whites into a mixture, first mix in one-fourth with a spatula to lighten batter. Fold in remaining whites by placing the spatula under all ingredients and bringing the bottom to the top in a circular folding motion.

Gruyère Grits

1 quart milk
1 cup regular grits
1 stick butter, cut in cubes
1 teaspoon salt
Dash Tabasco
¾ stick butter, melted
1 cup Gruyère cheese, grated

In large saucepan bring milk to boil; add grits and cubed butter. Cook over medium heat 5 minutes or until thickened, stirring frequently. Pour warm grits into large bowl of electric mixer; add salt and Tabasco; beat 5 minutes at fast speed. Pour into buttered 13 x 9-inch baking dish; cool. Preheat oven to 350 ° F. Cut grits into squares, do not remove from baking dish; top with melted butter and cheese. Bake 30 minutes. Wonderful with steak.

12 servings.

Preparation Time: 20 Minutes   *Cooking Time: 30 Minutes*

Country Grits and Sausage

½ teaspoon salt
1 cup regular grits
4 cups (1 pound) extra-sharp
    cheddar cheese, shredded
4 eggs, well beaten
1 cup milk
½ teaspoon dried whole thyme
½ teaspoon garlic salt
2 pounds mild bulk pork sausage,
    cooked, crumbled and drained

Night before: In large saucepan bring 4 cups water and salt to boil; stir in grits. Return to boil; reduce heat to medium. Cook 4 minutes, stirring occasionally. Add cheese; stir until cheese melts. Combine eggs, milk, thyme and garlic salt; mix well. Add small amount of hot grits to egg mixture, stirring well. Stir egg mixture into remaining grits. Add sausage, stirring well. Pour into 13 x 9 x 2-inch baking dish. Cover; refrigerate overnight.

Next morning: Remove from refrigerator 15 minutes before baking. Preheat oven to 350° F. Bake 50 to 55 minutes.

12 servings.

Preparation Time: 15 Minutes   *Cooking Time: 50 to 55 Minutes*

Treasure Tip: To bring out their flavor, grits must be cooked in salted water. Grits cooked without salt have little taste.

PASTA & RICE

The Gasparilla Distance Classic

Along the curve of Bayshore Boulevard, winds the world's longest continuous sidewalk. This is where we find the setting for our next treasure, the annual Gasparilla Distance Classic. Some 12,000 runners, joggers and wheel-chair athletes participate in 15K and 5K events along the 9.3 mile course. The race, one of the top in the country, attracts competitors from around the world.

A big drawing card is the race course itself. Bayshore Boulevard is a favorite place for residents to walk, jog, bicycle and roller skate or just sit and enjoy a panoramic water view. In the 1920's this boulevard, which we affectionately call "The Bayshore" became the setting for many of Tampa's finest residences. These stately homes still preside over Tampa's grandest boulevard.

Since the mild climate accommodates year-round sports, the avid sports enthusiast is rarely idle. Usually one can swing a golf club, hit a tennis ball, swim a lap or ride a polo pony without giving much thought to the weather. Baseball fans can attend major league spring training games and get a preview of next season's winners.

Our love of the outdoors extends itself to alfresco entertaining. Many homes feature terraces, pools and porches where guests can enjoy fresh foods surrounded by the sight and sound of tropical gardens. The Luncheon On The Terrace spotlights healthy pasta and rice combined with fresh vegetables and fruits, seafood, poultry and many different cheeses. Rice, that beloved Southern grain, is used in this section as a base for sophisticated risottos and pilafs. In the section look for local favorites like Saffron Lobster Risotto and Florida Orange Rice.

**The Distance Classic photograph was underwritten by
Memorial Hospital of Tampa**

PASTA & RICE

Luncheon On The Terrace

Pasta with Oriental Chicken and Snow Peas

Spaghetti Primavera

Indian Rice Almandine

Garlic Lime Marinated Shrimp

Amaretto Fruit Dip

**The menu photograph was underwritten by Guy and Co.
John Hancock Financial Services**

Pasta with Oriental Chicken and Snow Peas

12 ounces chicken breasts, boned, skinned, cut into 1-inch strips

3 tablespoons fresh lime juice, divided

⅓ cup, plus 1 tablespoon, peanut oil, divided

2 tablespoons soy sauce, divided

1 tablespoon fresh ginger, minced or grated (plus more for garnish)

¼ teaspoon crushed, dried red pepper

2 cloves garlic, crushed

6 ounces fresh snow peas, trimmed

12 ounces fettucini or linguini

1 teaspoon sesame oil

½ teaspoon salt (or to taste)

¼ cup whole green onions, thinly sliced

1 teaspoon sesame seeds, toasted 10 seconds in hot skillet

1 tablespoon fresh cilantro leaves (optional)

At least 1 hour before cooking: In bowl, place chicken, 1 tablespoon lime juice, 1 tablespoon peanut oil, 1 tablespoon soy sauce, ginger, red pepper and garlic; toss well to combine. Cover; refrigerate at least 1 hour. Meanwhile, steam snow peas about 3 minutes. Rinse with cool water; set aside. Cook fettucini in plenty of salted water until al dente. Drain; rinse with cool water; drain again.

Make dressing: Whisk together ⅓ cup peanut oil, 2 tablespoons lime juice, 1 tablespoon soy sauce, sesame oil and salt. Prepare hot fire in barbecue grill. After chicken has marinated, grill until browned and tender about 3 minutes per side; cool slightly. (Or cook in skillet over medium heat, 3 minutes per side.)

Combine snow peas, fettucini, chicken strips, dressing, green onions, sesame seeds and cilantro. Let sit a few minutes to blend flavors; serve on lettuce leaves; garnish with ginger. For buffet meals, cut chicken into bite-sized chunks after grilling.

6 servings.

Preparation Time: 30 Minutes   *Cooking Time: 6 Minutes*

Spaghetti Primavera

4 cups fresh broccoli florets
2 small zucchini, trimmed,
    quartered lengthwise and cut
    crosswise into 1-inch lengths
4 fresh asparagus spears, trimmed,
    cut into thirds
6 ounces fresh green beans,
    trimmed, cut into 1-inch
    lengths
½ cup fresh tiny new green peas
    (or frozen, thawed)
1 tablespoon peanut, vegetable or
    corn oil
6 ounces fresh mushrooms, thinly
    sliced
Salt and freshly ground black
    pepper to taste
1 teaspoon fresh red or green chile
    pepper, seeded and finely
    chopped
¼ cup fresh parsley, finely chopped
6 tablespoons olive oil, divided
1 teaspoon garlic, finely chopped
    and divided
1¼ pounds (about 3 cups) fresh
    ripe tomatoes, cut into 1-inch
    cubes
¼ cup fresh basil, chopped
1 pound spaghetti
½ stick unsalted butter
2 tablespoons chicken broth
½ cup heavy cream (more if
    necessary)
⅔ cup Parmesan cheese, freshly
    grated

Bring large, heavy saucepan of water to boil to cook spaghetti. Place broccoli, zucchini, asparagus, beans and peas in steamer; steam until crisp-tender, 2 to 3 minutes. Drain well; place in large bowl. Cook spaghetti in boiling water until al dente; drain; return to saucepan.

Heat peanut oil in large, heavy skillet. Add mushrooms, salt and pepper; cook about 2 minutes, shaking skillet. Stir in chile pepper and parsley; remove from heat. Add mushroom mixture to vegetables in bowl; set aside.

Heat 3 tablespoons olive oil in heavy saucepan over medium heat; add ½ teaspoon garlic and tomatoes. Reduce heat to low; cook, stirring gently, about 4 minutes. Stir in basil; set aside.

Heat remaining 3 tablespoons olive oil in large skillet over medium heat. Add ½ teaspoon garlic and vegetable mixture; stir gently just until heated through.

Melt butter in Dutch oven or large, heavy pot over medium heat. When foam subsides, add chicken broth, cream and Parmesan. Cook, stirring constantly, until mixture is smooth, 2 to 3 minutes. Add spaghetti; toss quickly to blend. Add half of vegetable mixture. Drain tomatoes, set aside, add juice to Dutch oven. Toss; stir over very low heat to combine. Add remaining vegetables, adding more cream if sauce seems too dry (sauce should not be soupy).

To serve, divide spaghetti evenly among warmed bowls. Spoon equal amount of tomatoes over each serving; serve immediately.

4 to 6 servings.

Preparation and Cooking Time: 1 Hour and 30 Minutes

Indian Rice Almandine

2 tablespoons butter
½ cup onion, thinly sliced
3 tablespoons slivered almonds
¼ cup currants or seedless raisins
2 cups hot, cooked long-grain rice

Melt butter over medium heat in small skillet; cook onions and almonds until golden. Add currants; heat through until they puff. Add to rice; mix lightly. Serve with broiled meat, chicken or curried dishes.   *5 servings.*

Preparation Time: 10 Minutes   *Cooking Time: 15 Minutes*

Garlic Lime Marinated Shrimp

3 pounds large fresh shrimp,
    peeled, tails left on
3 medium garlic cloves, crushed
1½ teaspoons salt
½ cup packed brown sugar
3 tablespoons grainy mustard
¼ cup cider vinegar
Juice of 1 lime
Juice of ½ large lemon
6 tablespoons olive oil
Black pepper to taste

Night before: Place shrimp in shallow bowl. Mix garlic, salt, brown sugar, mustard, vinegar, lime and lemon juices; blend well. Whisk in oil; add pepper; pour over shrimp. Cover; refrigerate overnight, turning once.

When ready to cook: Bring to room temperature. Grill over hot coals or under broiler 2 to 3 minutes per side. This marinade is also fantastic for chicken!   *6 servings.*

Preparation Time: 20 Minutes   *Cooking Time: 4 to 6 Minutes*

Amaretto Fruit Dip

1 pint sour cream
¼ cup brown sugar
2 to 4 tablespoons Amaretto

Mix all ingredients. Serve as dip with assorted fresh fruits.
                    Makes 2¼ cups.

Preparation Time: 5 Minutes

Treasure Tip: *Never depend on cooking time printed on the box when cooking pasta. Start testing fresh pasta after 30 seconds and dried pasta after 4 minutes. Perfect pasta "al dente" (to the tooth) should be firm but tender, with a slightly chalky center that sticks to your teeth. In many of our pasta dishes, timing is essential. Be sure to cook your pasta so that the pasta and sauce are ready to be combined when both are hot.*

Chicken-Fettucini Florentine

1 stick butter or margarine
1 onion, sliced
2 tablespoons fresh basil, chopped
   (or ½ teaspoon dried basil)
2 cloves garlic, minced
½ teaspoon dried red pepper flakes
1 pound boneless chicken breasts,
   skinned and cut into strips
2 (10-ounce) packages frozen
   chopped spinach, thawed and
   squeezed dry
Salt and pepper to taste
8 ounces fettucini, freshly cooked
2 cups Parmesan cheese, freshly
   grated
1½ tablespoons fresh orange juice

Melt butter in large, heavy skillet over medium heat. Add onion, basil, garlic and red pepper; cook until onion is soft, about 7 minutes. Add chicken; sauté, stirring frequently, until cooked through, about 10 minutes. Stir in spinach; season with salt and pepper. Place pasta in large bowl; add chicken mixture. Add Parmesan; toss thoroughly. Drizzle with orange juice; serve.

4 generous servings.

Preparation Time: 10 Minutes   **Cooking Time: 20 Minutes**

Chicken Fettucini Verde

¼ cup olive oil
1 small onion, julienned
4 fresh mushrooms, sliced
½ stick plus 2 tablespoons butter or
   margarine, divided
½ cup (about 2 ounces) julienned
   prosciutto
⅓ cup fresh tomato, peeled, seeded,
   chopped
1 cup julienned chicken breast,
   barely cooked
¼ cup heavy cream
Pinch nutmeg
Salt and pepper to taste
8 ounces green fettucini
Freshly grated Parmesan cheese

In a large, heavy pot, boil 3 quarts salted water. Meanwhile, heat olive oil in large skillet; add onion; sauté until golden. Add mushrooms; sauté 2 minutes. Add ½ stick butter, prosciutto and tomatoes; simmer 6 minutes. Stir in chicken, cream, nutmeg, salt and pepper. Bring to simmer, stirring, over high heat. Remove from heat; keep warm. Cook fettucini just until tender, about 8 minutes. Drain; toss with 2 tablespoons butter. To serve, pour sauce over pasta; sprinkle with Parmesan.

2 servings.

Preparation Time: 10 Minutes   **Cooking Time: 15 Minutes**

Treasure Tip: Cooked pasta can be kept in the refrigerator up to 2 days. Reheat it in the microwave; or place it in a colander and pour boiling water over it until strands will separate, or stir it in a skillet with a little olive oil and white wine.

Garlic Penne with Cauliflower

1 (1½-pound) head fresh
   cauliflower
⅓-½ cup olive oil
6 large cloves garlic, peeled and
   chopped
6 flat anchovy filets, chopped
¼ teaspoon hot red pepper flakes
1 pound penne or other macaroni
2 tablespoons fresh parsley,
   chopped
Salt to taste

Strip cauliflower of all but a few very tender leaves; rinse; cut in half. In large saucepan bring 4 to 5 cups water to boil. Add cauliflower; cook until tender but compact, 25 to 30 minutes. Drain; set aside.

Place oil, garlic and anchovies in medium skillet; sauté over medium heat until garlic is golden. Stir occasionally with wooden spoon, mashing anchovies. Add cauliflower; quickly break up with fork, crumbling to pieces no bigger than a peanut. Turn cauliflower thoroughly in oil, mashing part of it to a pulp. Add pepper flakes; turn up heat; cook a few more minutes, stirring frequently. Turn off heat.

Cook penne until al dente. Briefly reheat cauliflower mixture; pour over penne. Toss thoroughly; add parsley and salt; toss again; serve. Anchovies are a must in this dish. If they are not your favorite, use less. **6 to 8 servings.**

Preparation Time: 10 Minutes   ***Cooking Time: 1 Hour***

Shells Seafood Pasta At Home

From Shells' popular Florida seafood restaurants

1 pound linguini
2 tablespoons butter
4 ounces fresh mussel meat
6 ounces clams, chopped, cooked
   and drained
10 ounces fresh scallops
12 ounces fresh shrimp, peeled
¼ cup olive oil
¼ cup dry white wine
2 cups heavy cream
8 cloves garlic, finely chopped
Salt and pepper to taste
2 dashes soy sauce

Cook linguini with butter in salted water until al dente; set aside. Mix mussel meat, clams, scallops and shrimp in bowl. In large saucepan combine remaining ingredients; bring to boil. Add linguini and drained seafood mixture. Cook over medium heat, stirring gently, until seafood is done and sauce has creamy consistency, about 10 minutes. Serve immediately. **4 servings.**

Preparation Time: 20 Minutes   ***Cooking Time: 15 to 20 Minutes***

Treasure Tip: *Be prepared to serve this dish at once. If the sauce simmers too long after it is cooked, the seafood will become tough and lose its flavor.*

Fresh Tomato Garlic Pasta

4 large ripe tomatoes, diced
5 cloves garlic, chopped
1 large sprig fresh parsley, chopped
½ cup chopped fresh basil
½ cup extra-virgin olive oil
⅓ cup red wine vinegar
Salt and pepper to taste
6 ounces mozzarella cheese, cubed
   (optional)
1 pound pasta
Parmesan cheese, freshly grated
   (garnish)

Night before, or early in day: In large bowl combine all ingredients except pasta and Parmesan; stir well. Cover; refrigerate at least 2 hours (preferably overnight) but not more than 1 day, or sauce will congeal. Stir once or twice while in refrigerator.

When ready to serve: Prepare pasta. Coat with sauce; serve hot or cold with Parmesan. **4 to 6 servings.**

Preparation Time: 10 Minutes   *Cooking Time: 10 Minutes*

Treasure Tip: Light or thin sauces are usually served with the thinner pastas (angel hair, vermicelli, spaghettini, etc.) Heavier sauces go better with thicker pastas (fusilli, fettucini, linguini, shells, etc.)

Brie and Plum Tomato Pasta

⅔ pound ripe Brie, cubed
4 very ripe Italian plum tomatoes,
   cubed
1 cup fresh basil leaves, shredded
⅔ cup olive oil
3 cloves garlic, minced
Salt and pepper to taste
1 pound freshly cooked fusilli
Freshly grated Parmesan cheese

Combine Brie, tomatoes, basil, olive oil, garlic, salt and pepper. Toss with hot fusilli; serve with Parmesan. **6 servings.**

Preparation and Cooking Time: 25 Minutes

Treasure Tip: Fusilli, a twisted or spiral-shaped pasta, should be cooked 10 to 12 minutes.

Lobster Ravioli

Fresh pasta and lobster from Saltwaters Restaurant at Downtown Hyatt Regency

Pasta
³/₄ cup flour
¹/₄ cup semolina
3 eggs
¹/₄ cup extra-virgin olive oil

Lobster Mixture
2 pounds fresh lobster, in shell
2 tablespoons Parmesan cheese,
  freshly grated
1 teaspoon fresh basil, chopped
Pinch salt
Pinch pepper
2 tablespoons fresh mushrooms,
  finely chopped
¹/₂ teaspoon truffle, finely diced
  (optional)
Egg wash (1 beaten egg mixed
  with 1 teaspoon water)

Lobster Sauce
2 empty lobster shells, crushed
1 stick butter, divided
¹/₂ medium onion, sliced
¹/₂ carrot, peeled and sliced
2 stalks celery, chopped
¹/₄ cup brandy
1 teaspoon garlic, chopped
1 bay leaf
¹/₄ cup flour
Salt and pepper to taste

About 4 hours before serving, make pasta: Combine flour, semolina, eggs and olive oil in large bowl of electric mixer. Beat dough until it comes away from sides of bowl. Take dough out of bowl; let rest 2 hours.

While dough rests, make lobster mixture: Steam lobster about 4 minutes; remove meat from shell; cool. In small bowl mix Parmesan, basil, salt and pepper; set aside. Sauté mushrooms in small pan until liquid is absorbed. Chop lobster coarsely; add to mushrooms. Add truffle; mix with Parmesan mixture. Test for taste; season if needed; set aside.

Make lobster sauce: Sauté lobster shells in ¹/₂ stick butter in large skillet. Add onion, carrot and celery; sauté over high heat 15 minutes. Add brandy, garlic, bay leaf and 3 cups water. Reduce heat; simmer 30 minutes; strain sauce. Return sauce to pan; cook 10 minutes over medium heat until sauce is reduced by half. Keep warm. Roll out pasta dough very thin by hand or pasta machine; cut dough in half. Place 1 teaspoon lobster mixture in small piles on half of dough. Brush egg wash around lobster mixture before putting other half of dough on top. Once top layer is on, press around filling to seal; cut ravioli into shapes. Bring 2 quarts water to boil. Add ravioli; cook until al dente, about 4 minutes.

While ravioli cooks, finish sauce: Whisk in flour; season with salt and pepper; cook to thicken. Add ¹/₂ stick butter to melt; stir. Drain ravioli; serve immediately with sauce.   ***4 servings.***

Preparation Time: 3 Hours   ***Cooking Time: 1 Hour***

Treasure Tip: *When making ravioli by hand, be sure to press the inner and outer seams together well. This eliminates air bubbles in the seams and seals the ravioli. Cut down the middle of each seam with a pizza cutter or sharp knife to make each ravioli shape.*

Zesty Lobster Tetrazzini

Spice Mixture

1 tablespoon salt
1 tablespoon black pepper
1 tablespoon white pepper
1 tablespoon garlic powder
1 tablespoon onion powder
2 tablespoons paprika
2 tablespoons oregano

Lobster Filling

½ stick butter
1 tablespoon garlic, minced
2 pounds fresh lobster meat
2 cups heavy cream
1 pound linguini, cooked al dente
½ cup Parmesan cheese, freshly
    grated

To make spice mixture: Combine all ingredients. In large skillet over medium-high heat, melt butter with spice mixture. Add garlic and lobster; sauté briefly; add cream. Increase heat to high; cook, stirring, until cream is thick and liquid is reduced by half. Add linguini; toss to combine. Top with Parmesan; serve.

4 servings.

Preparation Time: 15 Minutes   *Cooking Time: 20 Minutes*

Treasure Tip: To shell cooked lobster, lay it on its back with the underside exposed. With a heavy knife, split it down the middle without going all the way to the back. Arch the tail backward to break it off. If meat from the tail doesn't come out easily, cut the underside with kitchen shears.

Cheese-and-Spinach-Stuffed Shells

24 jumbo pasta shells for stuffing
4 cups spaghetti sauce with
    mushrooms (a 32-ounce jar),
    divided
1 (10-ounce) package frozen
    chopped spinach, thawed and
    squeezed dry
2 cups ricotta cheese
2 cups mozzarella cheese, shredded
1 small onion, diced
¾ cup Parmesan cheese, freshly
    grated, divided
2 tablespoons fresh parsley,
    chopped
1 teaspoon dried oregano
Dash Tabasco
Dash nutmeg

Cook pasta shells; drain; set aside. Preheat oven to 350 ° F. Combine spinach, ricotta, mozzarella, onion, ½ cup Parmesan, parsley, oregano, Tabasco and nutmeg; mix well. Spoon 1½ tablespoons spinach mixture into each pasta shell. Spoon 1 cup spaghetti sauce into 13 x 9 x 2-inch baking dish. Arrange shells, spinach side up, in baking dish. Spoon remaining sauce over shells; sprinkle with ¼ cup Parmesan. Cover; bake until heated through, 30 to 40 minutes. Casserole can be prepared ahead up to baking time, and refrigerated or frozen. If frozen, bake 60 to 80 minutes.

6 to 8 servings.

Preparation Time: 20 Minutes   *Cooking Time: 30 to 40 Minutes*

Shrimp and Mushroom Linguini

8 ounces linguini or thin spaghetti
1 stick butter or margarine
     (or ½ cup olive oil)
4 to 6 cloves garlic, minced
12 fresh jumbo shrimp, peeled,
     deveined and diced
¼ pound fresh mushrooms, diced
6 tablespoons Romano cheese,
     freshly grated, more for garnish
½ teaspoon salt
Freshly ground pepper to taste
Parsley sprigs (garnish)

Cook linguini in rapidly boiling water 10 minutes. Drain; rinse with cold water; set aside. Melt butter in 10-inch skillet. Add garlic, shrimp and mushrooms; cook slowly 5 minutes. Add linguini; sprinkle with cheese, salt and pepper. Toss over low heat until linguini is very hot. Turn into warm serving dish; sprinkle with additional cheese; garnish with parsley.

4 servings.

Preparation Time: 15 Minutes   *Cooking Time: 20 Minutes*

Spaghetti Carbonara

6 slices lean bacon
¾ stick butter, divided
1 medium onion, minced
½ cup light cream
¼ cup dry white wine
2 egg yolks, beaten
½ cup Parmesan cheese, freshly
     grated, more for garnish
Salt and pepper to taste
8 ounces spaghetti
4 heaping tablespoons fresh
     parsley, minced

Fry bacon until crisp; drain; crumble; set aside. Melt 2 tablespoons butter in small skillet; sauté onion until soft; set aside. In top of double boiler, over hot water, combine cream, wine, egg yolks, cheese, remaining butter, salt and pepper; mix well. Cook until sauce is thick and smooth. Meanwhile, cook spaghetti in boiling salted water until al dente; drain. While spaghetti is very hot, toss lightly with cheese sauce. Garnish with crumbled bacon, sautéed onion, parsley and additional cheese, if desired.

4 servings.

Preparation Time: 30 Minutes   *Cooking Time: 15 Minutes*

Golden Baked Macaroni and Cheese

½ pound macaroni
1 tablespoon butter
1 egg, beaten
1 teaspoon dry mustard (or to taste)
1 teaspoon salt
1 teaspoon pepper (or to taste)
1 cup milk
3 cups cheese, grated (Monterey Jack or Gouda), divided

Preheat oven to 350° F. Boil macaroni until tender; drain. Add butter and egg; stir well to mix. In separate bowl mix mustard, salt and pepper with 1 tablespoon hot water; add to macaroni mixture. Add most of cheese; mix well. Lightly grease casserole dish with vegetable cooking spray; place macaroni mixture in dish; sprinkle with reserved cheese. Bake until custard is set and crusty, about 45 minutes. *8 servings.*

Preparation Time: 20 Minutes   *Cooking Time: 45 Minutes*

Treasure Tip: Hard cheeses such as cheddar can be frozen for up to 6 months. Freeze your left over cheeses to use in this tasty casserole.

Traditional Basil Pesto

2 cups fresh basil leaves, tightly packed
2 large cloves garlic
½ cup olive oil
2 tablespoons pine nuts
1 teaspoon salt
¼ cup Parmesan cheese, freshly grated
2 tablespoons Romano cheese, freshly grated
3 tablespoons butter, softened

Process basil and garlic in food processor or blender; with motor running, add oil in thin, steady stream. Add remaining ingredients; process long enough to make smooth paste. Pesto can be served over any kind of pasta or with chicken, meat or seafood. *Makes about 3 cups.*

Preparation Time: 15 Minutes

Treasure Tip: Here is a great way to serve pesto: Slice a loaf of French bread in half, lengthwise; top each half with pesto, cream cheese and sliced tomatoes; heat at 450° F. Slice; serve as appetizer or side dish.

Spinach Pesto

1 tablespoon vegetable oil
1 (10-ounce) package frozen,
  chopped spinach, thawed but
  not drained
¼ tablespoon garlic powder
⅛ teaspoon pepper
¾ cup cottage cheese
2 tablespoons Parmesan cheese,
  freshly grated
2 teaspoons fresh basil, minced (or
  ½ teaspoon dried)
2 tablespoons pine nuts or walnuts

Combine all ingredients in food processor or blender; process to blend. Pour into medium saucepan; heat thoroughly, stirring constantly. Serve hot with favorite pasta.   *Makes about 3 cups.*

Preparation Time: 20 Minutes   *Cooking Time: 15 Minutes*

Treasure Tip: Store Spinach Pesto in your freezer and bring it out for a quick, light pasta supper.

Red Wine Marinara Sauce

2 tablespoons olive oil
1 cup onion, chopped
6 large cloves garlic, minced
2 tablespoons fresh parsley, minced
1 teaspoon dried whole oregano
1 teaspoon dried whole basil
½ teaspoon dried whole thyme
1 teaspoon salt
¼ teaspoon pepper, freshly ground
2 bay leaves
1 (28-ounce) can whole tomatoes,
  undrained and chopped
2 (6-ounce) cans tomato paste
¾ cup dry red wine

Add oil to coat Dutch oven or large, heavy pot. Place over medium-high heat until oil is hot. Add onion and garlic; sauté until tender. Add parsley, oregano, basil, thyme, salt and pepper; cook, stirring, 1 minute. Add bay leaves, tomatoes, tomato paste, wine and ¾ cup water. Reduce heat; simmer, uncovered, 30 to 45 minutes, stirring often. Serve over pasta.
8 to 10 servings.

Preparation Time: 10 Minutes   *Cooking Time: 30 to 45 Minutes*

Treasure Tip: To dry fresh herbs, wash and air-dry them thoroughly. Place on a paper towel in the microwave oven; cook about 5 minutes on high; rotating after 2 minutes.

Straight-from-the-Pantry Sauce

2 tablespoons olive oil
3 cloves garlic, minced
1 medium onion, chopped
5 flat anchovy filets, finely
  chopped
1 (28-ounce) can Italian crushed
  tomatoes
1 tablespoon capers

Heat olive oil in large skillet; sauté garlic, onion and anchovies until garlic and onion are browned and anchovies appear to dissolve. Add tomatoes and capers; cook until warmed through. Serve over your choice of pasta.
2 servings.

Preparation Time: 5 Minutes   Cooking Time: 10 to 15 Minutes

Super Spaghetti Sauce

1 tablespoon olive oil
¾ cup onion, chopped
2 garlic cloves, minced
⅓ cup fresh parsley leaves, minced
4 teaspoons fresh basil, minced
1 (28-ounce) can crushed tomatoes
1 (6-ounce) can tomato paste
½ cup chicken stock or broth
¼ cup dry red wine
2 tablespoons sugar
½ teaspoon salt
½ teaspoon oregano
1 pound lean ground beef
½ pound fresh mushrooms, sliced

At least 30 minutes before serving, or night before: Heat oil in large, heavy saucepan; add onion and garlic. Cook over low heat, stirring, 2 minutes. Add parsley, basil, tomatoes, tomato paste, stock, wine, sugar, salt and oregano. Simmer, stirring occasionally, 30 minutes. (Flavor improves if chilled overnight.)

Shortly before serving: Brown ground beef and mushrooms in skillet; drain. Add to sauce; serve over hot cooked pasta. For a variation without meat, add your favorite vegetables.

6 servings.

Preparation Time: 10 Minutes   *Cooking Time: 45 Minutes*

Treasure Tip: A little sugar in spaghetti sauce cuts the acidity of the tomatoes.

Sun-Dried Tomato Cream Sauce

1 tablespoon olive oil
½ pound fresh mushrooms, sliced
1 (7-ounce) jar sun-dried tomatoes in oil
1 tablespoon oil from tomatoes
1½ cups light cream
1 tablespoon fresh basil, minced (or ¾ teaspoon dried basil)

Heat olive oil in large skillet; sauté mushrooms over low heat until tender. Cut about 15 sun-dried tomatoes in narrow strips; add to skillet. Add oil from tomatoes; stir to coat mushrooms. Add cream and basil; heat until warmed through. Serve over pasta of your choice.

2 servings.

Preparation Time: 5 Minutes   *Cooking Time: 10 to 15 Minutes*

Wild Mushroom-Shallot Sauce

1 pound chanterelle, shitake or porcini mushrooms (or a mixture)
1 stick unsalted butter
3 shallots, minced
Salt to taste
Freshly ground pepper to taste
3 tablespoons fresh parsley, chopped

Slice mushrooms lengthwise through cap and stem. (If mushrooms are dried, reconstitute them by soaking in hot water 30 minutes. Drain and clean before using.) Melt butter in large skillet; add mushrooms and shallots; sauté quickly over medium-high heat, shaking pan. Season with salt and pepper while cooking. Pour over freshly cooked pasta; mix well; sprinkle with parsley.

Makes about 2 cups.

Preparation Time: 10 Minutes   *Cooking Time: 5 to 10 Minutes*

Rice-Wild Mushroom Pilaf

¼ cup dried shitake or porcini
  mushrooms
2 tablespoons butter or margarine
1 shallot, finely chopped
1 cup basmati, Texmati or long-
  grain rice
1½ cups chicken broth
½ cup dry white wine or apple
  juice
½ cup celery, sliced
2 cups spinach leaves, torn
1 (2-ounce) jar diced pimentos,
  drained
½ to ¾ cup pecans, chopped
  (optional)

Soak mushrooms 30 minutes in enough hot water to cover. Drain mushrooms; remove and discard stems. Chop mushrooms; set aside. Heat butter in 2-quart saucepan; cook shallot until tender but not brown. Add rice; cook and stir over medium heat until rice is light brown, about 2 minutes. Carefully pour in broth and wine; add celery and chopped mushrooms. Bring to boil; reduce heat. Cover pan; simmer until rice is tender and liquid is absorbed, 20 to 25 minutes. Stir in spinach, pimentos and nuts; serve immediately.

6 to 8 servings.

Preparation Time: 35 Minutes   *Cooking Time: 30 Minutes*

Treasure Tip: *Basmati rice, a long-grain rice grown in India, Pakistan and Iran, is valued by chefs for its nutty aroma and taste. Texmati rice has similar qualities.*

Red Pepper Rice

5 slices lean bacon
1 large onion, chopped
½ cup celery, chopped
½ cup green pepper, chopped
1 cup long-grain rice
1 (16-ounce) can whole tomatoes,
  chopped, undrained
½ teaspoon salt
¼ teaspoon pepper
¼ teaspoon dried hot red pepper
⅛ teaspoon Tabasco

Preheat oven to 350° F. Cook bacon in skillet until crisp; drain on paper towels; reserve drippings in skillet. Crumble bacon; set aside. Sauté onion, celery and green pepper in skillet, until vegetables are tender. Stir in rice, tomatoes, ½ cup water, salt, pepper, red pepper and Tabasco. Spoon into lightly greased 1 ½-quart baking dish. Cover; bake until rice is tender about 25 minutes. After 15 minutes, stir rice and add ½ cup more water, if needed.   *6 to 8 servings.*

Preparation Time: 20 Minutes   Cooking Time: 35 to 40 Minutes

Treasure Tip: *Uncooked rice keeps better when stored in the refrigerator.*

Herbed Spinach Rice

3 cups cooked white rice
4 eggs
½ pound New York sharp cheddar
   cheese, grated
1 tablespoon Worcestershire sauce
1 cup milk
1 stick butter, softened
1 (10-ounce) package frozen
   chopped spinach, cooked and
   drained
2 tablespoons onion, chopped
½ teaspoon thyme
½ teaspoon marjoram
½ teaspoon rosemary
2 teaspoons salt

Preheat oven to 350° F. Mix all ingredients; place in casserole dish. Bake, uncovered, 35 minutes. **6 to 8 servings.**

Preparation Time: 20 Minutes   Cooking Time: 35 to 40 Minutes

Treasure Tip: Brown rice will enhance this recipe with a nutty flavor.

Pine Nut Rice and Vermicelli

1½ cups long-grain rice
1 stick butter or margarine
½ pound dried vermicelli, broken
   into ½-inch pieces
½ cup pine nuts
2 cups chicken stock
Salt and pepper to taste

About 1 hour before serving: Cook rice according to package directions. Melt butter in large skillet; add vermicelli and pine nuts ; sauté over medium heat until brown, 5 to 10 minutes. Add chicken stock, salt and pepper; boil 5 minutes. Stir in cooked rice. Cover; let stand about 30 minutes before serving. **6 servings.**

Preparation Time: 5 Minutes   Cooking Time: 15 Minutes

Saffron Lobster Risotto

¼ cup champagne or dry white
   wine
15 saffron threads
1 tablespoon olive oil
1 tablespoon butter
¼ to ⅓ cup onion, finely chopped
1 small clove garlic, minced
⅔ cup Arborio rice
Salt and freshly ground pepper to
   taste
2 cups hot chicken broth, divided
6 ounces fresh lobster meat (or
   fresh shrimp), cooked and
   chopped
1 tablespoon fresh flat-leaf parsley,
   chopped
2 tablespoons Parmesan cheese,
   freshly grated (optional)

In small saucepan heat champagne and saffron over medium heat until simmering; remove from heat; set aside. Heat oil and butter in heavy, medium saucepan over low heat. Add onion and garlic; cook, stirring frequently, until onion is golden, 8 to 10 minutes.

Add rice, salt and pepper; cook, stirring constantly, over medium heat until rice is completely coated and begins to look transparent, about 5 minutes. Add hot broth, about ⅓ cup at a time, until broth is absorbed. Cook, stirring constantly, until rice is tender and creamy, 18 to 20 minutes. About 2 to 3 minutes before rice is done, stir in champagne and lobster. Remove mixture from heat; stir in parsley, then cheese. Serve hot.   *2 servings.*

Preparation Time: 15 Minutes   ***Cooking Time: 45 Minutes***

Treasure Tip: *Arborio is a short-grain rice from Italy. It cooks to a tender, creamy consistency and is best suited for risottos. Don't rinse before cooking. The starch that coats the grains is essential for creamy rice. Any short-grained, full-starch rice may be substituted in recipe above.*

Creole Dirty Rice

A popular dish from Tampa's Mott & Hester Deli

1¼ cups white rice
¾ cup vegetable oil
2½ teaspoons fresh garlic, chopped
1½ cups red onion, chopped
¾ cup green bell pepper, chopped
¾ cup red bell pepper, chopped
½ pound ground beef
3½ ounces chicken livers
   (optional)
2 pounds eggplant, peeled, cubed
½ pound fresh mushrooms, sliced
1⅛ teaspoons poultry seasoning
½ teaspoon (heaping) crushed red
   pepper
1 tablespoon salt
2 teaspoons black pepper
7 tablespoons margarine, softened
¼ cup fresh parsley, chopped

Cook rice, omitting salt, as package directs; keep hot. Heat oil in large skillet; sauté garlic, onion and bell peppers until soft. Add beef and chicken livers; fry until beef is brown. Add eggplant; cook until brown and very soft. Add mushrooms, poultry seasoning, red pepper, salt and black pepper; mix well. Add margarine and parsley; mix well. Add hot cooked rice; mix well; serve.   *8 to 10 servings.*

Preparation and Cooking Time: 1 Hour

Treasure Tip: *Simmer rice in a heavy pan, so that the rice at the bottom doesn't scorch. Rice can be kept warm in a low oven or in a colander, over hot water, covered.*

Florida Orange Rice

2 tablespoons butter or margarine,
   melted
2 tablespoons onion, chopped
½ teaspoon orange rind, grated
½ cup fresh orange juice
1 teaspoon salt
⅛ teaspoon dried whole marjoram
⅛ teaspoon dried whole thyme
1 cup long-grain rice

Heat butter in large saucepan; sauté onion until tender. Add 2 cups water, orange rind and juice, salt, marjoram and thyme; bring to boil. Add rice; stir well. Cover; bring to boil; simmer until rice is tender and liquid is absorbed, about 20 minutes.

4 to 6 servings.

Preparation Time: 10 Minutes   ***Cooking Time: 25 to 30 Minutes***

Savory Beer Rice

½ stick butter or margarine, melted
½ cup onion, chopped
½ cup green bell pepper, chopped
   (for more color, use ¼ cup
   yellow and ¼ cup red bell
   pepper)
2 cups chicken stock (or 2 chicken
   bouillon cubes dissolved in 2
   cups boiling water)
1 cup long-grain rice
¾ cup beer
½ teaspoon salt
¼ teaspoon pepper (more to taste)
¼ teaspoon ground thyme or
   marjoram

Heat butter in deep saucepan; sauté onion and green pepper until tender but not brown. Add chicken stock or bouillon. Stir in rice, beer, salt, pepper and thyme. Bring to boil; cover. Reduce heat; simmer until all liquid is absorbed, 30 to 35 minutes.

4 servings.

Preparation Time: 10 Minutes   ***Cooking Time: 30 to 35 Minutes***

Treasure Tip: *To add interest to your table, try serving your rice in pretty molded shapes. Generously butter the sides and bottom of your mold. Spoon in the rice, pressing gently to eliminate air pockets. Let stand for about 5 minutes; carefully invert onto a serving platter or individual plates.*

Bloody Mary Rice

6 ounces Bloody Mary mix
2 to 3 dashes Tabasco
2 strips bacon, cooked and
   crumbled
3 tablespoons butter or margarine
½ teaspoon fresh garlic, chopped
   (not garlic salt)
¼ cup onion, chopped
1 stalk celery, chopped
½ cup long-grain rice

In medium saucepan combine Bloody Mary mix, ½ cup water, Tabasco, crumbled bacon, butter, garlic, onion and celery; bring to boil. Add rice; reduce heat to simmer; cover tightly. Simmer until rice is tender and liquid is absorbed, about 25 minutes.

3 to 4 servings

Preparation Time: 20 Minutes   ***Cooking Time: 30 Minutes***

Treasure Tip: *For an easy entrée, double the recipe and add 1 pound medium fresh shrimp, cooked.*

Fiesta Rice

1/3 cup olive oil
1 onion, chopped
1 clove garlic, minced
1 cup long-grain rice
1 teaspoon salt
1 teaspoon black pepper
1 tablespoon chili powder
1 (4-ounce) can sliced mushrooms
1 to 2 Spanish chorizos, sliced
   (Spanish sausage)
1 1/2 cups chicken broth

Preheat oven to 350° F. Heat oil in deep saucepan; sauté onion and garlic until tender. Add rice, salt, pepper, chili powder, mushrooms and chorizos; cook, stirring, until rice is lightly browned. Add chicken broth. Pour mixture into casserole with tight-fitting cover; cover; bake until rice is tender and liquid is absorbed, about 45 minutes. Serve with Mexican foods.

6 servings.

Preparation Time: 20 Minutes   *Cooking Time: 45 Minutes*

Southern Pecan Rice

1 cup celery, sliced
3/4 cup whole green onions, sliced
3/4 cup bell green pepper, chopped
   (optional)
2 3/4 cups chicken broth
1 teaspoon poultry seasoning
1/2 teaspoon salt
1/8 teaspoon pepper
1 1/2 cups long-grain rice
1/4 cup pecans, chopped and toasted

Preheat oven to 350° F. Lightly grease a large nonstick skillet. place over medium-high heat until hot. Add celery, green onions and green bell pepper; sauté until crisp-tender. Stir in broth, poultry seasoning, salt and pepper; bring to boil. Spoon rice into shallow 2-quart baking dish; add hot broth mixture. Cover; bake until rice is tender and liquid is absorbed, about 30 minutes. To serve, sprinkle with pecans.   *6 to 8 servings.*

Preparation Time: 20 Minutes   *Cooking Time: 30 Minutes*

VEGETABLES & FRUITS

Balloning Over Citrus Groves

The pristine stillness of the early morning sweeps by as brilliantly colored hot air balloons float silently over our next treasure, local agriculture. Hillsborough County's pastures, fields and groves provide pastoral vistas for balloon enthusiasts as well as a bountiful harvest for one and all.

Area groves produce a wide variety of citrus from grapefruit, tangelos and tangerines to navel, temple, valencia and hamlin oranges. No sangria would be complete without the zest of lemons and limes. Several of Florida's native lemon trees bear a fruit so large that the juice of just one will make a pie.

Plant City, our neighbor to the east, is famous for its luscious strawberries and the annual Strawberry Festival. Thousands of fairgoers line up for fabulous fresh strawberry desserts. During February and March, we can stop at roadside stands all over the county and pick or buy flats of glorious fresh berries.

Ruskin, just to the south, is renowned for tomatoes and Florida sweet onions. A short drive takes us to fields where we can pick tomatoes, green peppers, sweet corn, field peas, squash and other fresh delights. While many farmers raise traditional livestock, hundreds of acres are devoted to exotic tropical fish, ornamental plant and tree nurseries.

Most homes have at least one citrus tree in the yard and many have avocado, mango, banana, papaya or guava trees. With a year-round growing season, fresh produce is always in abundance. This section contains new recipes for many local favorites, including the black beans that are a staple of our Spanish restaurants. The menu highlights a Zucchini and Ham Frittata which is appealing to the eye as well as the palate and a Fruit Salad with Honey Lime Dressing. Sweet Raisin Bread is delicious when lavishly spread with the Strawberry Festival Butter.

The Ballooning photograph was underwritten by
Jean Ann Cone
Julianne Cone McKeel

VEGETABLES & FRUITS

POST-FLIGHT BREAKFAST

Zucchini-Ham Frittata

Elegant Rolled Spinach

Fruit Salad with Honey Lime Dressing

Sweet Raisin Bread

Strawberry Festival Butter

Fresh Fruit Pizza

**The menu photograph was underwritten by
Frances Protiva Kruse**

Zucchini-Ham Frittata

3 tablespoons vegetable oil
¾ cup green pepper, chopped
1½ cups fresh mushrooms, sliced
1½ cups zucchini, chopped
¾ cup onion, chopped
1 cup cooked ham, cubed
6 eggs, beaten
¼ cup half-and-half
8 ounces cream cheese, diced small
1½ cups cheddar cheese, shredded
2 cups fresh bread cubes
1 clove garlic, minced
1 teaspoon salt
¼ teaspoon pepper

Preheat oven to 350° F. Heat oil in large skillet over medium-low heat; sauté green pepper, mushrooms, zucchini, onion and ham until zucchini is crisp-tender, about 10 minutes. Cool slightly. Beat eggs with half-and-half; add vegetable mixture and remaining ingredients. Mix well; pour into well-greased 10-inch springform pan. Bake until center is set, about 1 hour. Cool 10 minutes before cutting. *8 servings.*

Preparation Time: 25 Minutes   *Cooking Time: 1 Hour 15 Minutes*

Treasure Tip: This colorful frittata is a wonderful way to use leftover ham and makes a superb brunch dish!

Elegant Rolled Spinach

Duxelles mixture

1 stick butter
1 pound mushroom caps, finely chopped
¼ cup shallots, finely chopped
1 teaspoon freshly ground pepper
1 garlic clove, minced
Juice of 1 lemon

Spinach Mixture

Vegetable oil
Bread crumbs
¼ cup Parmesan cheese, freshly grated
4 (10-ounce) packages frozen chopped spinach, cooked and squeezed dry
¾ stick butter, melted
1 teaspoon salt
Dash nutmeg
4 egg yolks, slightly beaten
4 egg whites, beaten stiff but not dry
8 ounces sour cream
Chopped red pepper (garnish)
Chopped onion (garnish)

Make duxelles: Melt butter in skillet; brown mushrooms and shallots over medium-high heat, stirring frequently, until liquid is absorbed. Add garlic and lemon juice; mix; set aside.

Preheat oven to 350° F. Brush cookie sheet with oil, line with heavy-duty foil; coat foil well with vegetable cooking spray. Sprinkle with bread crumbs, then Parmesan. Mix spinach, melted butter, salt, nutmeg and egg yolks; carefully fold in egg whites. Spread spinach mixture over bread crumbs; bake 12 to 15 minutes.

Spread with sour cream and duxelles; roll lengthwise; place on platter. If desired, garnish with chopped red pepper and onions; serve. *8 servings.*

Preparation Time: 30 Minutes   *Cooking Time: 12 to 15 Minutes*

Fruit Salad with Honey-Lime Dressing

1 head romaine lettuce, torn into pieces
1½ cups fresh pineapple chunks, or 1 (20-ounce) can pineapple chunks, drained
1 large Florida orange, peeled, sectioned, cut in chunks, or 1 (11-ounce) can mandarin oranges, drained
1 red apple, unpeeled, chopped
¼ cup raisins
¾ cup mayonnaise
¼ cup fresh lime juice
¼ cup honey
¾ teaspoon poppy seeds
Sliced almonds, toasted (optional)

Divide lettuce among four or six individual salad plates. Top with pineapple chunks, oranges, apple and raisins. Combine mayonnaise, lime juice, honey and poppy seeds in bowl; stir to blend. Drizzle dressing over salads; top with almonds, if desired. Serve remaining dressing separately.   **4 to 6 servings.**

Preparation Time: 20 Minutes

Treasure Tip: *This light, cool, pretty salad makes a marvelous summer luncheon entree. Serve with fruit muffins, sherbet and cookies.*

Sweet Raisin Bread

1½ cups golden raisins
Sherry or cognac
½ teaspoon mace
2 teaspoons fresh orange rind, grated
1 package dry yeast
2 cups warm milk, divided
⅓ cup sugar
1 tablespoon salt
3 tablespoons butter, softened
5 to 6 cups flour, divided
Melted butter
1 egg yolk, beaten with 2 tablespoons cream

Night before: Put raisins in bowl; pour sherry or cognac over them to cover; let soak and plump overnight.

When ready to make bread: Add mace and orange rind to raisins; set aside. Dissolve yeast in ¼ cup milk. In large bowl combine remaining milk, sugar, salt and softened butter. Add yeast; gradually beat in 3 cups flour; beat well. With hands or heavy wooden spoon, gradually stir in enough flour to make stiff dough. Turn out on floured surface; knead until smooth, elastic and glossy, about 10 minutes. Place in buttered bowl; turn well to coat all sides. Cover; allow to rise in warm place until doubled in bulk, about 2½ hours.

Punch dough down; knead 3 minutes. Return to bowl; let rise 30 minutes. Divide dough into two parts; roll each into rectangle, about 20 x 7 inches. Brush each with melted butter; sprinkle with raisin mixture. Roll dough tightly into two loaves, turning in ends slightly as you roll. Place in well-buttered 8½ x 4½-inch loaf pans. Cover pans; let loaves rise in warm place until dough fills pans and extends above pan tops. Brush with egg yolk and cream. Preheat oven to 400°F. Bake 20 minutes; reduce heat to 350° F. Continue baking until loaves sound hollow when tapped with knuckles, 20 to 30 minutes more. Remove loaves from pans; return to oven briefly, if desired, to brown bottom crust.

Makes 2 loaves, 8 to 10 servings each.

Preparation Time: 3 Hours 30 Minutes   **Cooking Time: 40 to 50 Minutes**

Strawberry Festival Butter

1 pint fresh strawberries, washed
   and stemmed
2 sticks unsalted butter, softened
1 cup powdered sugar

Place all ingredients in food processor or blender; blend until smooth, pink and creamy. Serve on raisin bread, toast or hot rolls. **Makes 2½ cups.**

Preparation Time: 5 Minutes

Fresh Fruit Pizza

1 (20-ounce) roll refrigerated sugar
   cookie dough
8 ounces cream cheese, softened
⅓ cup granulated sugar
1 teaspoon vanilla extract
Assorted colorful fresh fruit
   (strawberries, kiwi, peaches,
   blueberries, etc.)
1 (10-ounce) jar peach or apricot
   jelly

Early in day: Preheat oven to 350° F. Lightly grease round pizza pan or jelly roll pan. Cut cookie dough into ⅛-inch slices; seal dough edges together to make crust (dough expands when baked, so leave a little space at edge of pan, unless pan has sides). Bake until light brown, 10 to 12 minutes; cool.

In bowl combine cream cheese, sugar and vanilla; mix until smooth. Spread over cooled crust. Arrange fruit in decorative pattern on top of cream cheese mixture. Heat jelly until slightly runny. Carefully spoon over fruit to glaze. Refrigerate until ready to serve. Variation: Add ½ teaspoon of your favorite liqueur to cream cheese. **10 to 12 servings.**

Preparation Time: 25 Minutes   Cooking Time: 10 to 12 Minutes

Tiny Roman-Style Artichokes

12 baby artichokes (the smaller, the better)
Juice of 1 fresh lemon
¼ cup olive oil
2 medium onions, coarsely chopped
1 clove garlic, chopped
½ teaspoon dried basil
½ teaspoon marjoram
1 cup chicken broth
Salt and pepper to taste

Trim artichokes; halve lengthwise. Place artichokes and lemon juice in cold water to cover; let stand 10 minutes; drain well. Heat oil in heavy skillet; sauté artichokes and onion gently until golden. Add remaining ingredients. Cover; bring to boil over high heat. Reduce heat to low; simmer gently until tender, about 15 minutes. Season to taste. **4 to 6 servings.**

Preparation Time: 15 Minutes   **Cooking Time: 25 Minutes**

Treasure Tip: *Good fresh artichokes are bright green and somewhat silky, with tightly packed leaves. Very fresh baby artichokes, which may be eaten raw, are pretty on a crûdité platter.*

Artichoke Spinach Bake

1 (8½-ounce) can artichoke hearts, drained
2 (10-ounce) packages frozen chopped spinach, thawed and squeezed dry
8 ounces cream cheese
1 stick butter or margarine
8 slices bacon, cooked, drained and crumbled
Parmesan cheese, freshly grated
Slivered almonds or pecans, toasted (garnish)

Preheat oven to 350° F. Cut artichokes into quarters; place in large bowl; add spinach. Melt butter and cream cheese together in small saucepan (cream cheese will be lumpy). Mix with vegetables; spoon into 8 x 8-inch baking dish. Sprinkle bacon on top; sprinkle lavishly with Parmesan. Top with almonds or pecans, if desired. Bake until bubbly, about 30 minutes.

4 to 6 servings.

Preparation Time: 20 Minutes   **Cooking Time: 30 Minutes**

Horseradish-Sour Cream Asparagus

32 fresh asparagus spears
1½ cups sour cream
1 teaspoon garlic salt
1½ tablespoons horseradish
1½ tablespoons butter
¾ cup dry bread crumbs

Steam asparagus until crisp and tender, about 10 minutes; place in 9 x 13 x 2-inch baking dish. Mix sour cream, garlic salt and horseradish; spread over asparagus. Melt butter; add bread crumbs; sprinkle over asparagus. Broil until bread crumbs are browned. **8 servings.**

Preparation Time: 10 Minutes   Cooking Time: 20 to 25 Minutes

Green Beans Almandine

1 to 1½ pounds fresh green beans,
    trimmed
2 tablespoons butter or margarine
1 medium celery stalk, sliced
¼ cup slivered almonds
½ pound small, fresh mushrooms
Salt and pepper to taste

Cook beans 15 to 20 minutes, to desired tenderness; drain well. Melt butter in medium saucepan over medium heat; sauté celery, almonds and mushrooms until celery is tender and almonds and mushrooms are lightly browned, about 10 minutes. Add beans, salt and pepper; toss lightly. Heat through; serve. **4 to 6 servings.**

Preparation Time: 10 Minutes   *Cooking Time: 25 to 35 Minutes*

Fresh Green Beans Vinaigrette

2 pounds fresh green beans
6 whole green onions, chopped
1 clove garlic, minced
⅓ cup vegetable oil
3 tablespoons fresh lemon juice
1 teaspoon salt
1 teaspoon sugar
1 teaspoon dry mustard
¼ teaspoon dried basil
¼ teaspoon oregano
¼ teaspoon marjoram
¼ teaspoon pepper

Trim ends of beans; leave whole. Steam until crisp-tender, about 10 minutes. Meanwhile, to make dressing: Place green onions and all remaining ingredients in jar with tight-fitting lid; shake to mix thoroughly. Drain cooked beans; pour dressing over; serve. To serve cold, plunge cooked beans immediately into cold water; drain. Pour dressing over; cover; chill at least 2 hours, stirring several times. **6 to 8 servings.**

Preparation Time: 30 Minutes   *Cooking Time: 10 Minutes*

Treasure Tip: When buying green beans, look for the smallest and freshest ones of uniform size. Snap one to check its freshness.

Black Beans

Traditional Tampa dish from the Valencia Garden Restaurant

1 pound dried black beans
¼ cup olive oil
1 large onion, chopped
3 green peppers, chopped
1 clove garlic, minced
¼ ham bone (from cooked ham)
3 bay leaves
Salt to taste
1 ounce salt pork, chopped
½ cup wine vinegar
Additional oil, vinegar and
　chopped onion (garnish)

Night before: Wash and pick over beans; cover with 2 cups water; soak overnight.

When ready to cook: Leave beans in soaking water. Heat olive oil in skillet; sauté onion, green pepper and garlic lightly. Add to beans and liquid with ham bone, bay leaves, salt and salt pork. Bring to boil; reduce heat; simmer until beans are tender and liquid is thick, 2 to 2½ hours, adding vinegar about 5 minutes before serving. Serve over white rice. Place bowl of chopped onion and cruets of oil and vinegar on table for guests to add to beans, if desired. **6 servings.**

Preparation Time: 15 Minutes

Cooking Time: 2 Hours 30 Minutes

Black Beans with Rum Sauce

1 pound dried black beans
1 medium onion, sliced
1 bay leaf
¼ teaspoon thyme leaves
1 celery stalk, chopped
¼ pound salt pork, cubed
Salt to taste
1 teaspoon butter or margarine
1 teaspoon flour
Dash Tabasco
1 teaspoon salt
¼ cup dark rum

Night before: Place beans in pot; cover with water; refrigerate overnight.

About 3½ hours before serving: Rinse beans; place in 6-quart saucepan with 5 cups cold water. Add onion, bay leaf, thyme, celery and salt pork. Bring to boil; reduce heat; simmer, stirring occasionally, until beans are tender, 2 to 2½ hours. Taste beans; add salt if necessary. Drain; reserve 2 cups cooking liquid. Place beans in 2-quart casserole. Preheat oven to 350° F.

Make sauce: Melt butter in small saucepan; remove from heat; stir in flour, Tabasco, salt and reserved bean liquid. Return to heat; cook over low heat until bubbly. Stir in rum; pour over beans in casserole; stir to mix. Bake, uncovered, 25 to 30 minutes. If desired, top with sour cream. **10 to 12 servings.**

Preparation Time: 10 Minutes

Cooking Time: 3 Hours

Snow-Capped Broccoli Spears

1 large bunch fresh broccoli,
   trimmed, cut into spears
1 tablespoon butter, melted
2 egg whites
¼ teaspoon salt
¼ cup mayonnaise
Parmesan cheese, freshly grated

Cook broccoli until tender; drain well. Preheat oven to 350 ° F. Arrange broccoli in 9-inch pie pan with ends toward center; brush with melted butter. Combine egg whites and salt in small bowl of electric mixer; beat until stiff peaks form; fold in mayonnaise. Spoon mixture onto center of broccoli; sprinkle generously with cheese. Bake until egg mixture is golden brown, 12 to 15 minutes. Watch closely so that the top does not burn.   *6 servings.*

Preparation Time: 25 Minutes   Cooking Time: 15 to 20 Minutes

Bayshore Broccoli Soufflé

2 tablespoons butter
2 tablespoons onion, minced
2 tablespoons flour
½ teaspoon salt
½ cup milk
⅓ cup Parmesan cheese, freshly
   grated
4 eggs, separated
1½ cups fresh broccoli, chopped
   and cooked

Preheat oven to 350° F. Melt butter in large saucepan; sauté onion until tender. Whisk in flour and salt; cook, stirring, over medium heat about 3 minutes. Add milk; whisk until thick and bubbly. Remove from heat; stir in cheese. Beat egg yolks; stir small amount of sauce into eggs. Add egg mixture to remaining sauce, mixing well; stir in broccoli. Beat egg whites until stiff; fold into sauce mixture. Grease 1-quart casserole or soufflé dish; pour in broccoli mixture. Bake, uncovered, until knife inserted in center comes out clean, about 35 minutes. Serve immediately.
4 servings.

Preparation Time: 30 Minutes   Cooking Time: 35 Minutes

Sweet Red Cabbage

1 head fresh red cabbage, cored and
   sliced thin
½ cup orange marmalade
2 Granny Smith apples, peeled and
   sliced
2 pears, peeled and sliced
1 teaspoon cinnamon
¼ teaspoon ground cardamom
½ teaspoon ground cloves
3 tablespoons red wine vinegar
3 tablespoons Aji Mirin (sweet rice
   cooking wine)

In large stockpot combine all ingredients with 1 cup water; bring to boil. Cover; reduce heat to moderately low. Cook, stirring occasionally, until all liquid is absorbed, about 2½ hours. Serve immediately, or refrigerate and serve chilled.

About 30 servings.

Preparation Time: 30 Minutes

Cooking Time: 2 Hours 30 Minutes

Treasure Tip: Sweet red cabbage is a wonderful accompaniment to cold sliced meats on a buffet.

Horseradish Carrots

2 pounds fresh carrots, peeled and
   sliced
½ cup mayonnaise
2 tablespoons fresh onion, minced
1½ tablespoons prepared
   horseradish (or to taste)
Salt and pepper to taste
½ cup Saltine crackers, finely
   crushed
2 tablespoons butter or margarine
Fresh parsley, chopped
Paprika

Place carrots in enough salted water to cover; cook until crisp-tender, check after 10 minutes. Drain, reserving ¼ cup liquid. Preheat oven to 325° F. Place carrots in baking dish. Combine reserved liquid, mayonnaise, onion, horseradish, salt and pepper; pour over carrots. Sprinkle cracker crumbs on top; dot with butter; sprinkle with parsley and paprika. Bake until heated through, about 20 minutes. **8 to 10 servings.**

Preparation Time: 20 Minutes

Cooking Time: 20 Minutes

Chilled Marinated Carrots

2 pounds carrots, peeled and sliced
1 medium Florida sweet onion,
   chopped
1 small green pepper, chopped
½ cup vegetable oil
1 cup sugar
¾ cup cider vinegar
1 teaspoon Dijon mustard
1 teaspoon Worcestershire sauce

At least 12 hours before serving: Cook carrots until crisp-tender, 5 to 10 minutes; drain. While carrots are hot, add onion; keep covered. Combine remaining ingredients; pour over carrots and onions. Chill at least 12 hours, stirring occasionally.

10 to 12 servings.

Preparation Time: 15 Minutes

Cooking Time: 5 to 10 Minutes

Treasure Tip: This is a good dish for buffets or cookouts.

Baked Cauliflower Au Gratin

1 head fresh cauliflower
1 (3-ounce) jar marinated
    artichokes, drained
3/4 cup milk
1 cup sharp cheddar cheese, grated
1 cup Velveeta cheese, cubed
1 teaspoon garlic powder
Salt and pepper to taste

Preheat oven to 350°F. Cut cauliflower into florets; cook in water or steam until tender, about 10 minutes; drain. To make cheese sauce: Combine milk, cheeses, garlic powder, salt and pepper in microwave-safe bowl; microwave at 50% power 2 to 3 minutes. Check and stir; continue microwaving until cheese melts completely. Combine cauliflower with artichokes in casserole dish and pour cheese sauce over it; bake 30 minutes. This sauce can be used on baked potatoes and other vegetables, or anything that is complemented by a cheese sauce.

6 to 8 servings.

Preparation Time: 20 Minutes   *Cooking Time: 30 Minutes*

Minted Grilled Corn

6 ears fresh corn, husks and silks
    intact
6 tablespoons unsalted butter, cut
    into 12 equal pieces
6 sprigs fresh mint

1¼ hours before cooking: Soak corn in husks in large pot of salted water 1 hour; drain. Carefully peel husks back, without detaching at bottom; remove silk. Place 2 pieces butter and 1 sprig mint on each ear of corn; completely enclose with husks.

When ready to cook: Grill corn over moderately hot coals, turning frequently, until tender, 10 to 15 minutes.   *6 servings.*

Preparation Time: 1 Hour 15 Minutes   *Cooking Time: 10 to 15 Minutes*

Treasure Tip: This dish is excellent with grilled lamb!

Italian Eggplant Casserole

12 small, or 4 large, eggplants
Salt
12 ripe plum tomatoes or 6 large
  tomatoes
4 large cloves garlic, peeled and
  slivered
2 bunches fresh basil, stems
  removed, divided
¾ cup olive oil, divided
Black pepper, coarse ground to
  taste
Salt to taste
2 tablespoons fresh lemon juice,
  divided
1 cup Parmesan cheese, freshly
  grated, divided
6 tablespoons fresh thyme leaves or
  1½ tablespoons dried thyme,
  divided
¼ cup fresh parsley, coarsely
  chopped, divided

Cut off eggplant stems; halve eggplants lengthwise. Sprinkle with salt; place on paper towels for 30 minutes. (Moisture will come to eggplant surface.) Pat dry. Cut tomatoes into ½-inch slices; sprinkle with salt; place on paper towels. Pat dry.

Preheat oven to 425° F. Make lengthwise 2-inch slit in cut side of each eggplant half; insert garlic slivers and 1 basil leaf in each slit; push in well. Place eggplant on baking sheet, skin sides down. Drizzle with ¼ cup olive oil; sprinkle with pepper. Cover tightly with foil; bake 20 minutes. Remove from oven; reduce temperature to 350° F.

Layer half of eggplants and tomatoes in baking dish; drizzle with 1 tablespoon lemon juice, salt and pepper. Cover with ½ cup Parmesan and half of thyme. Cover with whole basil leaves; drizzle 2 tablespoons olive oil over top. Repeat layers; sprinkle top with 2 tablespoons parsley. Cover tightly with foil; bake 1 hour. Remove foil; bake until tender, about 10 minutes more. Garnish with remaining parsley. *8 servings.*

Preparation Time: 45 Minutes

*Cooking Time: 1 Hour
30 Minutes*

Luscious Leeks

4 large leeks
2 tablespoons butter
½ cup whipping cream
⅓ cup chicken broth
Freshly grated nutmeg to taste
Salt and white pepper to taste

Cut whole leeks into ½-inch slices; separate slices; soak in cold water 30 minutes; drain. In large skillet melt butter until foam begins to subside. Add leeks; stir to coat with butter. Add cream and broth; bring to boil. Stir; reduce heat to moderate. Cook, stirring occasionally, until thickened, 10 to 15 minutes. Season with nutmeg, pepper and salt; serve. *6 to 8 servings.*

Preparation Time: 40 Minutes

Cooking Time: 20 Minutes

Sautéed Onions and Mushrooms

2 large onions, sliced
1 pound whole fresh mushrooms
2 tablespoons butter or margarine
Soy sauce to taste
Garlic powder to taste
Italian seasoning to taste
Pepper and seasoned salt to taste
Sherry to taste (optional)

Cut each onion slice in half. Place mushrooms on cutting board, cap side down; cut into quarters through stems. Heat large skillet over high heat; add butter and onion; sauté quickly until onions are soft. Add mushrooms; add all other ingredients to taste. Stir quickly over high heat. Cook until done, about 3 minutes. Serve immediately. *4 to 6 servings.*

Preparation Time: 10 Minutes   **Cooking Time: 5 Minutes**

Treasure Tip: *When cleaning mushrooms, do not soak them in water. Just wipe them well with a damp cloth or paper towel.*

Curried Mushroom Strudel

2 tablespoons butter
1¼ pounds fresh mushrooms, minced
1 teaspoon salt
¼ teaspoon pepper
1 tablespoon curry powder
1 tablespoon white wine
2 tablespoons onions, finely chopped
¾ cup plus 2 tablespoons bread crumbs, divided
1 cup sour cream
1 (1-pound) box frozen strudel or phyllo dough
1 stick melted butter

Make filling: Melt 2 tablespoons butter in large skillet; sauté mushrooms, salt, pepper, curry powder, wine, onions and 2 tablespoons bread crumbs until mushrooms and onions wilt, about 15 minutes. Set aside; cool, then add ½ tablespoon bread crumbs and sour cream.

Preheat oven to 375° F. Spread dough on cool, damp cloth; unwrap carefully; keep covered with damp cloth. Lay out one layer; brush with melted butter; sprinkle with bread crumbs. Repeat until you have four or five layers. Spoon half of mushroom mixture into center; turn in sides about 1 inch; roll up. Brush with butter; repeat procedure.

Place on greased baking sheet; bake 25 to 30 minutes. Strudels can be frozen before baking. Do not thaw; bake frozen strudels 35 to 40 minutes at 375° F. *16 servings.*

Preparation Time: 30 to 45 Minutes   **Cooking Time: 25 to 30 Minutes**

Sherry-Glazed Onion Bake

5 medium Florida sweet onions,
  sliced (5 cups)
½ teaspoon honey (or more to
  taste)
¼ cup sherry, Marsala or Madeira
2 tablespoons butter, melted
Pinch salt
1 tablespoon fresh parsley, minced
¼ cup Parmesan cheese, freshly
  grated

Preheat oven to 350° F. Place onions in 2-quart casserole or baking dish. Mix honey, sherry, butter and salt; slowly pour over onions. Bake, covered, 25 minutes. Remove from oven; sprinkle with parsley and Parmesan. Bake, uncovered, 15 minutes more, until top browns and crisps.   **6 servings.**

Preparation Time: 10 minutes   **Cooking Time: 40 Minutes**

Harvest Stuffed Potatoes

4 large baking potatoes
1 cup raw carrots, grated
¼ cup fresh parsley, chopped (or 1
  teaspoon dried)
¼ cup whole green onions, minced
½ teaspoon prepared horseradish
  (or more to taste)
⅔ cup plain yogurt or sour cream
½ to 1 stick butter, melted
Salt and pepper to taste
Parmesan or cheddar cheese,
  freshly grated
Paprika

Preheat oven to 400° F. Scrub potatoes; bake 1 hour; reduce oven temperature to 350° F. Cut potatoes in half lengthwise. Without breaking skin, carefully scoop out as much pulp as possible. Place pulp in large bowl of electric mixer; add carrots, parsley, green onions, horseradish, yogurt and butter; whip until smooth and creamy. Season with salt and pepper. Fill potato skins with mixture; top with cheese and paprika. Bake until heated through, 10 to 15 minutes.   **8 servings.**

Preparation Time: 15 Minutes   **Cooking Time: 1 Hour
                                                  15 Minutes**

Treasure Tip: *For a crispy potato skin, rub lightly with olive oil before baking.*

Herb-Roasted Potatoes

18 new potatoes, cleaned, peels on,
  cut in quarters
⅓ cup extra-virgin olive oil
1 clove garlic, sliced thin
1 sprig fresh rosemary, chopped
1 sprig fresh thyme, chopped
Salt and pepper to taste

Preheat oven to 475° F. Place potatoes in baking dish; sprinkle with olive oil, rosemary, thyme, salt and pepper. Bake until tender, about 30 minutes.   **6 to 8 servings.**

Preparation Time: 10 Minutes   **Cooking Time: 30 Minutes**

Spinach-Cheese Timbales

½ stick butter or margarine
¼ cup flour
1 cup milk
1 teaspoon salt
¼ teaspoon black pepper
½ teaspoon nutmeg
2 (10-ounce) packages frozen
  chopped spinach, cooked,
  drained, squeezed dry
5 eggs, beaten
1 medium onion, grated
1 cup sharp cheddar cheese, grated
10 slices bread
Olive or vegetable oil
Mayonnaise (optional)
Tomato slices
Hollandaise sauce*
Paprika

*Use traditional sauce or make
Blender Hollandaise Sauce
from recipe on Page 123

Preheat oven to 350° F. Grease eight to ten individual 8-ounce salad molds or ramekins; set aside. Over medium heat, melt butter in large saucepan; add flour; whisk to combine. Stir in milk, salt, pepper and nutmeg; cook, whisking, until smooth and very thick. Cool 10 minutes.

Add spinach, eggs, onion and cheese. Mix well; pour into greased molds. Place molds in baking dish; add enough water to baking dish to come halfway up sides of molds. Cover pan with foil; bake until mixture is firm, 35 to 40 minutes.

Cut large rounds from bread. Heat about 2 tablespoons oil in skillet; fry bread rounds until lightly browned. Remove; drain; cool. Spread mayonnaise, if desired, on toast. Add 1 slice tomato to each piece of toast; turn out spinach mold on top. Top with Hollandaise; add dash of paprika; serve.   *8 to 10 servings.*

Preparation Time: 30 Minutes   Cooking Time: 35 to 40 Minutes

Spinach-Topped Tomatoes

2 (10-ounce) packages frozen
  chopped spinach, cooked,
  drained, squeezed dry
6 whole green onions, chopped
⅓ cup melted butter
¾ cup bread crumbs
3 eggs, beaten
½ cup Parmesan cheese, freshly
  grated
½ teaspoon thyme
1 teaspoon black pepper
¼ teaspoon cayenne pepper
  (optional)
8 slices ripe tomato

Preheat oven to 350° F. In large skillet, sauté spinach and onions in butter until onion is tender, 5 to 10 minutes. Remove from heat; add all other ingredients except tomatoes; mix thoroughly. Arrange tomatoes in buttered baking dish; top with mounds of spinach mixture. Bake until heated through, 15 to 20 minutes.

8 servings.

Preparation Time: 20 Minutes   Cooking Time: 20 Minutes

Treasure Tip: Serve this colorful vegetable dish as part of a holiday meal.

Ratatouille-Stuffed Zucchini

3 zucchini squash
1 yellow squash
1 whole red bell pepper
1 onion, thickly sliced
½ eggplant, cut lengthwise
4 fresh mushrooms, quartered
1 fresh tomato, sliced thick
Olive oil
1 clove garlic, chopped
1 tablespoon fresh basil, chopped
½ tablespoon fresh oregano,
    chopped
Salt and pepper to taste
Parmesan cheese, freshly grated

Start grill. Cut 2 zucchini in half lengthwise; hollow out; set aside. Cut yellow squash and remaining zucchini in half, lengthwise. Rub these squash halves, red bell pepper, onion slices, eggplant, mushrooms and tomato slices with olive oil; place on barbecue grill over hot coals. When grill marks are visible, turn vegetables; cook until grill marks appear on the other side. Remove; set aside.

Preheat oven to 400° F. Cut grilled vegetables into smaller pieces; add garlic, basil, oregano, 2 tablespoons oil, salt and pepper; toss to combine. Place vegetable mixture in reserved zucchini shells; sprinkle with cheese, if desired. Bake 15 minutes; serve immediately.   **2 to 4 servings.**

Preparation Time: 15 Minutes   **Cooking Time: 30 Minutes**

Treasure Tip: When grilling vegetables outdoors, make sure the grill rack is oiled and very clean. For delicious flavor, leave vegetables un-peeled. Slice larger ones to shorten cooking time. Since vegetables have no natural fat, always brush them with oil before grilling.

Southern Squash Puppies

5 medium yellow squash, trimmed
    and sliced
Salt and pepper to taste
1 egg, beaten
½ cup buttermilk
1 medium onion, chopped
¾ cup self-rising cornmeal
¼ cup flour
Vegetable oil

Place squash in covered pan; add ¼ cup water. Cook over medium heat until tender, about 20 minutes. Drain well; mash; drain again. Blend squash and remaining ingredients. Drop batter by scant tablespoons into hot oil (350° F.); brown on both sides until golden.   **4 to 6 servings.**

Preparation Time: 10 Minutes   **Cooking Time: 50 Minutes**

Treasure Tip: Since squash contains a lot of moisture, cook it in a small amount of water and drain it very well after cooking. When it will be cooked again, as in a casserole, cook it early and drain for an hour or so in a colander to extract all of the water.

Crunchy Peanut Sweet Potatoes

4 cups sweet potatoes, mashed
   (cooked or canned)
2½ cups granulated sugar
¼ cup creamy peanut butter
2 cups milk
4 eggs, slightly beaten
2 sticks butter, divided (soften 1
   stick)
1 teaspoon nutmeg
1 teaspoon cinnamon
1½ cup corn flakes, crushed
1 cup brown sugar, firmly packed
1 cup Spanish peanuts, chopped

Preheat oven to 400° F. Place mashed sweet potatoes in large bowl. Mix granulated sugar with peanut butter; add to sweet potatoes with milk, eggs, softened butter, nutmeg and cinnamon; mix well. Pour into two greased casseroles; bake 20 minutes.

While potatoes bake, make topping: Melt remaining butter; combine with corn flakes, brown sugar and peanuts. Spread over potatoes; bake 10 minutes more. **8 to 10 servings.**

Preparation Time: 10 to 15 Minutes   *Cooking Time: 30 Minutes*

Treasure Tip: *Baked sweet potatoes are an excellent accompaniment to pork or ham. Bake them just like white potatoes in a regular or microwave oven or on the grill.*

Ybor City Vegetable Paella

⅓ cup (or more) olive or vegetable
   oil
1 medium onion, diced
2 small zucchini squash (about 6
   ounces each), cut in bite-size
   pieces
½ pound medium mushrooms, cut
   in half or quartered
1 eggplant (about 1 pound), cut in
   half lengthwise, each half cut
   crosswise into ½-inch thick
   slices
2 medium-sized fresh tomatoes, cut
   in ¾-inch pieces
3 (14½-ounce) cans chicken broth
1 (16-ounce) package converted
   rice
1 (10-ounce) package frozen
   artichoke hearts, thawed
¾ teaspoon salt
½ teaspoon saffron threads,
   crushed (optional)
¼ teaspoon pepper
1 (16-ounce) can garbanzo beans,
   drained
1 (3-ounce) jar pimento-stuffed
   olives, drained
1 (10-ounce) package frozen peas
   (do not thaw)

About 1½ hours before serving: Preheat oven to 350° F. Heat oil in a 4 quart oven-proof saucepan over medium-high heat; cook onion until tender. Add zucchini and mushrooms; cook, stirring occasionally, until vegetables are golden brown. Add eggplant and 1 tablespoon oil, if needed; cook, stirring frequently, until eggplant is crisp-tender. Stir in tomatoes, broth, rice, artichoke hearts, salt, saffron and pepper; heat to boiling over high heat.

Place saucepan in oven; bake, uncovered, until rice is tender and liquid is absorbed, about 50 minutes. Remove from oven; stir in garbanzos, olives and frozen peas. Return to oven and heat through, about 15 minutes. **8 main-dish servings.**

Preparation Time: 25 Minutes   *Cooking Time: 1 Hour*
*   30 Minutes*

Treasure Tip: *This Spanish-style recipe, with its excellent blend of flavors, is perfect for a meatless main dish.*

Fresh Dill Tomatoes and Barley

1 teaspoon vegetable oil
1 cup whole barley (can be instant)
1¼ pounds fresh tomatoes, peeled
2 tablespoons pitted black olives, finely chopped
½ pound fresh mushrooms, sliced
2⅔ tablespoons fresh dill, chopped (or 2 teaspoons dried dill weed)
⅔ cup sour cream
1 cup cheddar cheese, grated, divided
Salt and pepper to taste

Heat oil in large saucepan over medium heat; fry barley 3 to 4 minutes. Add enough boiling water to cover barley by 2 inches; cover; simmer until tender, 50 to 60 minutes for whole barley; drain; set aside.

Preheat oven to 375° F. Coarsely chop half of tomatoes; add tomatoes, olives, mushrooms, dill, sour cream and half of cheese to barley. Salt and pepper to taste; place into lightly greased baking dish. Slice remaining tomatoes; arrange on top of casserole; sprinkle with remaining cheese. Bake until cheese melts and begins to brown, 10 to 15 minutes. **4 to 6 servings.**

Preparation Time: 1 Hour   *Cooking Time: 10 to 15 Minutes*

Treasure Tip: This dish is an unusual mixture of flavors for a meatless main course.

Rich Vegetable Pâté

Pâté

1¼ cups carrots, sliced
1¼ cup fresh spinach leaves, torn
1¼ cup cauliflower florets
1¼ cup fresh green beans, cut
4 eggs, divided
Salt and pepper to taste
Lettuce leaves
1 tomato, cut in wedges (garnish)

Dressing

1 egg yolk
1 tablespoon Dijon mustard
Salt and pepper to taste
½ cup vegetable oil
1 to 2 tablespoons wine vinegar
Cayenne pepper to taste

Night before, or several hours ahead: Cook carrots, spinach, cauliflower and beans separately. Preheat oven to 275 ° F. Spray loaf pan with vegetable cooking spray. Puree carrots, 1 egg, salt and pepper in food processor or blender; layer in bottom of loaf pan. Repeat procedure with spinach, cauliflower and beans, pureeing each with 1 egg, salt and pepper; layer, in order, on top of carrots. Place loaf pan in 12 x 9-inch baking dish filled with water. Bake 2½ hours; cover; refrigerate several hours or overnight.

To make dressing: Using food processor or blender, or whisking by hand, blend egg yolk and mustard; add salt and pepper. Very slowly add oil, a drop at a time, blending or whisking. Slowly add vinegar and cayenne; refrigerate.

When ready to serve: Place lettuce leaf on each of six or eight salad plates. Unmold pâté; cut in slices. Place on lettuce; top with dollop of dressing; garnish with tomato.

6 to 8 small servings.

Preparation Time: 45 Minutes   *Cooking Time: 2 Hours 30 Minutes*

Treasure Tip: This beautiful pâté is labor intensive, but worth it!

Curried Wine Sauce for Vegetables

1 cup mayonnaise
¼ cup dry white wine
1 teaspoon fresh lemon juice
¼ to ½ teaspoon curry powder

Combine all ingredients in small pan; place over low heat until heated through; do not boil. Serve over broccoli, cauliflower or other cooked vegetables. **Makes 1¼ cups.**

Preparation Time: 5 Minutes   **Cooking Time: 5 Minutes**

Broiled Florida Grapefruit

3 large Florida grapefruit
   (preferably seedless), halved
¼ cup plus 2 tablespoons firmly
   packed brown sugar
1 tablespoon cinnamon
¼ teaspoon ground mace
3 tablespoons butter or margarine
3 strawberries, halved (garnish)
Fresh mint sprigs (garnish)

Cut between sections to make grapefruit easy to eat; remove any seeds. Combine brown sugar, cinnamon and mace; mix well. Sprinkle over grapefruit halves; dot with butter. Broil grapefruit 4 inches from heat until lightly browned, 10 to 15 minutes. Transfer to individual serving dishes; garnish with strawberry half or fresh mint sprig. Serve warm. **6 servings.**

Preparation Time: 15 Minutes   **Cooking Time: 10 to 15 Minutes**

Spiced Orange Slices

4 Large Florida oranges, seeded
2 cups sugar
½ cup cider vinegar
5 whole cloves
1 (3-inch) stick cinnamon

Peel oranges; slice ¼ inch thick; discard small end pieces. Place in saucepan; cover with water. Bring to boil; reduce heat; simmer 30 minutes. Drain; rinse well. Return oranges to saucepan; add sugar, vinegar, ¼ cup water, cloves and cinnamon stick. Simmer; uncovered, 1 hour. Serve immediately, or pack into sterilized quart jar; seal. Serve with game or poultry. **4 to 6 servings.**

Preparation Time: 15 Minutes   **Cooking Time: 1 Hour 30 Minutes**

Beach Park Baked Fruit

Sauce

¹/₃ cup butter
³/₄ cup brown sugar
1 tablespoon curry powder
Dash apple pie spice
Splash of sherry or applejack brandy

Fruit

2 (30-ounce) cans pear halves
1 (30-ounce) can sliced peaches
1 (16-ounce) can pineapple chunks
1 (30-ounce) can plums
1 (16-ounce) can blueberries
1 (8-ounce) can mandarin oranges
1 (16-ounce) can apricot halves
³/₄ cup whole walnuts

Make sauce: Place all ingredients in small saucepan; heat on stove until dissolved. Preheat oven to 350° F. Drain fruits well; place in casserole dish. Pour sauce over fruit; cover; bake 1 hour, or microwave 30 minutes on medium high.   ***10 servings.***

Preparation Time: 15 Minutes   *Cooking Time: 1 Hour*

Cranberry Horseradish Delight

2 (16-ounce) cans jellied cranberry sauce
1 package plain gelatin
1 (5-ounce) jar prepared horseradish
¹/₂ teaspoon salt

Early in day, or night before: In saucepan melt cranberry sauce. Dissolve gelatin in ¼ cup cold water; add to hot cranberry sauce; cool. Add horseradish and salt; pour into decorative mold or individual molds. Chill several hours or overnight. When ready to serve, unmold; serve with turkey or wild game, or spread on turkey or chicken sandwiches.   ***Makes 2¹/₄ cups.***

Preparation Time: 25 Minutes

Treasure Tip: This makes a scrumptious spread on turkey or chicken sandwiches.

Cinnamon Baked Apples

8 McIntosh or Rome Beauty
    apples, unpeeled, cored, cut into
    eighths
½ cup brown sugar (to taste)
1 teaspoon cinnamon (to taste)
½ stick butter (optional)

Preheat oven to 350° F. Mix all ingredients; place in large glass baking dish. Cover; bake until apples are soft and tender, about 1 hour. As alternative, cook, covered, in microwave on high about 15 minutes, stirring every 4 minutes. Delicious with pork. **8 to 10 servings.**

Preparation Time: 10 Minutes   *Cooking Time: 1 Hour*

Golden Apple Cheddar Bake

2 pounds Granny Smith apples,
    peeled, cut into ¼-inch slices
½ cup raisins
½ teaspoon cinnamon
¼ cup fresh lemon juice
¾ cup dark brown sugar, firmly
    packed
½ cup flour
½ stick butter, cut into bits
1 cup extra-sharp cheddar cheese,
    finely grated

Preheat oven to 350° F. Arrange apple slices in well-buttered 2-quart rectangular baking dish; sprinkle with raisins, cinnamon and lemon juice. In small bowl combine brown sugar and flour; blend in butter until mixture resembles coarse meal; toss with cheddar. Sprinkle cheddar mixture over apple mixture; bake in upper third of oven until apples are tender, about 30 minutes. Serve immediately. **4 to 6 servings.**

Preparation Time: 15 Minutes   *Cooking Time: 30 Minutes*

A few favored fresh fruit combinations

Citrus Sections

Arrange orange and pink grapefruit sections together on a plate. Sprinkle fruit with Grand Marnier.

Tropical Fruits

Prepare a compote of pineapple cubes, mango cubes and papaya cubes. Sprinkle the compote with coconut milk and top with flaked coconut.

Melons

Slice thinly a honeydew melon and garnish with cantaloupe pared paper thin. Sprinkle melon slices with lime juice and garnish with a lime slice.

Berries

Combine strawberries, blueberries, raspberries and pitted fresh cherries. Sprinkle berries with brown sugar.

Treasure Tip: Sprinkle fresh fruit with grapefruit or orange juice in place of lemon juice to preserve freshness and color.

FISH & SHELLFISH

Fishing By the Bay

For those who love to fish, Tampa is the place to be. We are never far from water, an open bay, a quiet lake, a lazy river or the ever changing Gulf of Mexico. Whether from a pier, seawall, beach or boat, this Tampa treasure is frequently enjoyed by just about everyone.

In this tranquil setting, we cast our bait into Hillsborough Bay by the shrimp docks, with another spectacular Florida sunset framing the scene. Nearby coastal waters provide enough blue crabs, scallops and succulent Florida lobster to fill any seafood platter to overflowing. During the season, stone crabs claws, a Florida delicacy, are carefully collected and the harvest is celebrated with many a sumptuous feast.

Because local waters seldom get cold, something can usually be enticed to nibble. Inland, freshwater lakes are home to the Florida bass, bream and catfish. Saltwater varieties include Kingfish, mackerel, mullet, redfish, snapper, seatrout, grouper and pompano to name a few. In summer, tarpon is the prize for sport fishermen who compete for money and trophies. In recent years, the large and elusive Silver Kings have been tagged and released to be caught again.

While out on the water, it is a common sight to see playful porpoises racing along in the wake of the boat for a quick game of hide and seek. Returning fishermen are usually greeted by patient pelicans who fluff up from their naps and waddle over for handouts.

Seafood has long been a staple in Tampa's cuisine. With so many varieties of seafood readily available, recipes in this section represent a wealth of experience and enjoyment sure to be successful anywhere. Pompano in Papillote, with its subtle Spanish flavoring and steaming aromatic presentation, is a true Tampa classsic. Particularly with seafood, you will want to read the entire section before making your first selection.

The Fishing photograph was underwritten by
Tom and Pat Daley
Tony, Cindy, Carolyn and Julianne Coney

FISH & SHELLFISH

PICNIC AT THE BEACH

Caribbean Grilled Fish with Mango Butter

Stone Crabs with Mustard Sauce

Margarita Shrimp

Toasted Walnut Rice Florentine

Bibb Salad with Tropical Fruits

Lacy Oatmeal Cookies

**The menu photograph was underwritten by
Peninsular Paper Co.,
South Florida's Pioneer Paper Merchants**

Caribbean Grilled Fish with Mango Butter

1 pound margarine
1 (5-ounce) bottle Pickapeppa
    sauce
1 tablespoon garlic, chopped
¾ cup fresh basil leaves, chopped
1 tablespoon cracked black pepper
¼ cup white wine
8 (8-ounce) fillets fresh fish
    (grouper, snapper, mahi-mahi,
    sea trout)*
*Chicken, sea scallops or shrimp
    may be substituted

Mango Butter Sauce

Juice of 1 lime, rolled and squeezed
    by hand
1 ripe mango, peeled and coarsely
    chopped
¼ cup whipping cream
2 sticks unsalted butter, cubed in
    1-inch pieces
Salt and white pepper to taste

Night before: Melt margarine in medium saucepan over low heat. In medium bowl, combine Pickapeppa, garlic, basil, pepper and wine. Add hot margarine; mix thoroughly. Place fish in shallow pan so that fillets don't overlap. Pour remaining marinade evenly over fillets; marinate overnight in refrigerator. (If using chicken, scallops or shrimp, marinate 1 to 2 hours.)

Just before cooking fish, make Mango Butter Sauce: In medium saucepan combine lime juice, mango and cream; cook over low heat until reduced and thick. Cool until warm to touch; add butter, stirring, one cube at a time. Add salt and white pepper. Keep sauce warm in double boiler over simmering water until served. Remove fish from marinade. Grill over hot coals until fish flakes easily with fork, 5 to 6 minutes on each side for 1-inch-thick fillets. Serve with sauce.

8 servings.

Preparation Time: 20 Minutes   Cooking Time: 10 to 12 Minutes

Stone Crab Claws with Mustard Sauce

3½ teaspoons dry mustard
1 cup mayonnaise
2 teaspoons Worcestershire sauce
1 teaspoon A-1 sauce
2 tablespoons light cream
⅛ teaspoon salt
9 to 15 jumbo stone crab claws,
    cooked and cracked

In small bowl of electric mixer beat mustard, mayonnaise, Worcestershire, A-1, cream and salt for 3 minutes. Serve sauce in dipping bowls with warm or cold crab claws.

1¼ cups sauce

Preparation Time: 5 Minutes

Treasure Tip: Local markets sell stone crabs, in season, already cooked. To warm claws, drop in boiling water 1 minute, or heat in 300°F. oven 15 minutes.

Margarita Shrimp

5 tablespoons corn or olive oil
1½ pounds large fresh shrimp,
    peeled and deveined
½ cup whole green onions, minced
2 large cloves garlic, minced
¼ cup tequila
2 tablespoons fresh lime juice
1 teaspoon coarse or Margarita salt
Lime wedges (optional)

Heat oil in large skillet over medium-high heat. Add shrimp, green onion and garlic; cook 1 minute. Remove from heat; add tequila. Return to heat. Bring to boil, scraping up any browned bits in pan. Transfer to bowl; toss with lime juice and salt. Garnish with lime wedges; serve warm or cooled. If desired, serve with rice. **4 main-dish, 6 first-course servings.**

Preparation Time: 20 Minutes **Cooking Time: 5 Minutes**

Treasure Tip: This is a fun first course. Dip rims of six Margarita or sherbet glasses in lime juice, then in coarse salt. Place cooled shrimp in glasses; garnish with lime wedges.

Toasted Walnut Rice Florentine

1 (14-ounce) can beef broth
3 tablespoons butter
1 cup converted rice
1 cup onion, coarsely chopped
1 clove garlic, minced
2 tablespoons dry sherry
3 cups fresh spinach, shredded
⅓ cup heavy cream
½ cup walnuts, toasted, coarsely
    chopped
Black pepper to taste
¼ cup Parmesan cheese, freshly
    grated

Add water to broth to make 2¼ cups; set aside. Melt butter in large saucepan. Add rice, onion and garlic. Cook over medium heat, stirring constantly, 3 to 4 minutes. Add broth and sherry; bring to boil. Reduce heat; cover tightly; simmer 20 minutes. Remove from heat. Stir in spinach and cream; let stand, covered, until all liquid is absorbed, about 5 minutes. Stir in walnuts; sprinkle with pepper and cheese. **6 servings.**

Preparation Time: 15 Minutes **Cooking Time: 30 Minutes**

Treasure Tip: Converted, or parboiled, rice is a long-grain rice that has been steamed under pressure before milling, retaining most of its natural nutrients. Converted rice is almost foolproof; it cooks up fluffy with separate, distinct grains.

Bibb Salad with Tropical Fruits

Lime and Cilantro Vinaigrette

1 whole egg
5 tablespoons olive oil
1 tablespoon sugar
3 tablespoons fresh cilantro,
    chopped
1 teaspoon fresh garlic, chopped
1/4 teaspoon white pepper
Kosher salt to taste
Juice of 4 Persian limes

Salad

2 Large Florida oranges
2 Florida avocados, peeled
1 medium papaya
2 ripe tomatoes
1 medium Florida sweet onion
1 cucumber, peeled and seeded
3 tablespoons fresh cilantro,
    chopped
6 tablespoons olive oil
1 teaspoon white pepper
Kosher salt to taste
3 heads Bibb lettuce

Early in the day, make vinaigrette: Using wire whisk, beat egg and olive oil to blend. Add sugar, cilantro, garlic, pepper and salt; whisk in lime juice. Serve or refrigerate.

Up to 6 hours ahead, make salad: Peel oranges; cut off white membrane; dice into 1/2-inch pieces; place in large bowl. Dice avocado, papaya, tomatoes, onion and cucumber into 1/2-inch pieces; add to bowl. Sprinkle with cilantro, olive oil, pepper and salt; toss. Refrigerate until serving time, or serve at once. To serve, arrange lettuce leaves on platter; cover with fruit mixture. Serve with vinaigrette on side.   *4 to 6 servings.*

Preparation Time: 20 Minutes

Treasure Tip: *A ripe avocado yields slightly under pressure from your finger. To ripen a hard avocado, place it in a brown paper bag in a kitchen cabinet; check daily. If you are using only half an avocado for your meal, leave the avocado seed in the other half and wrap tightly with plastic wrap.*

Lacy Oatmeal Cookies

1/2 cup sifted flour
1/4 teaspoon baking powder
3/4 cup sugar (1/2 granulated,
    1/2 brown)
1/2 cup quick-cooking oats
2 tablespoons cream
2 tablespoons light corn syrup
1 teaspoon vanilla extract
1 stick butter, melted

Preheat oven to 375° F. Mix all ingredients in large bowl. Lightly grease cookie sheet. (Make sure the cookie sheet has sides, because cookies are runny.) Drop dough from teaspoon, about 4 inches apart, onto cookie sheet. Bake 6 to 8 minutes. Cool on cookie sheet just until they do not scrunch up when nudged with spatula; remove with spatula. Cookies will crumble if you cool them completely before removing.

Makes 24.

Preparation Time: 10 Minutes   *Cooking Time: 6 to 8 Minutes*

Fillets en Papillote

8 small, or 4 large, flounder fillets
½ pound fresh small mushrooms
3 tablespoons butter or margarine
½ pound small fresh shrimp, peeled
    and deveined
1 teaspoon salt
Pepper to taste
1½ tablespoons fresh lemon juice
Dash paprika (garnish)
Fresh parsley, chopped (garnish)

Seasoned White Sauce

2 tablespoons butter or margarine
2 tablespoons flour
1 cup milk
1 tablespoon fresh lemon juice
Salt and pepper to taste

Cut four pieces of foil, each 14 inches long. Place one portion fish (1 large or 2 small fillets) in center of each. Remove and chop mushroom stems. Melt butter in small saucepan; lightly sauté mushroom stems and caps. Distribute shrimp and mushrooms equally on top of fillets. Season with salt, pepper and lemon juice.

Make sauce: Melt butter in medium saucepan over low heat. Stir in flour; cook, stirring constantly, until smooth and bubbly. Slowly whisk in milk; cook over medium heat, stirring constantly, until thick. Add lemon juice, salt and pepper.

Preheat oven to 425° F. Spoon one-fourth of white sauce over each fish portion; sprinkle with paprika and parsley. Bring edges of foil together in double fold to make tight seal. Double-fold ends to form a tent shaped square bag. Place on cookie sheet; bake 20 to 30 minutes. Place foil bags on serving plates; snip through foil with scissors to form criss-cross pattern on top; fold back foil; serve. **4 servings.**

Preparation Time: 45 Minutes   Cooking Time: 20 to 30 Minutes

Treasure Tip: Looks complicated, but is easy to make and spectacular to serve to guests.

Lemon-Dill Flounder

3 tablespoons butter or margarine
1 tablespoon fresh dill, chopped
2 tablespoons fresh lemon juice
¼ teaspoon seasoned salt
¼ teaspoon white pepper
2 whole medium green onions,
    chopped
1 pound fresh flounder fillets

Melt butter in 10-inch skillet over medium-low heat. Add dill, lemon juice, seasoned salt, pepper and green onions. Sauté 5 minutes, stirring occasionally. Add flounder; cook, basting occasionally with pan juices, until firm and flaky, 10 to 15 minutes. **4 servings.**

Preparation Time: 25 Minutes   Cooking Time: 10 to 15 Minutes

Taste-of-the-Islands Grouper

1 ripe papaya
1 ripe mango
¹/₄ ripe pineapple
1 to 2 jalapeño or serrano peppers
¹/₂ tomato, peeled, seeded and diced
¹/₃ cup Spanish wine vinegar
¹/₂ red onion, diced small
1 tablespoon olive oil
¹/₃ cup fresh cilantro or mint leaves,
    coarsely chopped
1 cup peanut or vegetable oil
¹/₃ cup soy sauce
Juice of 1 orange
10 whole black peppercorns,
    slightly bruised
2 bay leaves
4 (8-ounce) grouper fillets, cut on
    extreme bias

Up to 6 hours before serving, prepare salsa: Peel papaya and mango; remove seeds; cut into small cubes. Remove outside skin from pineapple; core; remove eyes. Cube one-fourth of the pineapple. Wearing rubber gloves, remove and discard stems, seeds and ribs from jalapeños; chop fine. In large bowl combine papaya, mango, pineapple, jalapeños, tomato, vinegar, onion, olive oil and cilantro; toss gently to combine. Keep at room temperature up to 6 hours.

Shortly before cooking, prepare marinade: In medium bowl combine peanut oil, soy sauce, orange juice, peppercorns and bay leaves; keep at room temperature.

When ready to cook: Preheat broiler or prepare charcoal grill with hot fire; grease grill rack. Place fish into marinade for about 3 minutes; grill fish or broil in broiler pan until just cooked through. Place fish on warm plates; top with salsa to taste.   *4 servings.*

Preparation Time: 20 Minutes   *Cooking Time: 15 Minutes*

Treasure Tip: If the fish in this recipe marinates any longer than the 3 minutes suggested, the orange juice in the marinade will begin to cook the fish.

Grouper Royale

A favorite recipe from Chavez at the Royal Restaurant

³/₄ to 1 cup oil and butter
    combined, divided
6 (6-ounce) grouper fillets
1 large bunch whole green onions,
    chopped
1 pound fresh mushrooms, sliced
8 ounces fresh blue or lump
    crabmeat
Salt and pepper to taste
Bread crumbs
2 cups Hollandaise sauce*

*Use traditional sauce or make Blender Hollandaise Sauce on Page 123

Preheat oven to 250° F. Lightly coat grouper fillets with bread crumbs. Melt 2 tablespoons oil-butter mixture in large skillet; sauté grouper fillets until just done. Season with salt and pepper; place in single layer in baking dish; set aside. In separate skillets melt more oil and butter; sauté green onions and mushrooms separately; combine. Layer a portion of crabmeat, then vegetables, on each fillet; cover with foil. Bake fish until warm enough to serve, about 20 minutes. Just before serving, pour ¹/₃ cup Hollandaise over each fillet.   *6 servings.*

Preparation Time: 20 Minutes   *Cooking Time: 20 Minutes*

Treasure Tip: Owner Helen Chavez says, "Please remember, prepared dishes vary with the cook. If you plan to serve this for company, please cook it at least once first and make adjustments to your taste." This is a good rule to follow for any recipe.

Red Snapper with Roasted Red Peppers

Roasted Red Peppers

6 red bell peppers
½ cup olive oil
Freshly ground black pepper
Garlic cloves to taste (optional)

Red Pepper Vinaigrette

3 roasted red bell peppers, finely
  chopped
¼ cup oil-cured black olives,
  chopped
2 tablespoons capers, drained
2 tablespoons olive oil
1 garlic clove, crushed
2 tablespoons fresh parsley,
  chopped
1½ teaspoons fresh lemon juice
⅛ teaspoon salt
¼ teaspoon red pepper flakes
4 red snapper fillets (leave skin on)
Olive oil

4 hours, or several days before serving, make Roasted Red Peppers: Preheat broiler. Wash peppers; cut in half; remove seeds. Lay pieces, skin side up, on broiling pan; broil until skin is charred. Remove from oven; place in paper bag to steam 10 minutes. Remove from bag, one at a time; peel off skin. Slice into narrow strips; marinate in olive oil and pepper at least 30 minutes.

At least 3 hours, or up to 3 days before, make Red Pepper Vinaigrette: In medium bowl combine chopped roasted peppers and remaining ingredients; stir well. Let stand at room temperature 3 hours, or cover and refrigerate up to 3 days. (If refrigerated, bring to room temperature before serving with fish.)

When ready to cook: Prepare medium-hot coals in charcoal grill. Brush both sides of snapper fillets with oil. Place skin-side down in oiled, hinged grill basket or directly on oiled grill rack, 4 to 6 inches from coals. Grill, turning once, until fish is barely opaque in center, about 3 minutes per side. Place on individual serving plates; top with Red Pepper Vinaigrette.   *4 servings.*

Preparation Time: 45 Minutes   Cooking Time: 6 to 10 Minutes

Treasure Tip: Any kind of fresh peppers can be roasted by the method in this recipe. Peppers will keep in tightly covered jar in refrigerator several weeks. Add a few garlic cloves, if desired. Use in pasta, salads, pizzas or sandwiches, or purée for use in sauces and soups.

Grilled Catfish with Dijon Sauce

4 catfish fillets
3 tablespoons margarine, melted
2 teaspoons Worcestershire sauce,
  divided
1 teaspoon lemon pepper seasoning
½ cup sour cream
1 tablespoon Dijon mustard

Rinse fillets; blot dry with paper towels. Combine margarine, 1 teaspoon Worcestershire sauce and lemon pepper. Brush both sides of fillets with butter mixture; place on broiler pan or grill. Broil 6 inches from heat, turning once, until fish flakes easily with fork, 10 to 12 minutes. (Fish can be grilled for same amount of time using heavy-duty foil on grill rack over medium coals.)

While fish is cooking, make sauce: Combine 1 teaspoon Worcestershire, sour cream and mustard in small saucepan. Heat until warm. Serve 2 tablespoons sauce over each catfish fillet.   *4 servings.*

Preparation Time: 5 Minutes   Cooking Time: 15 Minutes

Grilled Grouper with Honey-Jalapeño Sauce

1 cup honey
¼ cup white wine vinegar
1½ teaspoons ground cinnamon
4 ounces sliced canned jalapeño
    peppers with juice
½ cup light brown sugar
Dash Tabasco (optional)
¼ cup cornstarch
4 (8-ounce) fresh grouper fillets, or
    any fish or chicken fillets
1 large red bell pepper, julienned

Up to 2 days ahead, make sauce: Place honey, vinegar, cinnamon, jalapeños and juice, ½ cup water, brown sugar and Tabasco in 1-quart saucepan; bring to gentle boil. Put cornstarch in measuring cup, add ½ cup cold water to dilute, stir to dissolve well. With wire whisk, slowly add diluted cornstarch to honey mixture; cook over medium heat to thicken slightly. Strain sauce through sieve; discard solids. Refrigerate until ready to serve. (Flavor of sauce improves with time.)

When ready to cook: Oil barbecue grill rack. Heat sauce on stovetop. Grill fillets over hot coals until done. Top fillets with sauce; sprinkle with julienned pepper; serve.   ***4 servings.***

Preparation Time: 15 Minutes   *Cooking Time: 15 Minutes*

Almond Crabmeat Mahi-Mahi

2 to 3 pounds fresh mahi-mahi
    (dolphin) fillets
Corn or wheat flour
2 tablespoons margarine
Juice of 1 lemon
1 medium onion, chopped fine
½ cup celery, chopped
1 to 2 sticks butter
½ bunch parsley, chopped fine
2 bunches whole green onions,
    chopped, divided
1 pound fresh crabmeat
1 cup toasted almond slices
Juice of 2 lemons

Clean mahi-mahi fillets; cut into 6- to 8-ounce portions; dust with flour. In large skillet over medium-high heat, melt margarine; add lemon juice. Fry fillets until golden brown on both sides, at least 15 minutes; set aside in warm oven.

Prepare crabmeat topping: In large saucepan, over medium heat, melt butter. Sauté celery and onion until cooked, but not brown. Add parsley and most of green onions (save part of chopped green tops for garnish). Stir together to warm. Add crabmeat; heat through. Place 1 piece of fish on each warm dinner plate; sprinkle with almonds; top with portion of crabmeat mixture. Sprinkle with lemon juice; garnish.

3 to 6 servings.

Preparation Time: 25 Minutes   *Cooking Time: 15 to 20 Minutes*

Shrimp and Mushroom-Stuffed Snapper

1 (4-pound) fresh red snapper fillet
1 clove garlic, crushed
1 stick butter or margarine,
    softened
1 teaspoon salt
1/8 teaspoon pepper
1/2 teaspoon dried thyme leaves
1 teaspoon flour
1/2 pound large shrimp, shelled and
    deveined
1/2 pound fresh mushrooms, sliced
3 tablespoons fresh lemon juice,
    divided
1/2 cup dry white wine, divided
1 teaspoon lemon peel, grated
1/4 cup fresh parsley, chopped
Lemon slices for garnish

Preheat oven to 375°F. Slit snapper lengthwise to form cavity; rinse inside and out under cold running water. Dry well on paper towels. In small bowl combine garlic, butter, salt, pepper, thyme and flour; mix well.

Place fish on double thickness of 24 x 18-inch heavy-duty foil. In cavity of fish place 1 tablespoon garlic mixture, 4 shrimp and 1/2 cup mushrooms. Sprinkle with 1 tablespoon lemon juice and 1/4 cup wine. Dot top of fish with remaining garlic mixture.

Arrange remaining shrimp and mushrooms over top; sprinkle with remaining lemon juice, wine and lemon peel. Bring long sides of foil together over fish; secure with double fold. Fold both ends of foil upward several times; place on cookie sheet. Bake 40 minutes or until fish flakes easily with fork. Open foil; spoon juices over fish; sprinkle with parsley. Serve with lemon slices.

4 to 6 servings.

Preparation Time: 30 Minutes   *Cooking Time: 40 Minutes*

Grouper Dijonnaise

2 tablespoons butter
1 small onion, chopped
2 tablespoons flour
1/3 cup dry white wine
Salt and pepper to taste
1 tablespoon Dijon mustard
1/3 cup milk or light cream
1/3 cup mozzarella cheese, grated
1 tomato, peeled, seeded and
    chopped
2 pounds grouper fillets
2 tablespoons butter, melted
2 tablespoons fresh lemon juice

Make sauce: Melt butter in small saucepan over medium heat. Sauté onion 3 to 5 minutes; whisk in flour; cook 2 minutes. Add wine, 1/4 cup water, salt, pepper and mustard; whisk until thickened. Add milk and cheese; stir until cheese melts. Add tomato; remove from heat. Cover; keep warm.

To cook fish. Preheat broiler. Arrange fillets on broiler pan, turning under thin ends. Brush with melted butter. Sprinkle with lemon juice; season to taste. Broil 4 inches from heat 8 to 10 minutes, until fish flakes with fork. Cover fillets with sauce; return to broiler until sauce is lightly browned, 2 to 3 minutes.

4 servings.

Preparation Time: 15 Minutes   *Cooking Time: 10 to 13 Minutes*

Treasure Tip: Let frozen fish fillets thaw in milk for 30 minutes or longer. This makes the fish taste fresher, milder, and more moist.

Red Snapper Papillote

A terrific Tampa classic from the Columbia Restaurant!

1 stick plus 2 tablespoons butter,
    melted, divided
1 onion, chopped fine
1 cup flour
2 cups milk, brought to boil
2 eggs
Dash nutmeg
Dash Tabasco
2 tablespoons sauterne wine
½ pound fresh shrimp, cooked and
    chopped
½ pound crawfish meat, cooked
    and chopped
Salt to taste
2 (1-pound) red snapper fillets,
    skinned
Parchment paper

Preheat oven to 350° F. In large saucepan melt 1 stick butter; sauté onion 5 minutes. Slowly add flour to form paste; cook, stirring constantly, over low heat until mixture is dry. Slowly whisk in milk; stir and cook over medium heat until thickened and bubbly; remove from heat.

In small bowl beat eggs with nutmeg, Tabasco and sauterne; fold into sauce. Add shrimp, crawfish and salt. On buttered piece of parchment paper spread one-third of sauce; top with 1 red snapper fillet. Top, in order, with one-third of sauce, 1 red snapper fillet and remaining sauce. Fold paper to form bag with crimped edges; brush paper with 2 tablespoons melted butter. Bake 30 minutes.   *4 servings.*

Preparation Time: 45 Minutes   ***Cooking Time: 30 Minutes***

Trout, Russian Style

A favorite fish presentation from the Valencia Garden Restaurant

6 to 9 fresh trout, filleted
½ teaspoon salt
¼ teaspoon white pepper
2 eggs, well beaten
¼ cup milk
1½ cups toasted bread crumbs,
    finely crushed
2 tablespoons corn or peanut oil
1 stick butter, softened
2 hard-boiled eggs, finely chopped
⅓ cup fresh parsley, finely
    chopped
2 tablespoons pimento, finely
    chopped
2 lemons, thinly sliced

Season trout with salt and pepper. In medium bowl mix beaten eggs and milk; dip trout in mixture, then roll gently in bread crumbs. Heat oil to medium on griddle or 300° F. in electric skillet. Use just enough oil to keep fish from sticking. Make a paste by combining butter, hard boiled eggs, parsley and pimento. Fry trout until golden, 5 to 6 minutes per side; remove to heated platter. Spread butter paste over each piece; top each with 2 to 3 slices lemon. Serve immediately.   *6 to 8 servings.*

Preparation Time: 15 Minutes   Cooking Time: 10 to 12 Minutes

Treasure Tip: *For juicy, tender fish, avoid overcooking. As a rule of thumb, cook fish 10 minutes per inch of thickness. Fish is done when it loses its translucency and becomes flaky.*

Snapper with Olive Spread

1 stick butter
2 tablespoons fresh parsley,
  chopped
4 teaspoons fresh lime juice
1/4 cup green olives with pimento,
  chopped
2 pounds red snapper fillets, cut
  into 4-inch-long pieces

Make olive spread: Melt butter in small saucepan over low heat; stir in parsley, lime juice and olives. Mix well; transfer to serving bowl. Prepare medium-hot coals in charcoal grill. Oil grill rack; oil snapper pieces on both sides; place on grill rack. Grill until fish just begins to flake with fork, 3 to 4 minutes per side. Remove from heat immediately. Divide fish evenly among four warm dinner plates; spoon small amount of olive spread over each serving. **4 servings.**

Preparation Time: 10 Minutes   *Cooking Time: 6 to 8 Minutes*

Garlic Peppered Shrimp

5 pounds large fresh shrimp,
  unpeeled
2 cups olive oil
6 cloves garlic, chopped
3 tablespoons salt
3 tablespoons pepper
Juice of 4 lemons
Juice of 4 limes
1 1/4 cups dry vermouth

Wash and drain shrimp. Heat oil in large skillet; sauté garlic until soft. Add shrimp, salt, pepper, lemon and lime juices. When shrimp begin to turn pink, add vermouth; stir; remove from stove. Let guests peel their own shrimp and serve cooking sauce in individual bowls. **10 servings.**

Preparation Time: 15 Minutes   *Cooking Time: 5 to 10 Minutes*

Treasure Tip: For a casual outdoor feast, use hollowed out lemon or lime halves to serve sauces.

Hickory-Smoked Shrimp

2 cups hickory chips
2 pounds jumbo fresh shrimp,
  unpeeled
1 cup vegetable oil
Salt and pepper to taste
Your favorite barbecue sauce for
  dipping

3 hours before cooking: Place hickory chips in bucket; cover with water; soak 3 hours.

2 1/4 hours before cooking: Wash shrimp; drain; pat dry. In large bowl combine oil, salt and pepper; add shrimp; mix well. Refrigerate 2 hours, stirring occasionally.

When ready to cook: Preheat grill to low flame; place wet hickory chips on top of charcoal. Remove shrimp from marinade, drain well to remove excess oil. Place shrimp on grill; cover; smoke 5 minutes. Turn shrimp; smoke 5 more minutes. Allow to cool 5 to 10 minutes until they can be handled; serve. Let guests peel their own and dip in barbecue sauce.

4 servings.

Preparation Time: 10 Minutes   *Cooking Time: 10 Minutes*

rg's Grilled Marinated Shrimp

From Tampa's rg's Restaurants

1 pound margarine, melted
½ cup white wine
¼ cup olive oil
1 (5-ounce) bottle Pickapeppa
  sauce
1 (5-ounce) bottle Tiger Sauce
2 tablespoons fresh basil, chopped
1 tablespoon garlic powder
2 tablespoons dried tarragon
24 to 36 large fresh shrimp, peeled
  and deveined

About 1 hour before cooking: Preheat charcoal grill. Place all ingredients except shrimp in large bowl or baking dish; mix well. Add shrimp; marinate 30 to 45 minutes. Remove shrimp from marinade; charcoal broil, turning once, until done, 10 to 15 minutes, or sauté in large skillet until shrimp turn pink, about 5 minutes. **2 to 4 servings.**

Preparation Time: 30 Minutes   *Cooking Time: 5 to 15 Minutes*

Herb Baked Shrimp

5 pounds large fresh shrimp, peeled
  and deveined
½ pound butter
½ pound margarine
⅓ cup Worcestershire sauce
2½ tablespoons rosemary
2 teaspoons salt
2 to 3 cloves garlic, sliced
2 lemons, sliced

Preheat oven to 400° F. Wash and drain shrimp. In deep saucepan melt butter and margarine; add Worcestershire, rosemary, salt and garlic. Place shrimp in large, flat baking dish; pour butter sauce over; mix well. Cover shrimp with lemon slices. Bake uncovered 20 to 25 minutes. Serve as is or drain shrimp. Either way, reserve sauce for dipping with Cuban or French bread. **10 servings.**

Preparation Time: 5 Minutes   *Cooking Time: 20 to 25 Minutes*

Shrimp de Jonghe

3/4 cup butter
3 cloves garlic, sliced
1/4 teaspoon tarragon
1 tablespoon parsley, chopped
Dash salt
1/2 teaspoon nutmeg
1/2 teaspoon thyme
1/4 teaspoon instant minced onion
1/4 cup dry sherry
1/4 cup chicken broth
1 cup seasoned bread crumbs
2 pounds extra-large fresh shrimp,
   peeled, deveined and partially
   butterflied

Preheat oven to 400° F. Melt butter in small saucepan over medium-high heat; add garlic; cook until browned. Remove garlic and discard. Add tarragon, parsley, salt, nutmeg, thyme, onion, sherry and broth to butter; stir to combine. Place bread crumbs in small bowl; add 1/4 cup butter mixture; stir to combine. Put shrimp in baking dish; pour remaining butter mixture over them; mix. Sprinkle buttered crumbs over shrimp. Bake until crumbs are brown, 20 to 25 minutes.   **4 servings.**

Preparation Time: 30 Minutes   Cooking Time: 20 to 25 Minutes

Treasure Tip: Leftover shrimp can be served as a shrimp cocktail for dinner the next night, or made into a salad.

Tarpon Springs Baked Shrimp

3/4 stick unsalted butter
3 large cloves garlic, minced
36 large fresh shrimp, peeled and
   deveined
3/4 teaspoon dried oregano,
   crumbled
1/4 teaspoon dried red pepper flakes
Pinch salt
3/4 cup dry vermouth
3/4 pound fresh plum tomatoes
   cored, seeded, diced into 1/2-inch
   pieces
3 ounces feta cheese, crumbled
1/4 cup loosely packed fresh parsley
   leaves, minced

Preheat oven to 350° F. In heavy skillet large enough to hold shrimp in single layer (use two skillets if necessary), over medium-high heat, melt butter. Add garlic, shrimp, oregano, pepper flakes and salt. Cook, turning once, until shrimp are almost pink, about 2½ minutes. With slotted spoon, transfer shrimp to large shallow baking dish or six (6-inch diameter) gratin dishes.

Add vermouth to skillet; boil until reduced by half, about 3 minutes. While boiling, add any juices accumulated in shrimp casserole. Add tomatoes; stir until heated through, about 30 seconds. Top shrimp with tomato mixture; place crumbled cheese on top. May be prepared to this point up to 1 day in advance. Cool; cover; refrigerate. Before baking, let stand until at room temperature. Bake until cheese is bubbly, 8 to 9 minutes. Sprinkle with parsley; serve.

6 servings.

Preparation Time: 30 Minutes   Cooking Time: 8 to 9 Minutes

Shrimp Baked with Blue Cheese

8 ounces blue cheese, softened
8 ounces cream cheese, softened
1 tablespoon chives, chopped
1 tablespoon parsley, chopped
1 clove garlic, finely chopped
3/4 cup dry white wine
2 pounds fresh shrimp, shelled and
  deveined
4 slices lemon

Preheat oven to 400° F. In small bowl of electric mixer blend blue cheese, cream cheese, chives, parsley and garlic; add wine; blend to thin mixture. Cut four large squares aluminum foil; heap one-fourth of cheese mixture on each square. Top each with one-fourth of shrimp and 1 lemon slice. Bring edges of foil up over shrimp; fold together. Fold up ends of foil to make tight package. Place on baking sheet; bake 20 minutes.   *4 servings.*

Preparation Time: 25 Minutes   ***Cooking Time: 20 Minutes***

Shrimp Scampi

1/3 cup butter, melted
2 tablespoons olive oil
1 large clove garlic, minced fine
1 pound jumbo fresh shrimp,
  peeled and deveined
1/4 cup plus 1 tablespoon fresh
  lemon juice
1 1/2 tablespoons fresh parsley,
  minced
1/4 cup white wine
3/4 cup fresh mushrooms, sliced
5 tablespoons unseasoned bread
  crumbs
1/3 cup Parmesan cheese, freshly
  grated
Dash pepper

Preheat oven to broil. In large skillet heat butter and oil over medium heat. Sauté garlic until tender but not brown. Add shrimp; sauté both sides until golden brown, 3 to 4 minutes. Remove shrimp; place in shallow pan. Add lemon juice, parsley and wine to skillet; stir; heat on medium-high 1 minute. Pour over shrimp; add mushrooms. Sprinkle bread crumbs, cheese and pepper over shrimp. Broil until cheese melts and browns, 3 to 5 minutes.   *2 to 4 servings.*

Preparation Time: 35 Minutes   ***Cooking Time: 3 to 5 Minutes***

Evander Preston's Shrimp with Pungent Fruit Sauce

1 (12-ounce) can beer
1½ cups flour
1 teaspoon baking soda
Salt and pepper to taste
Paprika
1 egg yolk
1 cup orange marmalade
¼ cup prepared horseradish
Juice of ½ lemon
48 large fresh shrimp, peeled and
    deveined
Vegetable oil for deep frying

About 1½ hours before serving: Pour beer into large bowl of electric mixer; let stand until flat. Add flour, baking soda, salt, pepper, paprika (enough to color batter) and egg yolk; whip until smooth.

Make sauce: In small bowl combine marmalade, horseradish and lemon juice; set aside. Heat oil to 375° F. Dip shrimp in batter; fry in batches until golden and puffy, 3 to 5 minutes. Drain on paper towels; serve immediately with sauce.

6 to 8 servings.

Preparation Time: 10 Minutes   Cooking Time: 12 to 20 Minutes

Charcoal Marinated Shrimp

2 pounds jumbo shrimp, peeled
    and deveined
3 medium garlic cloves, crushed
½ cup packed brown sugar
3 tablespoons grainy mustard
½ cup cider vinegar
Juice of 1 lime
Juice of ½ lemon
6 tablespoons olive oil
Salt and pepper to taste

Early in the day. Mix the garlic, sugar, mustard, vinegar, lime and lemon juices. Blend well. Whisk in the olive oil and add salt and pepper. Pour over the shrimp and refrigerate several hours, covered. Turn once.

Remove from the refrigerator 30 minutes before you want to cook it. Prepare grill. Grill the shrimp for approximately 2 minutes per side, or until done. Be careful not to overcook. These can also be broiled for the same amount of time.

Serves 6.

Preparation time: 20 minutes   Cooking Time: 5 minutes

Sautéed Crab Vermouth

1 stick butter
2 tablespoons cornstarch
1¼ cups dry vermouth, divided
1½ cups chicken broth
2 tablespoons fresh parsley,
   chopped
1 tablespoon garlic, minced
1 tablespoon soy sauce
1 tablespoon lemon juice
1 teaspoon sugar
1 pound fresh crabmeat, cartilage
   removed

Melt butter in large saucepan over medium heat; add cornstarch, stirring constantly. Slowly add chicken broth and 1 cup vermouth. Add parsley, garlic, soy sauce, lemon juice and sugar; simmer 10 minutes. Add fresh crabmeat; continue simmering until crab is warm. Just before serving, stir in remaining vermouth. Serve over cooked rice. *3 to 4 servings.*

Preparation Time: 10 Minutes   Cooking Time: 15 to 20 Minutes

Ybor City Deviled Crab

A Columbia Restaurant recipe

Croquette Dough

*3 loaves stale white bread, crusts
removed*
*1 loaf stale Cuban bread, ground
very fine and sifted*
1 level tablespoon paprika
1 teaspoon salt

Crabmeat Filling

5 tablespoons olive or vegetable oil
3 onions, finely chopped
*½ red or green bell pepper, finely
chopped*
*4 cloves garlic, mashed or chopped
fine*
*1 level teaspoon crushed hot red
pepper*
2 bay leaves
½ teaspoon sugar
1 level teaspoon salt
1 (6-ounce) can tomato paste
*1 pound fresh claw crabmeat, shell
and cartilage removed, shredded*

Croquettes

2 eggs, well beaten
½ cup milk
Salt to taste
Pinch black pepper
1 cup cracker crumbs, crushed
½ cup flour
Vegetable oil for deep frying

About 4 hours before serving, make dough: Break white bread into pieces; place in large bowl; cover with water; soak 15 minutes. Drain water and squeeze soaked bread until almost dry; return to bowl. Gradually add sifted Cuban bread until mixture reaches dough consistency. Add paprika and salt; mix thoroughly. Form dough into ball; refrigerate about 2 hours.

Make filling: Heat olive oil in large skillet; reduce heat to low. Add onion, bell pepper, garlic and hot red pepper; sauté very slowly 15 minutes. Add bay leaves, sugar, salt and tomato paste; stir. Cover; cook 15 minutes over low heat. Add crabmeat; cook uncovered 10 minutes; remove bay leaves. Place mixture on platter; refrigerate 2 hours.

After dough and filling have chilled, make croquettes: With your hands, take about 3 tablespoons bread dough; press; add 1 tablespoon crab filling; seal dough around filling like a croquette with pointed ends. In small bowl mix eggs, milk, salt and pepper. In another small bowl mix cracker crumbs and flour. Roll croquettes first into cracker mixture, then into egg mixture, then into cracker mixture again. Refrigerate 2 hours.

When ready to cook: Heat oil in deep, heavy saucepan or deep-fat fryer. Place croquettes, a few at a time, in hot oil; fry until light brown. ***Makes about 24.***

Preparation Time: 1 Hour 30 Minutes   *Cooking Time:
30 Minutes*

Treasure Tip: Miniature deviled crabs make great appetizers.

Crab Chilau

24 large live blue crabs or 2
    pounds of fresh crabmeat
$1/4$ cup olive oil
1 large onion, chopped
1 large green pepper, chopped
1 clove garlic, minced
1 (48-ounce) jar plain spaghetti
    sauce
1 (6-ounce) can tomato paste
1 tablespoon Tabasco
2 bay leaves
2 pound spaghetti, cooked and
    drained

About 2½ hours before serving: Heat large, heavy pot full of water to rapid boil. Using tongs, carefully plunge crabs into boiling water until they turn pink; cool in cold water. Place crabs on their backs on cutting board; use sharp knife to break off back shells. Wash loose matter away with water, discard lungs. With mallet crack claws, body and legs. Place in bowl; cover; refrigerate.

In large pot heat olive oil; add onion, green pepper and garlic; sauté until tender. Add spaghetti sauce, tomato paste, 6 ounces water, measured in tomato paste can, Tabasco and bay leaves. Bring to boil; reduce to simmer; cook, stirring occasionally, until thick, 1 hour. Add crabs to sauce 20 to 25 minutes before end of cooking time. Serve over cooked spaghetti.   **6 to 8 servings.**

Preparation Time: 45 Minutes   *Cooking Time: 2 Hours*

Treasure Tip: This dish is commonly known as Crab Enchilada, but to everyone in Tampa, it has always been called Crab Chilau. Since it is very messy to eat, it is a good dish for eating outdoors, with bibs and lots of Cuban bread.

Stone Crab Claws with Butter Sauce

9 to 12 jumbo stone crab claws,
    cooked and cracked
2 sticks butter, melted
2 tablespoons fresh lemon or lime
    juice
Generous dash Tabasco

Thaw crabs, if frozen. Preheat oven to 300° F. Place crabs in baking dish; heat 15 minutes. Meanwhile, prepare sauce: Mix butter, lemon juice and Tabasco; place in individual dipping bowls. Serve crabs on a table covered with newspaper.
   3 to 4 servings.

Preparation Time: 10 Minutes   *Cooking Time: 15 Minutes*

Treasure Tip: Florida stone crabs are unique in that only one claw from each crab is harvested. The live crab is returned to the water to grow another claw during the seven months in which stone crabs are out of season.

Spicy Southern Crab Cakes

¾ cup milk
3 whole slices white bread
2 tablespoons fresh parsley, chopped
½ cup mayonnaise
1 tablespoon Worcestershire sauce
½ teaspoon cayenne pepper
1 teaspoon dry mustard
2 tablespoons Old Bay seasoning
2 tablespoons prepared horseradish
1 teaspoon paprika
½ teaspoon onion salt
2 to 4 whole green onions, chopped
2 pounds fresh lump crabmeat
1½ to 2 cups soda cracker crumbs
2 tablespoons olive oil
2 tablespoons margarine

About 5 hours before serving: In large bowl place milk and bread to soak. Add parsley, mayonnaise, Worcestershire, cayenne, mustard, Old Bay, horseradish, paprika, onion salt and green onions; stir together. Add crabmeat; blend very gently. Using an ice cream scoop, make balls of mixture; slightly flatten. Place on plate; refrigerate about 4 hours.

When ready to cook: Heat oil and margarine in large skillet over medium heat. Coat crab cakes with cracker crumbs. Fry crab cakes, turning and reforming with spatula (they tend to fall apart at first but eventually stick together), until golden brown, 6 minutes per batch. ***Makes 16 good-sized cakes.***

Preparation Time: 30 Minutes   ***Cooking Time: 12 Minutes***

Treasure Tip: *Lump crabmeat refers to large pieces of white meat from the body. It is usually the most expensive crabmeat. Meat from the claw is brownish in color and usually less expensive.*

Cognac Scallops with Lime Rice

4 to 5 cups cooked rice
Grated peel of 1 lime
¼ cup fresh lime juice, divided
2 tablespoons olive oil, divided
1 red bell pepper, seeded, cut in 1-inch long julienne strips
6 green onions (include half of green tops), cut diagonally into 1-inch pieces
1 tablespoon dry white wine
1 pound bay scallops (or sea scallops, quartered)
2 tablespoons cognac
2 teaspoons fresh tarragon, chopped
Salt and pepper to taste

Make lime rice: In large rice steamer or double boiler, over hot water, heat rice. Add lime rind and 2 tablespoons lime juice; stir; keep hot while preparing scallops. Cook scallops: In large skillet heat 1 tablespoon oil over medium heat; sauté red peppers and green onions about 5 minutes, stirring occasionally. Add wine; cook 3 more minutes; remove to small bowl.

Heat remaining tablespoon oil in same pan over medium-high heat; add scallops, Cognac, 2 tablespoons lime juice and tarragon. Cook about 2 minutes, shaking pan. Add red pepper-green onion mixture; cook 1 more minute. Salt and pepper to taste. Serve immediately with rice. ***4 servings.***

Preparation Time: 10 Minutes   ***Cooking Time: 12 Minutes***

Grilled Marinated Scallops

2 pounds sea scallops
Juice of 8 to 10 limes or lemons
½ cup olive oil
2 cloves garlic, finely chopped
¼ cup whole green onions, finely
    chopped
¼ cup canned green chilies, finely
    chopped
¼ cup fresh parsley, chopped
1½ teaspoons salt
1 to 2 dashes Tabasco

Up to 1 hour before cooking: In large bowl pour lime juice over scallops to cover completely; add all other ingredients; let stand in refrigerator 30 minutes to 1 hour.

When ready to cook: Drain scallops; grill over hot fire just until browned, 1 to 2 minutes; serve. If desired, you can serve scallops uncooked, as seviche. Marinate in refrigerator 24 hours, during which texture will change and scallops will cook.

4 to 6 main-dish, 6 to 8 first-course servings.

Preparation Time: 15 Minutes   *Cooking Time: 1 Minute*

Light Coquilles St. Jacques

1 cup dry white wine
5 tablespoons unsalted butter or
    margarine
1 small onion, chopped
3 sprigs parsley, with stems
½ teaspoon thyme
1 bay leaf
1 tablespoon fresh lemon juice,
    strained
1½ pounds sea scallops
1 teaspoon cornstarch, mixed with
    3 tablespoons cold water
2 to 3 tablespoon Parmesan cheese,
    freshly grated

In large saucepan place wine, butter, onion, parsley, thyme, bay leaf and lemon juice; bring to boil. Reduce heat; add scallops; simmer until tender, about 5 minutes. Remove scallops with slotted spoon; set aside; keep warm. Boil liquid in pan 5 minutes. Reduce to simmer; add cornstarch-water mixture; stir until sauce thickens. Remove from heat; strain. Place scallops in four individual ovenproof shells or single baking dish. Top with sauce; sprinkle with Parmesan; broil until cheese is nicely browned.

4 servings.

Preparation Time: 10 Minutes   *Cooking Time: 20 Minutes*

Treasure Tip: *By cooking quickly, scallops will be very tender.*

Florida Lobster with Orange Butter

1 cup plus 2 tablespoons dry white
    wine, divided
¾ cup whipping cream
4 sticks butter, softened
Salt and freshly ground pepper to
    taste
1 cup frozen orange juice
    concentrate, thawed
4 fresh Florida lobsters (2 to 2½
    pounds total) or 4 small lobster
    tails (about 7½ ounces each),
    cooked
1 to 2 large Florida oranges, peeled
    and sectioned

Make Orange Butter: In medium saucepan over medium heat, reduce 6 tablespoons wine to about 1½ tablespoons. Add cream; reduce until thickened. Whisk in butter, 1 tablespoon at a time, incorporating each piece completely before adding the next. Remove from heat; season with salt and pepper. Place orange juice in small saucepan over medium heat; reduce by half. Whisk juice into butter mixture; remove from heat; keep warm.

Cut lobsters in half; remove meat from tails. Cut meat from each tail into 5 slices. Transfer to 10-inch skillet, keeping each tail together. Add enough wine to cover bottom of skillet. Cover skillet; warm lobster over low heat. To serve, transfer lobster to four warm plates. Top each with one-fourth of warm Orange Butter and 3 orange sections.   ***4 servings.***

Preparation Time: 45 Minutes   ***Cooking Time: 5 Minutes***
36 fresh oysters on the half shell

Baked Oysters Macadamia

2 sticks unsalted butter, softened
2 tablespoons garlic, finely
    chopped
2 tablespoons shallots, finely
    chopped
1 tablespoon fresh parsley, chopped
½ cup macadamia nuts, finely
    chopped
2 tablespoons fine, fresh bread
    crumbs
Salt and freshly ground black
    pepper to taste

Preheat oven to 450° F. Place oysters in shallow pan. In blender or food processor combine remaining ingredients; blend well. Spoon equal amounts of butter mixture over oysters; place in oven. Bake until tops are lightly browned, 6 to 8 minutes. Serve immediately.   ***6 servings.***

Preparation Time: 15 Minutes   ***Cooking Time: 6 to 8 Minutes***

Treasure Tip: *Macadamia butter is great on other seafood!*

Oyster-Stuffing Casserole

3 cups oysters, drained
²/₃ cup onion, chopped
1 cup celery, finely chopped
1 cup herb stuffing crumbs
1 stick butter
2 tablespoons fresh lemon juice
Tabasco to taste
Crushed red pepper flakes to taste
¹/₂ teaspoon dry mustard
1 tablespoon Worcestershire sauce

Preheat oven to 350° F. Place oysters in baking dish; spread onion and celery on top; cover with stuffing crumbs. Melt butter; add lemon juice, Tabasco, red pepper, mustard and Worcestershire; mix well. Pour over contents of casserole. Bake uncovered, about 15 minutes. **6 servings.**

Preparation Time: 10 Minutes   *Cooking Time: 15 Minutes*

Treasure Tip: Freshly opened raw oysters are extremely perishable and should be eaten right away.

Fresh Dill Sauce

1 teaspoon dry mustard
1 tablespoon onion, minced
1 tablespoon sugar
³/₄ teaspoon salt
1 heaping tablespoon fresh dill, chopped
2 tablespoons tarragon vinegar
¹/₂ cup cucumber, chopped
1 cup sour cream
Dash Tabasco

In small bowl stir mustard into 1 teaspoon water; let stand 10 minutes. In medium bowl combine onion, sugar, salt, dill and vinegar. Add remaining ingredients; mix well; chill. **Makes 1¹/₂ cups.**

Preparation Time: 10 Minutes

Treasure Tip: This dill-cucumber sauce is delightful on poached, broiled or baked fish. It can also be used to dress a salad.

Irish Shrimp Sauce

¹/₂ cup mayonnaise
Dash Tabasco
1 tablespoon catsup
¹/₂ ounce Irish whiskey
2 tablespoons heavy cream
1 tablespoon fresh parsley, chopped

Mix all ingredients; use as shrimp cocktail or dipping sauce. **Makes ³/₄ cup.**

Preparation Time: 5 Minutes

Treasure Tip: This whiskey-cream sauce is a tasty change from the standard tomato-horseradish cocktail sauce.

Blender Hollandaise Sauce

6 egg yolks
6 ounces cream cheese, cubed and
  softened
Dash cayenne pepper (or to taste)
2 sticks butter or margarine
2 tablespoons fresh lemon juice
Salt and pepper to taste

Place egg yolks, cream cheese and cayenne in blender container. Cover; blend at low speed just until cheese is smooth, about 5 seconds. In small saucepan heat butter and lemon juice until butter melts and almost boils. Turn blender on high speed. With lid ajar, slowly pour in butter, blending until thick and fluffy, about 30 seconds. Pour into saucepan or top of double boiler over warm water. Season to taste; keep warm. **Makes 2½ cups.**

Preparation Time: 10 Minutes

POULTRY

Sailing Into the Sunset

Charting a course for the coves where pirates once buried their riches, we find the next treasure, Tampa Bay sailing. The sleek boats silhouetted against the sunset are competing in the Thursday Night Series, a weekly regatta during the spring, summer and fall.

For the most avid sailors, racing continues throughout the winter. The Southern Ocean Racing Conference held in February attracts yachtsmen and boats from all over the world. The enjoyment of the competition is enhanced by Tampa's crisp winter breezes, brilliant blue skies and bright sunshine. The consistent winds serve to propel the boats southward on their course from Tampa to the Florida Keys and then eastward to the Bahamas.

More relaxed sailors find "gunkholing" the way to go. Just stow some provisions, hop on board and set an easy course for a quiet harbor, pristine beach or intercoastal island. Gunkholers like to drop anchor for the night, enjoy spectacular sunsets and rise with the peaceful dawn to set sail for another port. A favorite pastime is watching the many varieties of exotic water birds, eagles and hawks along the way, or hoping to catch a glimpse of a gentle manatee. "Gunkholing" is a wonderful way to discover a little bit of Tampa paradise.

There is nothing like sun and fun to whet the appetite. Cookouts, on a boat or on the beach, are favorite Florida pastimes. Poultry is a great entree for outdoor entertaining. Chicken can be grilled with fresh herbs or enhanced with tropical sauces. Carrying on Florida's pioneer day traditions, we share with you delicious secrets for cooking the quail and doves that abound in the orange groves, woods and ranches nearby.

The Sailing photograph was underwritten by
Jim and Anne Comer
Jim and Lesley Lee

POULTRY

SUPPER ON BOARD

Fresh Herb Grilled Chicken

Cumin Rice Timbales

Sour Cream Rolls

Roasted Succotash

Lemon Cream Pastry

**The menu photograph was underwritten by
Clewis and Winkie Howell**

Fresh Herb Grilled Chicken

8 large whole chicken breasts,
  halved
½ cup olive oil
½ cup fresh lemon juice
1 teaspoon Dijon mustard
4 cloves garlic, crushed
¼ cup fresh parsley, chopped
1 tablespoon fresh rosemary,
  chopped
1 tablespoon fresh tarragon,
  chopped
1 tablespoon fresh sage, chopped
1 tablespoon fresh oregano,
  chopped
1 tablespoon fresh chives, chopped
½ teaspoon salt
Freshly ground pepper to taste

At least 2 hours before cooking: Place chicken in 9 x 13-inch baking pan. Combine remaining ingredients; pour over chicken. Marinate in refrigerator at least 2 hours.

When ready to cook: Drain chicken, reserving marinade. Grill chicken, brushing frequently with marinade, about 10 minutes per side or until done. Discard remaining marinade.

8 to 12 servings.

Preparation Time: 15 Minutes   *Cooking Time: 20 Minutes*

Treasure Tip: Make your own herb vinegar by adding your favorite fresh herbs to the vinegar bottle and letting them sit two weeks, swirling the bottle occasionally. Add herbs to butter and use on vegetables, fish or meats. To make herb oil, add dried (never fresh) herbs to the bottle; let it sit two weeks. Strain the oil; add more herbs; let it sit two more weeks.

Cumin Rice Timbales

2 tablespoons olive oil
½ cup onion, minced
1 teaspoon cumin seeds
⅛ teaspoon dried hot red pepper
  flakes
1 cup converted rice
1 cup chicken broth
¼ teaspoon salt
1 tablespoon fresh parsley, minced
½ teaspoon cumin seeds, lightly
  toasted (garnish)

In deep, heavy saucepan, heat oil over moderately low heat. Sauté onion, cumin seeds and red pepper flakes, stirring, until onion softens. Add rice; cook, stirring, 1 minute. Stir in broth, 1 cup water and salt; bring to boil; reduce heat to low. Cover pan; cook until liquid is absorbed, 18 to 20 minutes. Remove from heat; fluff rice with fork; stir in parsley. Let stand, covered, 5 minutes. Pack rice into six lightly oiled ¼-cup timbale molds or custard cups. To serve, unmold timbales on plate; sprinkle with toasted cumin seeds.

6 servings.

Preparation Time: 10 Minutes   *Cooking Time: 25 Minutes*

Sour Cream Rolls

¼ cup sugar
2 teaspoons salt
1 package dry yeast
4¾ cups flour, divided
2 cups sour cream
1 egg, beaten

About 2½ hours before serving: In large bowl of electric mixer combine sugar, salt, yeast and 1 cup flour. Heat ⅓ cup water until very warm, 120 ° to 130° F. With mixer at low speed, gradually beat water into dry ingredients, just until blended. Increase speed to medium; beat 2 minutes, scraping bowl occasionally with rubber spatula. Beat in sour cream and 1 cup flour to make thick batter; continue beating 2 minutes, scraping bowl often. With wooden spoon, stir in 2 cups flour to make soft dough.

Place dough on lightly floured surface; knead until smooth and elastic, about 10 minutes, working in more flour, ½ to ¾ cup while kneading. Shape dough into ball; place in large greased bowl, turning dough to grease top. Cover; let rise in warm place, away from draft, until doubled, about 1½ hours. Punch down dough; place on lightly floured surface. Cover dough with bowl; let rest 15 minutes. Grease 2 large cookie sheets.

Preheat oven to 400° F. With floured rolling pin, roll dough ½ inch thick. Using 3-inch-round cookie cutter, cut dough into circles; reserve trimmings. Using metal spatula, place circles 1 inch apart on cookie sheets. Using pastry brush, brush circles with a little beaten egg. Fold each circle almost in half. With tip of spoon firmly press edges together to seal. Brush tops again with beaten egg.

Re-roll trimmings; continue to cut and shape until all dough is used. Bake until lightly browned, about 15 minutes; serve warm. Note: Rolls may be made 1 day ahead. Cool on wire rack; wrap in single layer with foil. Just before serving, reheat wrapped rolls in preheated 400° F. oven 10 minutes or until warm.

Makes 24.

Preparation Time: 20 Minutes
(Plus Rising)

Cooking Time: 15 Minutes

Treasure Tip: To make light tender rolls, the dough should be as soft as can be handled without sticking to your hands or work surface.

Roasted Succotash

6 large ears corn, in husks
String
1 (10-ounce) package frozen lima
  beans, cooked
1 large tomato, seeded and diced
1/4 pound smoked Gouda cheese,
  shredded (1 cup)
3 tablespoons butter or margarine,
  melted
1 teaspoon sugar
1/2 teaspoon lemon pepper
  seasoning
1/2 teaspoon salt

About 1½ hours before serving: Carefully pull husks back from each ear of corn. Remove ears of corn and silk, leaving husks attached to stems. Place husks in deep saucepan; cover with water. Cut six 10-inch-long pieces of string; place in pan with husks; set aside. Boil 3 to 4 ears of corn until tender. With sharp knife, cut kernels from 3 to 4 ears of corn (enough to measure 3 cups); place in large bowl. Save the other ears to cook later. Stir in lima beans and remaining ingredients.

When ready to cook: Preheat oven to 425° F. Remove husks and string from water; shake excess water from husks. Carefully peel ¼ of husk from stem. Tie open end of each husk tightly with string to make boot shape; cut off loose ends of string. Carefully place about 1 cup succotash mixture into each husk. Place husks on jelly roll pan; bake until heated through, about 15 minutes. Serve succotash in husks. *6 servings.*

Preparation Time: 45 Minutes   *Cooking Time: 25 Minutes*

Lemon Cream Pastry

Lemon Curd

8 egg yolks
1½ cups superfine sugar
1 cup fresh lemon juice
¼ cup lemon peel, freshly grated

Pastry

*1 (17½-ounce) package frozen puff
 pastry, thawed*
1 egg, beaten
2 cups whipping cream, chilled
*Superfine sugar (enough to
 sweeten cream)*
2 pints strawberries, thinly sliced
*Fresh raspberries and powdered
 sugar for garnish*

Up to several days ahead, make Lemon Curd: In medium bowl of electric mixer, beat egg yolks and sugar until pale and thick, about 5 minutes; blend in lemon juice and peel. Place mixture in double boiler over low heat. Cook, whisking frequently, until lemon curd is texture of custard, 25 to 30 minutes. Work mixture through fine mesh strainer into bowl. Omit this step if you like the way it looks and tastes with peel in it. Cover; refrigerate until needed.

About 1 hour before serving: Preheat oven to 400° F. Refrigerate mixing bowl and beaters. Roll puff pastry out on lightly floured surface to ¼-inch thickness. (If pastry is pre-rolled, omit this step. Pastry could become tough if rolled twice.) Cut out eight 6 x 3-inch rectangles of pastry. Place on cookie sheet; brush tops with beaten egg. Score edge of tops with tines of fork. Bake until crisp and light brown, about 12 minutes. With serrated knife, split rectangles horizontally.

Remove bowl and beaters from refrigerator. Place cream in bowl; beat until stiff peaks form, adding enough superfine sugar to sweeten. Spread each serving plate with thin layer of lemon curd; place bottom half of pastry in center of each plate; spread with thin layer of lemon curd. Spread 1-inch-thick layer of whipped cream on pastry; top with other half of pastry. Spread with thin layer of lemon curd; cover with another layer of whipped cream. Decorate with strawberry slices; scatter raspberries in lemon curd on plates. Dust with powdered sugar; serve immediately.   *8 servings.*

Preparation Time: 45 Minutes   *Cooking Time: 45 Minutes*

Herb-Roasted Chicken with Perfect Giblet Gravy

1 (5 pound) roasting chicken

Herb Butter

⅓ cup butter or margarine,
  softened
2 teaspoons fresh lemon juice
2 tablespoons fresh parsley,
  chopped
1 tablespoon green onion, chopped
½ teaspoon salt
⅛ teaspoon pepper

Stuffing

1 stick butter or margarine
½ cup celery, chopped
½ cup whole green onions, chopped
4 cups day-old white bread cubes
2 tablespoons fresh parsley,
  chopped
½ teaspoon thyme
½ teaspoon salt
⅛ teaspoon pepper

Perfect Giblet Gravy

Chicken giblets and neck
1 onion, peeled and halved
Celery top from 1 stalk
2 whole black peppercorns
Salt to taste
1 (10½-ounce) can chicken broth,
  undiluted
¼ cup pan drippings
¼ cup flour

About 2½ hours before serving: Remove giblets from chicken. Wash chicken with cold running water; pat dry, inside and out, with paper towels.

Make herb butter: In small bowl beat all ingredients with fork, combining well. Using rubber spatula, carefully loosen skin from either side of chicken breast (don't break skin). With spatula carefully insert herb butter between breast meat and skin on both sides, pushing butter in as far as it will go.

Make stuffing: Melt butter in large saucepan; sauté celery and green onion until golden. Remove from heat; add remaining ingredients; toss to combine well. Preheat oven to 350° F. Stuff neck and body cavities of chicken. Bring neck skin over back; tuck wings under. Close body cavity with poultry pin; truss with string. Place chicken in uncovered roasting pan. Place meat thermometer in thigh. Roast 1¾ to 2 hours, until meat thermometer reads 180° F, basting occasionally with pan drippings. Place chicken on warm platter; remove pins and twine; let chicken stand 15 minutes before carving.

As soon as chicken is in oven, make gravy: Rinse giblets; place all except liver in deep saucepan (refrigerate liver until later). Add neck, onion halves, celery top, peppercorns, salt and broth. Add ¾ cup water. Bring to boil; reduce heat to low; cover pan; simmer 1¼ hours. Add liver; simmer 15 minutes more. Strain; add water to make 2 cups. Chop giblets fine; set aside until chicken is done. After placing chicken on platter, pour off pan drippings, reserving ¼ cup. Return reserved drippings to pan. With wire whisk, stir in flour until smooth. Place pan on stove; add broth. Bring to boil, stirring; add giblets. Reduce heat; simmer 1 minute. Season to taste; serve. **6 servings.**

Preparation Time: 25 Minutes   **Cooking Time: 2 Hours**

Rosemary Garlic Chicken

1 (4-pound) roasting chicken
2 large, or 4 small, lemons
1 head garlic cloves
Fresh rosemary sprigs
Olive oil
2 pounds small red potatoes
   (optional)

Preheat oven to 425° F. Wash chicken under cold water; pat dry, inside and out, with paper towels. Cut lemons in quarters. Separate garlic into cloves. Smash cloves with flat side of heavy knife; remove skin. Stuff chicken cavity with lemon quarters and garlic; tie legs together. Tuck rosemary sprigs between thighs and breast. Rub chicken with olive oil; place in roasting pan; roast 30 minutes. Reduce heat to 375° F.; place potatoes around chicken, if desired. Roast until juices run clear when chicken is pricked with fork, 35 to 45 minutes longer. To keep meat from breaking apart when carved, let chicken rest 10 to 15 minutes before serving. **4 servings.**

Preparation Time: 10 Minutes   **Cooking Time: 1 Hour 15 Minutes**

Treasure Tip: Poached chicken makes an excellent base for chicken salads and casseroles. For a moist, succulent poached chicken, keep your poaching liquid (water or chicken stock) at a gentle simmer. Remove chicken when breast is firm and drumsticks barely move.

Chicken and Yellow Rice

A favorite dish in Tampa's Spanish restaurants

About ¼ cup olive oil, divided
1 cut-up frying chicken, or 6 pieces
   chicken
1 medium Spanish onion, chopped
½ large green pepper, chopped
2 to 3 cloves garlic, minced
¼ cup tomato sauce
1 bay leaf
1 teaspoon crushed oregano
2 teaspoons salt
Pepper to taste
1 (14½-ounce) can low-salt chicken
   broth, mixed with water to make
   3 cups
1 (1-gram) envelope Vigo Spanish
   flavoring and coloring
Juice of ½ lemon (about 1
   tablespoon)
2 cups long-grain rice
1 (8½-ounce) can small early peas
   (optional, but traditional)

In heavy skillet over medium-high heat, heat enough oil to cover bottom of pan. Brown chicken pieces on both sides; remove from pan. While chicken browns, heat about 2 tablespoons oil (enough to cover bottom of pan lightly) in large, heavy saucepan over medium-high heat. Sauté onion, green pepper and garlic until clear but not brown. Turn down heat, if necessary. Add tomato sauce, bay leaf, oregano, salt and pepper; stir well. Add chicken broth, Spanish flavoring and lemon juice. Add chicken; bring to boil. Reduce heat to medium; cover pan; cook 30 minutes.

Remove chicken; add rice to pot; stir well. Place chicken on top of rice; return to rapid boil. Cover pot; turn off heat. Let sit covered 30 minutes (do not peek, or rice will stop steaming). When ready to serve, garnish with heated peas. Note: This can be prepared up to 1 day in advance. To reheat, place chicken and rice in casserole; cover; place in pre-heated 350° F. oven 20 minutes or until hot. Garnish; serve. **4 to 6 servings.**

Preparation Time: 20 Minutes   **Cooking Time: 1 Hour**

Chicken à la Duxelles

Brown Sauce

½ stick butter
1 heaping tablespoon flour
1 onion, finely chopped
1 shallot, finely chopped
1 clove garlic, chopped
1 carrot, peeled and chopped
1 heaping teaspoon tomato paste
1 teaspoon B-V seasoning
   (concentrated beef broth)
2 cups strong chicken stock
Bouquet garni (1 stalk celery,
   chopped, 1 sprig fresh thyme or
   ½ teaspoon dried thyme and 1
   bay leaf, tied together or put in
   cheesecloth bag)
Crushed pepper to taste

Duxelles

1 stick butter
1 pound fresh mushroom caps,
   finely chopped
¼ cup shallots, chopped fine
1 teaspoon freshly ground pepper
1 clove garlic, crushed
Juice of 1 lemon

Chicken

4 boneless chicken breasts with
   skin
Salt and pepper to taste
¼ cup plus about 2 teaspoons
   brandy, divided
3 tablespoons butter, divided
¾ cup dry white wine

At least 2 hours ahead, make brown sauce: In large saucepan over medium heat melt butter; add flour; stir constantly until flour browns. Gradually whisk in chicken stock. Add remaining ingredients; reduce heat; simmer 1½ hours, stirring occasionally.

Make duxelles: In large skillet over high heat, melt butter; add mushrooms, shallots and pepper; heat, stirring, until liquid evaporates. Add garlic and lemon juice; remove from heat; set aside until needed. Slice pockets in chicken breasts; fill each with duxelles. Sprinkle salt, pepper and brandy over each breast.

Melt 1 tablespoon butter in second large skillet over medium-high heat. Add chicken breasts, skin side down; cover with foil; weight foil down with heavy pot. Brown 1 minute. Turn breasts over; repeat procedure.

Remove breasts from pan; cover to keep warm. Add ¼ cup brandy to pan; deglaze over high heat. Add remaining butter to melt; add 1 cup brown sauce and wine. Bring to boil; add chicken; cover. Simmer 15 minutes, or until chicken is cooked. Serve chicken with sauce.

4 servings.

Preparation Time: 40 Minutes   *Cooking Time: 2 Hours*

Treasure Tip: Duxelles is a basic preparation of finely chopped mushrooms, shallots and/or onions sautéed in butter. It can be frozen in small containers and may be used in place of chopped mushrooms.

Chicken Piccata

1 cup flour
1 teaspoon pepper
1 teaspoon salt
½ teaspoon basil
1 teaspoon garlic powder
6 ounces beer
3 to 4 whole chicken breasts,
    halved, boned and skinned
¼ cup olive oil
¼ cup dry sherry
Juice of 1 lemon

In small bowl mix flour, pepper, salt, basil and garlic powder; pour beer into another bowl. Heat oil in large skillet over medium-high heat. Dip chicken pieces into beer; dust with flour mixture. Brown chicken 5 minutes per side. Remove chicken; add sherry and lemon juice to skillet; cook over medium-high heat 1 minute. Return chicken to pan; cover. Cook over low heat until chicken is done, about 15 minutes. To serve, pour sauce over chicken.

6 to 8 servings.

Preparation Time: 15 Minutes   *Cooking Time: 25 Minutes*

Cognac Mushroom Chicken

4 whole chicken breasts, halved,
    boned and skinned
Salt and pepper to taste
Italian seasoning
Flour for dredging
2 to 4 tablespoons butter
3 tablespoons cognac
1½ tablespoons butter
1½ tablespoons flour
¾ cup white wine
1½ teaspoons chicken bouillon
    powder
½ pound fresh mushrooms, sautéed
    until soft
Fresh parsley, minced

Place chicken breasts between two sheets of waxed paper. Pound with meat mallet to flatten slightly; sprinkle with salt and pepper. Coat with Italian seasoning; lightly dredge with flour. Melt 2 tablespoons butter in large, flat skillet over medium-high heat; brown chicken on both sides. Add more butter as needed to brown all chicken. Add cognac; using long match, ignite cognac; let flame burn out. Remove chicken to heated platter.

Melt 1½ tablespoons butter in same skillet; add 1½ tablespoons flour; cook and stir over low heat until flour browns. Dissolve bouillon in 1 cup boiling water; add with wine to skillet. Stir; bring to simmering. Add chicken; cook over low heat, 8 to 12 minutes. Add mushrooms and parsley; cook 5 minutes more.

6 to 8 servings.

Preparation Time: 10 Minutes   *Cooking Time: 25 to 30 Minutes*

Sherried Sesame Chicken

1 tablespoon instant minced onion
¼ cup plus 2 tablespoons soy sauce
1 tablespoon sugar
3 tablespoons sherry
3 tablespoons peanut or vegetable oil
¼ teaspoon ground ginger
Dash red pepper
3 whole chicken breasts, halved and skinned
1½ teaspoons sesame seeds

Preheat oven to 350° F. In small bowl combine all ingredients except chicken and sesame seeds. Place chicken in lightly greased baking dish. Pour sauce mixture over chicken. Cover; bake 30 minutes. Turn chicken; sprinkle with sesame seeds. Bake, uncovered, 10 minutes more or until done.

4 to 6 servings.

Preparation Time: 10 Minutes   *Cooking Time: 40 Minutes*

Country Manor Chicken

3 to 4 pounds skinned chicken pieces
1 (16-ounce) jar orange marmalade
⅓ cup prepared mustard
1 teaspoon curry powder
½ teaspoon salt
2 tablespoons lemon juice
1 lemon, thinly sliced
2 tablespoons cornstarch

Preheat oven to 350° F. Arrange chicken in shallow baking dish. In small saucepan over medium-low heat, heat marmalade, mustard, curry powder and salt until marmalade melts. Add lemon juice; pour over chicken. Cover with foil; bake 40 minutes. Remove foil; baste; top with lemon slices. Bake 20 minutes more. Remove chicken from oven; keep warm. Pour sauce back into saucepan. Combine ½ cup water and cornstarch; blend into sauce. Cook until thickened; pour over chicken to serve.

4 to 6 servings.

Preparation Time: 10 Minutes   *Cooking Time: 1 Hour*

Chicken in Champagne

2 tablespoons butter or margarine
4 whole chicken breasts, halved, skinned and boned
1 cup fresh mushrooms
⅔ cup champagne*
⅔ cup sour cream
¼ teaspoon salt
¼ teaspoon white pepper

*Chill the rest and serve with dinner.

Preheat oven to 350° F. In large skillet melt butter; add chicken; brown. Remove chicken to 2-quart baking dish; leave drippings in skillet. Add mushrooms to skillet; sauté. Remove; set aside to keep warm. Stir champagne into skillet drippings; simmer until heated through. Pour over chicken; bake 20 minutes. Remove chicken to heated platter, leaving liquid in casserole. Add sour cream, salt and pepper to liquid; whisk until smooth. Pour over chicken; top with mushrooms; serve.

4 to 6 servings.

Preparation Time: 20 Minutes   *Cooking Time: 40 Minutes*

Curried Chicken with Currants and Apples

1 whole chicken (3½ to 4 pounds)
½ stick butter or margarine
1 small onion, chopped
1 small apple, chopped
½ cup currants
1 to 2 teaspoons curry powder
⅛ teaspoon ginger
½ cup slivered almonds
¼ teaspoon salt
1½ cups cooked rice

Preheat oven to 375° F. Wash chicken; pat dry; set aside. In large skillet melt butter; sauté onions, apples, currants and curry powder until onions and apples are tender. Remove from heat; stir in ginger, almonds, salt and rice; mix well. Stuff chicken cavity with mixture; place any extra stuffing in small covered casserole. Bake chicken 1½ hours; extra stuffing 30 minutes.

4 servings.

Preparation Time: 30 Minutes

Cooking Time: 1 Hour 30 Minutes

Chicken Dressed in Blue

2 tablespoons butter or margarine
4 whole chicken breasts, halved and boned
1 medium white onion, quartered
⅓ cup fresh green pepper, chopped
3 ounces dry vermouth
1 cup sour cream
¼ cup bleu cheese (about 1¼ ounces), crumbled
1 tablespoon fresh lemon juice
½ teaspoon salt
Dash garlic salt
Dash pepper
Dash tarragon
Dash paprika
Paprika and fresh parsley, chopped (garnish)

Preheat oven to 350° F. Melt butter in 10-inch skillet over medium-high heat; sauté chicken, turning several times, until lightly browned. Place chicken in 2-quart casserole dish; reserve pan juices. In food processor or blender place pan juices, onion and remaining ingredients; combine well. Pour over chicken; bake, covered, 1 hour. Garnish; serve. *4 to 6 servings.*

Preparation Time: 30 Minutes

Cooking Time: 1 Hour

Treasure Tip: Chicken is among the most perishable of meats. Take it straight home from the supermarket and refrigerate it with plans to use it within 1 or 2 days or freeze it. After cutting up chicken, always wash your hands, knife and cutting board with soap and hot water.

Honey Chicken with Rosemary

2 tablespoons fresh rosemary, finely chopped
¼ cup honey
2 tablespoons grainy mustard
2 small cloves garlic, finely chopped
¼ cup olive oil
2 teaspoons fresh lime or lemon juice
¼ teaspoon pepper, freshly ground
Salt to taste
4 whole chicken breasts, cut in half

Several hours before cooking: Combine all ingredients except chicken; pour over chicken in shallow dish. Marinate several hours. Grill, basting with marinade, 40 to 45 minutes over low-burning coals. *4 to 6 servings.*

Preparation Time: 10 Minutes   Cooking Time: 40 to 45 Minutes

Treasure Tip: To get more juice out of a lime or lemon, let it come to room temperature or place under hot water before squeezing.

Brandied Chicken Macadamia

1 (3½-ounce) jar macadamia nuts
2 tablespoons butter
2 eggs
2 tablespoons peanut or vegetable oil
2 tablespoons soy sauce
1 teaspoon powdered ginger
¼ teaspoon pepper
2 tablespoons brandy
1 medium onion, minced
½ cup flour
¼ cup cornstarch
3 whole chicken breasts, halved
Peanut or vegetable oil for frying

Sweet and Sour Sauce
½ medium green pepper, diced
½ medium red bell pepper, diced
1 chicken bouillon cube
3 tablespoons dark brown sugar
3 tablespoons cider vinegar
4 teaspoons cornstarch
½ cup sugar
3 ounces pineapple juice

About 30 minutes before cooking: Preheat oven to 350° F. Place macadamias and butter in shallow baking pan. Bake, stirring frequently, until light brown, about 15 minutes. Be careful not to scorch nuts. Into food processor or blender put eggs, peanut oil, soy sauce, ginger, pepper, brandy, onion, ¼ cup cold water, flour and cornstarch; blend well. Place chicken in shallow pan; add batter; soak chicken in batter at least 20 minutes.

When ready to cook: Heat enough oil in large skillet, and panfry chicken until done, about 20 minutes.

While chicken fries, make Sweet and Sour Sauce: Place peppers and 1 cup water in medium saucepan. Bring to boil; reduce heat; simmer 1 minute or longer. Add bouillon cube and brown sugar. Combine vinegar and cornstarch to make smooth paste; slowly add paste to simmering liquid. Cook until sauce is thick and clear, 1 to 2 minutes. Add sugar and pineapple juice. To serve, place chicken on heated platter; cover with sauce; top with toasted macadamia nuts. *4 to 6 servings.*

Preparation Time: 40 Minutes   Cooking Time: 20 Minutes

Treasure Tip: Cornstarch must be dissolved in cold liquid before adding to a hot mixture, or it will lump. Cornstarch, used frequently in Oriental cooking produces the glazed, translucent sheen often associated with Chinese food.

Ybor Chicken

About ½ cup flour
1 whole chicken, cut up
Salt and pepper to taste
2 tablespoons olive oil
1 green pepper, cut in large pieces
1 large onion, cut in large pieces
1 large clove garlic, minced
1 large tomato, chopped
1 bay leaf
1 cup raisins
1 cup pimento-stuffed green olives,
    sliced
1 cup dry red wine
1 chorizo (Spanish sausage),
    chopped

Mix flour, salt and pepper; coat chicken in mixture. Heat olive oil in large skillet over medium heat; brown chicken slowly. Preheat oven to 325° F. Remove chicken to casserole dish. In oil remaining in skillet, sauté green pepper, onion, garlic, tomato, bay leaf, raisins and olives. Add wine; simmer 5 minutes. Pour over chicken in casserole; add chorizo. Cover; bake until chicken is tender, 1¼ to 1½ hours. Serve with white rice.

4 servings.

Preparation Time: 30 Minutes

**Cooking Time: 1 Hour
30 Minutes**

Treasure Tip: *"Chorizo" is the Spanish word for sausage. In Tampa's Spanish restaurants and markets, chorizo is a dried, highly spiced link sausage.*

Sizzling Chicken-Walnut Sauté

2 whole chicken breasts, skinned,
    boned, cut into bite-size pieces
3 tablespoons vegetable oil
3 to 4 whole green onions, chopped
2 medium celery stalks, chopped
1 tablespoon butter
¾ cup walnuts, coarsely chopped
1 teaspoon lemon peel, chopped
2 tablespoons soy sauce
1 tablespoon fresh lemon juice

In large skillet or wok, heat chicken and oil over medium heat until sizzling hot. Add onions and celery; stir-fry quickly until chicken is brown. Add butter, walnuts and lemon peel. Cook, uncovered, several minutes, stirring often. Turn off heat; add soy sauce and lemon juice. Stir until chicken is well coated. Serve at once with rice.

4 servings.

Preparation Time: 15 Minutes

Cooking Time: 15 Minutes

Treasure Tip: *The principle of stir-frying is to put the ingredients that need longer cooking in the skillet or wok first, followed by the other ingredients. The method originated centuries ago in China from the need to save fuel.*

Lime Chicken with Black Bean Sauce

1/4 cup fresh lime juice
1/2 cup vegetable oil
1/2 teaspoon cayenne pepper
1 clove garlic, crushed
4 whole chicken breasts, halved,
　skinned and boned
2 tablespoons red onion, chopped,
　parboiled
1 red bell pepper, diced and
　parboiled
Several sprigs fresh cilantro
　(garnish)

Black Bean Sauce

2 tablespoons balsamic vinegar
1/2 cup fresh orange juice
1 clove garlic, crushed
1 cup cooked black beans, drained
　and rinsed
Salt and freshly ground pepper to
　taste

Night before, or at least 8 hours before cooking: In large glass, ceramic or stainless bowl (or large plastic bag) mix lime juice, oil, cayenne and 1 clove crushed garlic. Add chicken breasts; marinate overnight or at least 8 hours.

When ready to cook: Preheat oven to 350° F. Lightly grease outdoor grill grate and heat grill to medium high heat. Remove chicken from refrigerator and drain. Quickly grill chicken on both sides to seal in juices; remove to shallow baking dish. Place in oven 15 minutes to finish cooking. While chicken is in oven, fill small saucepan with water; bring to boil. Add onion and red bell pepper; return water to boil. Immediately drain onion and pepper; rinse under cold water to blanch.

Make Black Bean Sauce: Place vinegar, orange juice, garlic and black beans in food processor or blender; purée; add salt and pepper to taste. Warm on stovetop or in microwave. To serve, spoon a little black bean sauce onto warm serving platter; arrange chicken on top of sauce. Sprinkle tops of chicken breasts with onion and bell pepper; garnish platter with cilantro. Serve with our Fiesta or Savory Beer Rice, salad and Cuban bread. *4 to 6 servings.*

Preparation Time: 30 Minutes　　　*Cooking Time: 20 Minutes*

Blackened Chicken with Tomato-Olive Butter

³/₄ teaspoon oregano
³/₄ teaspoon garlic powder
¹/₂ teaspoon cayenne pepper
¹/₂ teaspoon freshly ground black
  pepper
3 whole chicken breasts, halved,
  boned and skinned (or 6 turkey
  cutlets, about 4 ounces each)
1¹/₂ tablespoons olive oil

Tomato-Olive Butter

3 tablespoons unsalted butter
¹/₂ cup onion, chopped
1¹/₂ teaspoons garlic, chopped
1¹/₄ cups fresh tomatoes, peeled,
  seeded and chopped
¹/₂ cup chicken broth
12 black Calamata olives, pitted
  and sliced
6 green olives, pitted and sliced

About 40 minutes before cooking: In small bowl mix oregano, garlic powder, cayenne and black pepper. Rub mixture on both sides of chicken breasts. Cover; let stand 30 minutes.

Make Tomato Olive Butter: Melt butter in large skillet over medium-high heat. Add onion; sauté until softened, about 5 minutes. Add garlic and tomatoes; sauté 2 minutes. Add stock and olives; cook 5 minutes, stirring frequently. Set aside; keep warm. Melt olive oil in large, heavy skillet over high heat. Add chicken; sauté until golden brown, about 5 minutes per side. Remove chicken to warm platter; tent with foil to keep warm. Pour any juices from chicken platter into sauce; mix. Spoon sauce over chicken to serve. **4 to 6 servings.**

Preparation Time: 40 Minutes   *Cooking Time: 20 Minutes*

Treasure Tip: Greek Calamata olives, pickled in wine vinegar, have a very different flavor from California black olives. They add a unique flavor to this dish.

Orange Sherried Chicken

6 chicken breast halves (or 1 whole
  chicken)
¹/₂ cup onions, sliced
¹/₄ cup green pepper, chopped
1 cup fresh mushrooms, sliced
1 cup fresh orange juice
3 tablespoons sherry
1 tablespoon brown sugar
1 teaspoon salt
¹/₄ teaspoon freshly ground black
  pepper
1 tablespoon flour
1¹/₂ tablespoons fresh parsley,
  chopped

Preheat oven to 375° F. Place chicken, skin side up, in shallow baking pan. Add onions, green pepper and mushrooms. In shallow saucepan over moderate heat, combine remaining ingredients and ¹/₂ cup water. Cook, stirring, until mixture thickens and bubbles. Pour over chicken. Bake uncovered, 1 to 1¹/₄ hours, basting often with pan juices. **4 to 6 servings.**

Preparation Time: 15 Minutes   *Cooking Time: 1 Hour*
                                                 15 Minutes

Fiery Mexican Chicken

4 whole chicken breasts, halved,
  skinned and boned
1 (7-ounce) can green chiles
4 ounces Monterey Jack cheese, cut
  in 8 strips
1/2 cup fine dry bread crumbs
1/4 cup Parmesan cheese, freshly
  grated
1 tablespoon chili powder
1/2 teaspoon salt
3/4 teaspoon ground cumin, divided
1/4 teaspoon black pepper
2 tablespoons plus 2 teaspoons
  melted butter, divided
1 (16-ounce) can tomato sauce
1/3 cup whole green onions, sliced
Salt, pepper and Tabasco to taste

At least 4 hours before cooking: Place chicken pieces between two sheets of waxed paper; pound with meat mallet to about 1/4-inch thickness. Place about 2 tablespoons chiles and 1 strip Monterey Jack in center of each chicken piece; roll up; tuck ends under. In small bowl combine bread crumbs, Parmesan, chili powder, 1/4 teaspoon cumin and pepper. Place 2 tablespoons melted butter in shallow bowl. Dip each chicken roll in butter; roll in crumb mixture. Place chicken rolls, seam side down, in oblong baking dish; drizzle with 2 teaspoons melted butter. Cover; refrigerate at least 4 hours.

When ready to cook: Preheat oven to 400° F. Bake uncovered until done, about 20 minutes.

While chicken is cooking, make sauce: In small saucepan combine tomato sauce, remaining cumin, onions, salt, pepper and Tabasco; heat. Makes about 2 cups sauce to serve over chicken rolls.   *4 to 6 servings.*

Preparation Time: 20 Minutes   *Cooking Time: 20 Minutes*

Curry Chicken Cakes

From Mise en Place Restaurant, known for its "Floribbean flair".

2 (8-ounce) chicken breasts
Salt and pepper to taste
3 to 4 tablespoons olive oil
1 small onion, diced
1 stalk celery, diced
1 green pepper, diced
1 red bell pepper, diced
1 fresh jalapeño pepper, diced
3 tablespoons mayonnaise
2 eggs
2 tablespoons curry powder
1/4 teaspoon cayenne pepper
About 1/4 cup fresh bread crumbs
3 tablespoons vegetable oil
About 1/4 cup flour
Mango or tomato chutney

About 2 hours before serving: Preheat oven to 400° F. Season chicken with salt and pepper; rub with olive oil; place in shallow baking dish. Bake until tender, 20 to 25 minutes; cool. Finely julienne chicken; set aside. Heat 2 tablespoons olive oil in small skillet; sauté onion, celery and peppers 3 minutes; cool.

When ready to cook: In large mixing bowl combine chicken, onion mixture, mayonnaise, eggs, curry powder and cayenne; blend together. Add enough bread crumbs to bind mixture. Roll into 2-ounce patties, about 3 inches in diameter. Lightly dredge in flour, shaking off excess. Heat vegetable oil in nonstick pan; sauté patties until golden brown on both sides. Serve immediately with chutney.   *4 servings.*

Preparation Time: 20 Minutes   *Cooking Time: 30 minutes*

Chicken with Basil Cream Sauce

Basil Cream Sauce
2 shallots, chopped
¾ cup heavy cream
¼ cup chicken broth
About 20 fresh basil leaves,
 julienned

4 boneless chicken breast halves,
 skin intact
2 to 4 ounces chèvre (amount
 depends upon size of chicken
 breasts)
12 to 20 fresh basil leaves, washed
 and patted dry
Salt and freshly ground pepper to
 taste

Make sauce: In medium saucepan, simmer shallots with cream and broth until reduced by two-thirds; strain; set aside.

Make chicken: Carefully cut 1 x 2-inch pocket in meaty part of center of breasts. Wrap ½ to 1 ounce chèvre in 2 or 3 basil leaves (cheese should fit easily in pocket of breast). Place basil-wrapped cheese in pocket; gently close flap (do not sew or use skewers). Place 1 to 2 basil leaves directly under skin on top side of chicken breast; close skin over. Season to taste.

Grill breasts over medium-hot coals until juices run clear, 7 to 8 minutes per side (or sauté in light film of olive oil over moderate heat 6 to 10 minutes per side). Keep chicken warm while finishing sauce. Warm sauce; stir half of julienned basil leaves into sauce. With very sharp knife cut each breast into ⅓- to ½-inch slices. Divide sauce evenly among four warm plates; overlap chicken pieces on top of sauce. Garnish with remaining julienned basil. *4 servings.*

Preparation Time: 30 Minutes   *Cooking Time: 15 Minutes*

Kung Pao Chicken

1 pound chicken breast, boned and
    cut in 1-inch cubes
1/4 cup plus 2 tablespoons soy
    sauce, divided
1½ tablespoons plus 1 teaspoon
    cornstarch, divided
1/4 teaspoon garlic salt
4 dried red chiles (or more to taste)
2 tablespoons white wine or sherry
2 tablespoons sugar
1 teaspoon salt
2 teaspoons sesame oil
Peanut or vegetable oil for stir-
    frying
1 medium onion, diced
1/4 cup green bell pepper, chopped
1/4 cup red bell pepper, chopped
1/2 cup fresh mushrooms, sliced
2 teaspoons fresh ginger, peeled,
    chopped
1 (8-ounce) can bamboo shoots,
    drained and diced
1 (8-ounce) can water chestnuts,
    drained and chopped
1 (7-ounce) jar baby corn, drained
1/2 cup salted peanuts

30 minutes before cooking: Thoroughly combine chicken, 1/4 cup soy sauce, 1½ tablespoons water, 1½ tablespoons cornstarch and garlic salt in bowl. Marinate 30 minutes. Remove tips and seeds from chiles; cut in 1-inch pieces. In small bowl combine 1/2 cup soy sauce, wine, sugar, 1 teaspoon cornstarch, salt and sesame oil. In wok or large, heavy skillet, heat 2 to 3 inches oil to 400° F. Add chicken; fry 30 seconds.

Remove chicken; add onion, green and red peppers and mushrooms. Cook until crisp-tender. Remove vegetables; drain off all oil except 2 tablespoons. Fry chiles until black in reserved oil. Add ginger, chicken, bamboo shoots, water chestnuts and corn, stirring and tossing together. Add vegetables and soy-wine mixture; cook, stirring, just until thickened. Remove from heat; sprinkle with peanuts. Serve over rice.   *4 servings.*

Preparation Time: 30 Minutes   *Cooking Time: 5 Minutes*

Treasure Tip: Although stir-frying looks difficult, the only trick to it is split-second timing. Have every ingredient prepared and within reach before you start to cook. Once you have started, there is no time to stop and look for a sauce or seasoning.

Lemon Dill Peppered Chicken

1 (14-ounce) can chicken broth
1½ tablespoons cornstarch
2 tablespoons fresh lemon juice
2 teaspoons dill weed
1 teaspoon freshly ground black
    pepper
1/8 teaspoon salt
1 egg, beaten
1/4 cup flour, mixed with 1/4
    teaspoon salt
2 whole chicken breasts, halved,
    boned and skinned
1 tablespoon butter
1 tablespoon vegetable oil

In medium saucepan combine broth and cornstarch; stir to mix well. Add lemon juice, dill weed, pepper and salt; place over medium heat. Cook, stirring, until mixture comes to full boil. Reduce heat to low; cook 1 minute longer. Dip chicken in egg, then in flour-salt mixture. Melt butter and oil in large skillet over medium heat; brown chicken. When chicken has browned, pour sauce over it; simmer until chicken is done, about 10 minutes. Serve.   *2 to 4 servings.*

Preparation Time: 10 Minutes   *Cooking Time: 25 Minutes*

Low-Calorie Chicken Picante

½ cup medium-hot chunky taco
*   sauce*
¼ cup Dijon mustard
2 tablespoons fresh lime juice
3 whole chicken breasts, halved,
*   skinned and boned*
¼ cup olive oil
¼ cup plus 2 tablespoons plain
*   yogurt, divided*
1 lime, peeled, sliced into 6
*   sections, membrane removed*

At least 40 minutes before cooking, make marinade: In large bowl mix taco sauce, mustard and lime juice. Add chicken, turning to coat. Marinate at least 30 minutes.

When ready to cook: Heat oil in large skillet over medium heat. Remove chicken from marinade; reserve marinade. Sauté chicken, turning, until brown on all sides, about 10 minutes. Add marinade; cook until fork goes into chicken easily and marinade is slightly reduced and beginning to glaze chicken, about 5 minutes more. Transfer chicken to warm platter. Raise heat to high; boil marinade 1 minute; pour over chicken. Place 1 tablespoon yogurt on each breast; top with piece of lime.

4 to 6 servings.

Preparation Time: 10 Minutes   *Cooking Time: 20 Minutes*

Treasure Tip: This chicken makes fabulous fajitas!

Festive Roast Turkey

1 turkey (18 to 20 pounds)
6 to 8 garlic cloves, sliced
4 to 6 small sprigs fresh rosemary
½ stick butter, softened
Salt and freshly ground pepper to
*   taste*
1 cup chicken broth
About 1½ cups dry white wine or
*   champagne*

Preheat oven to 500° F. Clean turkey, removing any pinfeathers and fat. Discard neck and giblets. Place garlic slices and rosemary sprigs under skin around breast, thighs and legs. Rub softened butter all over outside of turkey. Tie or skewer legs together; close neck. Sprinkle salt and pepper all over. Place turkey, breast side down, on rack in roasting pan. Add chicken broth; place in oven. Turn heat down to 350° F.; cook 30 minutes.

Turn bird breast side up; insert meat thermometer in thick part of thigh, away from bone. Roast 2 to 3 hours, basting with pan juices every 15 to 20 minutes, until internal temperature reaches 185° F. (If breast browns before turkey is done, make loose tent of foil to cover bird.) Remove turkey to heated platter; let stand 15 minutes before carving. Save juices in roasting pan.

While turkey rests, make reduction sauce: Place roasting pan over medium to medium-high heat. Pour in wine; scrape up any brown bits in pan. Cook, stirring, until mixture boils down to about 1 cup and becomes rich tasting. Season to taste; serve with turkey.

12 to 16 servings.

Preparation Time: 30 Minutes   *Cooking Time: 2 to 3 Hours*

Garlic Marinated Turkey

1 ready-to-cook turkey, any size

For each pound of turkey, use:

1 small clove garlic, crushed
1 teaspoon salt
1/2 teaspoon red wine vinegar
1/2 teaspoon crushed oregano
1 tablespoon olive oil

Night before: Discard neck and giblets from turkey. Combine garlic, salt, vinegar, oregano and olive oil in small bowl. Rub turkey well, inside and out, with marinade, using all the mixture. Wrap turkey in heavy-duty foil; refrigerate overnight.

Next day: Preheat oven to 325° F. Place foil-wrapped turkey in roaster or large baking pan, breast side up. For the last 30 to 45 minutes of roasting time, remove foil to allow turkey to brown. Serve warm or cold.

Preparation Time: 10 Minutes   Cooking Time: Depends on Size of Turkey

Treasure Tip: This is great to make at home and take to the beach for vacation. It makes wonderful sandwiches and superb turkey salad.

Hickory-Smoked Turkey Breast

1 turkey breast (5 to 6 pounds)
1 teaspoon plus 1 tablespoon
    seasoned salt, divided
1 teaspoon crushed red pepper
1 1/2 teaspoons dried whole basil
1 teaspoon paprika
Hickory chips

About 4 hours before serving: Rinse turkey breast with cold water; pat dry. Slit breast through center to lay flat on grill. Combine 1 teaspoon seasoned salt and red pepper; sprinkle on breast. Combine 1 tablespoon seasoned salt, basil and paprika; sprinkle on breast. Grease breast to prevent sticking.

Prepare charcoal fire in one end of grill; let burn 15 to 20 minutes. Soak hickory chips in water while grill is heating. Spread coals to one side of grill; place hickory chips on coals. Insert meat thermometer into breast, not touching bone. Place breast on grill opposite hot coals; cook 3 to 3 1/2 hours, until meat thermometer reaches 185° F. Turkey can be smoked in gas or electric grill over medium indirect heat, turning breast once.

12 servings.

Preparation Time: 15 Minute

*Cooking Time 3 Hours
30 Minutes*

Jalapeño-Grilled Hens

6 Rock Cornish game hens (about
    1½ pounds each)
½ stick butter or margarine
⅔ cup jalapeño jelly*
2 tablespoons fresh lime juice
Salt and pepper to taste

*Purchased, or make your own
from recipe on Page 272

Cut game hens in half; rinse; pat dry. In small pot combine butter and jelly; stir over medium heat until melted. Stir in lime juice; set aside. Salt and pepper birds; place skin-side-up, on grill over medium coals. Cook until meat near thighbone is no longer pink, 30 to 40 minutes; cut to test. Turn several times during cooking; baste often with jelly mixture. **6 to 8 servings.**

Preparation Time: 15 Minutes   *Cooking Time: 30 to 40 Minutes*

Ricotta-Stuffed Cornish Hens

1 tablespoon olive oil
3 tablespoons unsalted butter,
    divided
½ cup plus 2 tablespoons shallots,
    chopped
¾ pound fresh mushrooms,
    chopped
¾ pound fresh spinach, rinsed and
    drained, or 1 (10-ounce)
    package frozen leaf spinach
½ cup ricotta cheese, or ¼ cup
    ricotta and ¼ cup feta
2 tablespoons Parmesan cheese,
    freshly grated
1 egg yolk
½ teaspoon dried thyme, crumbled
½ teaspoon salt
Freshly ground pepper to taste
2 ounces pistachio nuts, toasted,
    coarsely chopped
2 Rock Cornish hens (about 1½
    pounds each), split, backbones
    removed
6 small red new potatoes (optional)

Heat olive oil and 1 tablespoon butter in medium skillet over medium heat. When foam subsides, add shallots; cook until softened, about 2 minutes. Add mushrooms; cook, stirring frequently, until mushrooms are browned and liquid evaporates, 7 to 8 minutes. Remove from heat.

Preheat oven to 400° F. Place fresh spinach in steamer over boiling water; cover. Steam until tender, 3 to 5 minutes; drain. (If using frozen spinach, cook as package directs; drain.) When spinach is cool enough to handle, squeeze as dry as possible; chop coarsely. In medium bowl, thoroughly combine mushrooms, shallots, spinach, ricotta, Parmesan, egg yolk, thyme, salt and pepper; stir in pistachios.

Place hens flat on work surface, skin sides up and drumsticks facing you. With hands, open up skin from breast meat. Work half of the stuffing mixture under skin of each hen. Tie drumsticks together with string.

Heat remaining 2 tablespoons butter in small saucepan over low heat. Place hens, skin sides up and wings tucked under, in roasting pan. Add potatoes, if desired. Brush hens and potatoes with butter; salt and pepper to taste. Cook, basting every 10 minutes with pan drippings, until hens are golden brown and potatoes are tender, about 35 minutes. Let stand 5 minutes before serving. **2 servings.**

Preparation Time: 25 to 30 Minutes   *Cooking Time:
35 Minutes*

Cornish Hens with Hot Brandied Fruit

1 teaspoon poultry seasoning
1 teaspoon dried whole thyme
1 teaspoon salt
1 teaspoon pepper
½ teaspoon garlic powder
6 Rock Cornish game hens (about
    1½ pounds each)
4 to 6 tablespoons unsalted butter
1 to 2 tablespoons peach brandy
2 tablespoons butter or margarine
2 (16-ounce) cans peach halves,
    drained
24 white or green seedless grapes,
    sliced lengthwise

Combine poultry seasoning, thyme, salt, pepper and garlic powder. Lightly sprinkle all sides of hens with ice water, then with half of seasoning mixture. Repeat procedure; set aside. In large skillet (two, if necessary) melt unsalted butter. Add hens; cook over low heat 40 to 45 minutes or until done, turning occasionally. If necessary, add more butter to prevent sticking.

Transfer to warm serving platter; sprinkle with brandy; keep warm. Melt 2 tablespoons butter in skillet; add peach halves and grapes. Cook over medium heat, turning once, until lightly browned and thoroughly heated. Arrange fruit around hens on platter; serve.   *6 servings.*

Preparation Time: 15 Minutes   *Cooking Time: 50 Minutes*

Grapefruit Marinated Doves

15 to 20 doves, skinned
1 (11¼-ounce) jar whole jalapeño
    peppers
1 pound bacon
1 quart fresh grapefruit juice
¼ cup soy sauce
1 tablespoon Worcestershire sauce
Garlic powder to taste
Green oak or hickory pieces
2 (12 ounce) cans cola beverage,
    optional

Night before: Using small, sharp knife, carefully cut away both breasts from each dove; discard bones. Cut jalapeños into strips about ¼ inch wide; discard seeds. Cut bacon strips in half; wrap 1 dove breast and 1 pepper strip in each bacon piece; secure with toothpicks. In large bowl mix grapefruit juice, soy sauce, Worcestershire and garlic powder; add dove breasts. Cover; refrigerate overnight.

4 to 4½ hours before serving: Prepare wet smoker for at least 4 hours of cooking time. Remove dove pieces from marinade; reserve some marinade for basting doves. Add rest of marinade to water pan or, for a sweeter taste, add 2 (12-ounce) cans cola-flavored beverage to water in pan. Place doves on rack; cover smoker; cook 2 hours. Baste doves with marinade; cover again. Add green oak or hickory pieces to coals. Smoke at least 2 hours more.   *4 to 6 servings.*

Preparation Time: 1 hour 30 Minutes   *Cooking Time: 4 Hours*

Spicy Grilled Doves

8 doves
½ cup Worcestershire sauce
¼ cup Pickapeppa sauce
1 teaspoon garlic powder
¼ teaspoon marjoram
¼ teaspoon thyme
¼ teaspoon crushed black pepper
Pinch salt

At least 4 hours before cooking: In medium bowl mix Worcestershire and Pickapeppa. Dip doves in mixture; place, breast side down, in baking dish. Pour sauce mixture over birds (birds won't be fully covered). Mix garlic powder, marjoram, thyme, pepper and salt; sprinkle over birds. Cover pan with foil; refrigerate at least 4 hours. Grill over medium-high coals until done, about 30 minutes. **2 to 4 servings.**

Preparation Time: 15 Minutes   Cooking Time: 30 to 45 Minutes

Doves Marsala

8 doves
¼ cup fresh lemon or lime juice (2 to 3 lemons or limes)
Salt and pepper to taste
About ¾ cups flour, divided
¼ cup vegetable oil
1½ sticks unsalted butter, divided
1 cup onion, chopped
1 pound fresh mushrooms, sliced
1 cup Marsala
1½ cups chicken stock or broth
⅔ cup heavy cream

Rub doves inside and out with lemon juice, salt and pepper; roll in flour. Heat cast-iron Dutch oven or large, heavy pot over medium-high heat; add oil and ½ stick butter to melt. Brown birds on all sides; drain on paper towels. Add another ½ stick butter to pan; sauté onions 5 minutes. Add mushrooms; sauté just until tender. Remove; set aside.

In same pan melt remaining butter, scraping up brown bits from pan. Add ½ cup flour; reduce heat; cook slowly until butter and flour begin to foam. Remove from heat; whisk in Marsala, stock and cream. Preheat oven to 350° F. Return doves, onions and mushrooms to pan, stirring to settle. Cover with tight-fitting lid; bake 30 to 40 minutes. **2 to 4 servings.**

Preparation Time: 30 Minutes   Cooking Time: 30 to 40 Minutes

Orange Cranberry Quail

6 quail (about 3 pounds total)
2¾ cups fresh orange juice, divided
Hickory chips
Olive oil
1 (32-ounce) bottle cranberry juice
   (if using smoker)
½ stick unsalted butter, melted
1 tablespoon brown sugar
2 Florida navel oranges, peeled and
   sliced

Night before, or at least 8 hours before cooking: Place quail in shallow dish; add 2 cups orange juice. Cover; refrigerate 8 hours or overnight.

When ready to cook: Soak hickory chips in water at least 15 minutes. Prepare charcoal fire in smoker or covered grill with tight-fitting lid; let burn 10 to 15 minutes. Place hickory chips on coals. Place water pan in smoker; fill with cranberry juice. Combine butter, brown sugar and ¾ cup orange juice in small bowl. Place quail on smoker rack; brush with glaze. Close smoker lid; cook 1 to 1½ hours or until quail is done. (Or place quail on rack of covered grill; brush with glaze. Cook, covered, 1 to 1½ hours, basting every 15 to 20 minutes with glaze). Garnish with orange slices.   *4 servings.*

Preparation Time: 15 Minutes   *Cooking Time 1 Hour
                                                    30 Minutes*

Corn Stuffing Nuggets

1½ sticks butter, melted, divided
½ small onion, chopped
1 cup celery, chopped
1 (16-ounce) can cream-style corn
1 (8-ounce) package herb stuffing
   mix
3 egg yolks, slightly beaten

Preheat oven to 375° F. Melt ½ stick butter in medium saucepan; sauté onion and celery until soft. Remove from heat; add corn and ¾ cup water; stir. Bring to boil; remove from heat. Place stuffing mix in large bowl; pour corn mixture over; mix lightly. Add egg yolks. Shape into 10 to 12 balls. Spray shallow baking dish with vegetable cooking spray; place balls in dish. Pour 1 stick melted butter over balls. Bake until brown, about 20 minutes. Can be made ahead and refrigerated or frozen. If made ahead, do not add melted butter until ready to bake. If frozen, thaw before baking.   *6 to 8 servings.*

Preparation Time: 15 Minutes   *Cooking Time: 20 Minutes*

Wild Mushroom-Herb Stuffing

4¹/₂ ounces dried shitaki or porcini
  mushrooms
1¹/₂ (1-pound) loaves white
  sandwich bread, cut into ¹/₂-inch
  cubes
2¹/₄ sticks butter, plus a little more
3 large red onions, chopped
³/₄ pound fresh button mushrooms,
  sliced
3 cups celery, chopped
1 cup fresh parsley, chopped
3 tablespoons fresh rosemary,
  minced (or 2 teaspoons dried)
3 tablespoons fresh tarragon,
  minced (or 2 teaspoons dried)
Salt and pepper to taste

Up to 1 day ahead: Place dried mushrooms in bowl; add 3 cups boiling water. Soak until softened about 30 minutes. Drain; reserve liquid. Squeeze mushrooms to remove excess liquid. Cut out stems; slice mushrooms.

While mushrooms soak, prepare bread cubes: Preheat oven to 250° F. Spread bread cubes on cookie sheet. Bake until dry but not hard, about 40 minutes; stirring occasionally. Place in large bowl. Generously butter 4-quart baking dish. In large heavy skillet, melt butter over medium heat. Add onions; cook until tender. Add button mushrooms; sauté until tender. Add shitaki mushrooms and celery; sauté 1¹/₂ minutes. Add mushroom mixture to bread; mix in parsley, rosemary and tarragon. Season with salt and pepper; add ³/₄ cup reserved mushroom soaking liquid; blend well. Transfer to greased baking dish; cover with foil. (If making ahead, refrigerate).

When ready to cook: Bring stuffing to room temperature. Preheat oven to 350° F. Bake stuffing, covered, until heated through, about 1 hour.

12 servings.

Preparation Time: 1 Hour   *Cooking Time: 1 Hour*

ONE-DISH ENTERTAINING

Tampa's Flying Tradition

Training over the southernmost tip of Tampa's Interbay Peninsula, F-16 fighters lead us to the next treasure, MacDill Air Force Base. Since its 1941 opening as an Army Air Force base, MacDill has been an important part of the local scene. Thousands of pilots have trained here in bombers, cargo planes and jet fighters.

The air force base's annual open house draws hundreds of thousands of people to view the latest aircraft and breathtaking flying demonstrations by the visiting Thunderbirds or Blue Angels. Probably MacDill's most visible worldwide role was as headquarters for General H. Norman Schwarzkopf and the U.S. Special Operations and Southern Command, leaders of Operation Desert Storm.

Long before MacDill was built, this area earned a lasting place in aviation history. On New Year's Day 1914, a barnstorming aviator named Tony Jannus flew his Benoist wood and fabric "Flying Boat" from St. Petersburg to Tampa, cutting travel time between the two cities from two hours by steamboat to 23 minutes by air. Jannus' flight was the first scheduled commercial airline run. For a few months, his Airboat Line flew people and cargo across Tampa Bay. The modern airline industry was born.

Tampa continues its commercial aviation prominence with Tampa International Airport, a huge complex near Old Tampa Bay. Airline passengers consistently vote the airport one of the nation's best. Its innovative design allows travelers easy connections and gives them comfortable facilities and excellent ground services.

This section features dishes appropriate for a picnic, party, family reunion, church supper or buffet dinner at home. Discover new and interesting combinations of your favorite foods. Enjoy the make ahead recipes which allow the chef to enjoy the festivities. The menu highlights treasures like Tampa-Style Black Bean Chili, Creamy Corn Bread and our native Florida Grapefruit Cake.

**The MacDill photograph was underwritten by
Beverly and Al Austin**

ONE-DISH ENTERTAINING

FOURTH OF JULY REUNION

Tampa-Style Black Bean Chili

Chinese Noodles and Chicken

Cranberry-Apple Crunch

Creamy Cornbread

Brenda Schwarzkopf's Sour Cream Peach Pie

Florida Grapefruit Cake

**The menu photograph was underwritten by
Chuck and Hilary Davis**

Tampa-Style Black Bean Chili

24 ounces dried black beans, or 6
    (15-ounce) cans black beans
2 tablespoons olive or vegetable oil
1 large onion, chopped
8 garlic cloves, minced
2 to 4 pounds ground beef
2 (28-ounce) cans tomatoes
2 large green peppers, chopped
3 tablespoons chili powder, to taste
3 tablespoons cumin, to taste
8 to 10 dried chile peppers, to taste
6 to 12 ounces beer
Sour cream (garnish)
Diced fresh tomato (garnish)
Chopped cilantro or parsley
    (garnish)

About 6½ hours before serving: Soak and cook dried black beans according to package directions; drain. (Or drain canned beans, reserve some bean liquid to thin chili, if desired.) Heat oil in 8-quart stockpot; add onion and garlic; cook until soft. Add ground beef; brown; drain liquid. Add tomatoes, green peppers, chili powder, cumin and chile peppers; cook over low heat 10 minutes. Add drained beans, with some bean liquid, if desired. Simmer over low heat about 3 hours, stirring frequently. If chili is getting too thick, add up to 12 ounces beer during cooking. Serve garnished with sour cream, diced tomato and chopped cilantro or parsley. *16 servings.*

Preparation Time: 45 Minutes   *Cooking Time: 3 Hours*

Treasure Tip: There is no controversy over whether to serve this chili with or without beans—the beans make the chili! To complete the Ybor City flavor, serve with Cuban bread.

Chinese Noodles and Chicken

1 large whole chicken breast
1 cup fine egg noodles
2 tablespoons peanut or corn oil
2 tablespoons sesame oil, divided
3 tablespoons tahini (sesame seed
    paste)*
1 tablespoon white vinegar
1 tablespoon chile oil*
1 teaspoon sugar
2 teaspoons ground ginger
2 teaspoons garlic, chopped
½ teaspoon hot bean paste*
    (optional)
¼ cup, plus 2 tablespoons, soy
    sauce
2 cups bean sprouts, drained
2 tablespoons scallions, chopped
1 tablespoon peanuts, chopped
Red or yellow bell pepper, chopped
    (garnish)

*Available at Oriental markets and some supermarkets.

Cook chicken breast in water until done, about 15 minutes; shred chicken. Boil noodles; drain. Add peanut oil and 1 tablespoon sesame oil to noodles; set aside.

Make sauce: In food processor or blender place tahini, vinegar, chile oil, sugar, ginger, garlic, bean paste, 1 tablespoon sesame oil and soy sauce; blend well.

To assemble: Spread bean sprouts on serving platter; top with noodles; spread with chicken. When ready to serve, pour sauce over chicken; top with scallions and peanuts. If desired, garnish with chopped bell pepper. *4 servings.*

Preparation Time: 35 Minutes   *Cooking Time: 25 minutes*

Treasure Tip: If you can not find tahini to use in this dish, you may substitute peanut butter.

Cranberry-Apple Crunch

3 cups unpeeled apples, cut in bite-
   size pieces
Fresh lemon juice
2 cups whole fresh cranberries
1 cup sugar
1 ½ cups quick-cooking oats,
   uncooked
½ cup brown sugar, firmly packed
⅓ cup flour
⅓ cup pecans, chopped
1 stick butter or margarine, melted

Preheat oven to 300° F. In large bowl place apples; sprinkle with lemon juice. Add cranberries and sugar; mix well. Place in 2-quart casserole. In medium bowl mix sugar, oats, brown sugar, flour, pecans and butter. Place sugar mixture on top of apple mixture. Bake uncovered until bubbly and lightly browned, about 1 hour. Serve hot. **8 to 10 servings.**

Preparation Time: 15 Minutes   *Cooking Time: 1 Hour*

Creamy Cornbread

2 cups self-rising cornmeal
2 cups sour cream
½ cup corn or vegetable oil
4 eggs
1 (16 ½-ounce) can white or golden
   creamed corn
1 teaspoon salt (optional)

Preheat oven to 375° F. In large bowl combine all ingredients; mix well. Place in lightly greased 8-inch square baking dish; bake 35 minutes. Cut in squares; serve hot. **12 to 15 servings.**

Preparation Time: 10 Minutes   *Cooking Time: 35 Minutes*

Brenda Schwarzkopf's Sour Cream Peach Pie

2 pounds fresh peaches (or a 30-
   ounce can sliced peaches)
2 tablespoons cornstarch (use only
   with fresh peaches)
¼ cup apple juice (use only with
   fresh peaches)
⅓ cup flour
½ cup sugar
¼ teaspoon salt
1 cup sour cream
1 (9-inch) deep-dish pie shell,
   unbaked
1 tablespoon sugar and ¼ teaspoon
   cinnamon, mixed
Peach slices for garnish

Preheat oven to 350° F. Peel and slice fresh peaches, (10 to 12 slices each); place in large bowl. If using fresh peaches, mix cornstarch and apple juice until smooth. Pour over peaches; toss gently to coat. Let stand 10 to 15 minutes. (Or drain canned peaches thoroughly; place in bowl.) Mix flour, sugar, salt and sour cream. Arrange peaches in pie shell; top with sour cream mixture. Sprinkle with sugar and cinnamon. Bake 30 to 40 minutes, until crust edge is lightly browned. Garnish with peach slices, if desired. **10 servings.**

Preparation Time: 25 Minutes   *Cooking Time: 30 to 40 Minutes*

Florida Grapefruit Cake

⅔ cup butter or margarine,
  softened
1¾ cups sugar
2 eggs
3 cups cake flour, sifted
2½ teaspoons baking powder
½ teaspoon salt
½ cup fresh grapefruit juice
¾ cup milk
1 tablespoon grapefruit peel, grated
1½ teaspoons vanilla extract

Preheat oven to 350° F. Cream butter in large bowl of electric mixer. Gradually add sugar, beating well. Add eggs one at a time, beating well after each addition. Combine flour, baking powder and salt; add to creamed mixture alternately with grapefruit juice, beginning and ending with flour mixture. Gradually add milk; stir in grapefruit peel and vanilla; mix well. Pour into greased and floured tube or bundt cake pan. Bake 45 to 50 minutes, or until toothpick comes out clean. Cool in pan 10 minutes; remove from pan and cool completely on wire rack.   **10 to 12 servings.**

Preparation Time: 30 Minutes   **Cooking Time: 50 Minutes**

Treasure Tip: *A richly textured cake with a unique sweet and tangy citrus flavor.*

Sesame Chicken with Crispy Angel Hair Pasta

½ cup sesame oil, divided
¼ tablespoon crushed red pepper
¼ teaspoon ground ginger
¼ teaspoon Szechwan pepper
1 tablespoon curry powder
2 cloves garlic, minced
½ teaspoon dry mustard
1 tablespoon red wine vinegar
2 tablespoons soy sauce
2 tablespoons brown sugar
2 cups chicken broth
Cornstarch to thicken
Dry sherry to taste
Salt to taste
8 ounces angel hair pasta
*3 pounds boneless chicken breasts,
   skinned, cut in strips*
Flour
1 red bell pepper, julienned
3 to 4 scallions, sliced diagonally
8 mushrooms, quartered
Sesame seeds

Make sauce: Heat 2 tablespoons sesame oil in medium saucepan. Add red pepper, ginger, Szechwan pepper, curry powder, garlic and mustard; sauté 1 minute. Add vinegar, soy sauce, brown sugar and chicken broth. Bring to boil; simmer 10 to 15 minutes. Place cornstarch in small bowl; add enough sherry so that mixture will coat a spoon. Mix well; stir into sauce. Add salt and more red pepper, if desired. Set aside.

Prepare pasta: Cook and drain pasta. In large skillet heat ¼ cup sesame oil until very hot. Carefully place pasta evenly in pan; cook until golden brown. Turn pasta over; cook until golden brown. Remove from pan; pat pasta dry.

Prepare chicken: Heat 2 tablespoons sesame oil in wok or skillet. Lightly flour chicken strips; sauté until golden brown. When chicken is almost done, remove from pan; set aside. Add red bell pepper, scallions and mushrooms to pan; sauté a few minutes. Add chicken and sauce; cook a few more minutes until chicken is done. To serve, place pasta on plates; spoon chicken mixture over pasta. Sprinkle with sesame seeds; serve immediately.   *4 to 6 servings.*

Preparation Time: 30 Minutes   *Cooking Time: 30 Minutes*

Treasure Tip: If you like, add other vegetables, such as snow peas, celery or bamboo shoots, to this spicy dish. A new and different way to prepare chicken.

Chicken Cobb Salad

6 chicken breast halves, skinned
 and boned

Marinade

½ cup olive or vegetable oil
⅓ cup tarragon vinegar
1 teaspoon salt
1 teaspoon sugar
1 clove garlic, crushed
1 (20-ounce) can pineapple chunks
½ teaspoon basil
½ teaspoon dill weed
½ teaspoon dry mustard
½ teaspoon paprika
⅛ teaspoon pepper

Salad

2 cups lettuce, shredded
2 cups romaine leaves, torn
2 cups fresh spinach leaves
3 tomatoes, chopped
2 avocados, peeled and cut into
 pieces
8 slices bacon, cooked and
 crumbled
4 ounces bleu cheese, crumbled
¼ cup whole green onions, sliced

Night before: Cook chicken; cut into chunks. In large bowl combine oil and remaining marinade ingredients. Add chicken; refrigerate overnight.

Just before serving: Place lettuce, romaine, spinach, tomatoes, avocados, bacon, bleu cheese and onions in large bowl. Add chicken and marinade; toss. Serve at once.   *8 to 10 servings.*

Preparation and Cooking Time: 1 Hour 15 Minutes

Treasure Tip: When using dried herbs, rub them gently in the palms of your hands, crushing them to release their flavor. If you are using a spice or herb that is new to you, use less than the recipe calls for and taste (you can always add more). The flavors of herbs and spices intensify with heat.

Corn-Sour Cream Enchiladas

3 tablespoons vegetable oil, divided
2 cloves garlic, minced
1 onion, chopped
1 pound ground chuck
1½ cups green chile salsa
1½ teaspoons dried oregano,
    crumbled
1½ teaspoons chili powder
1½ teaspoons ground cumin
Salt and black pepper to taste
1 tablespoon unsalted butter
2 cups fresh corn kernels, cut from
    about 4 ears
¼ cup red bell pepper, julienned
¼ cup green bell pepper, julienned
6 (7-inch) corn tortillas
2 cups sour cream
2 cups Monterey Jack cheese,
    grated
¼ cup pitted black olives, sliced

Heat 2 tablespoons oil in large skillet; cook garlic and onion over moderately low heat, stirring until softened. Add ground chuck; cook over moderate heat, stirring and breaking up meat, until no longer pink; drain. Stir in salsa, oregano, chili powder, cumin, salt and black pepper; bring to boil; turn down heat; simmer 5 minutes.

Preheat oven to 375° F. In another skillet melt butter and 1 tablespoon oil; add corn. Cook, stirring, over moderately low heat, 3 minutes. Add bell peppers, salt and pepper; cook, stirring, 2 minutes or until bell peppers are softened.

Place 2 tortillas, side by side, in an oval 2-quart gratin dish. Top with one-third of meat mixture, one-third of sour cream and one-third of cheese. Repeat layers twice; sprinkle olives over top. Spoon corn mixture around edge of dish; bake 20 minutes.

6 servings.

Preparation Time: 30 Minutes   ***Cooking Time: 20 Minutes***

Spinach Rotolo

2 cups fresh or frozen chopped
    spinach
2 cups ricotta cheese
½ cup imported prosciutto,
    chopped
2 eggs, beaten
¼ cup fresh parsley, chopped
½ teaspoon salt
¼ teaspoon black pepper, freshly
    ground
3 to 4 drops Tabasco
16 lasagna noodles, cooked
4 cups marinara sauce
Parmesan cheese, freshly grated

Preheat oven to 350° F. Boil spinach in small amount of water 1 minute; drain; squeeze to remove remaining moisture. In bowl combine spinach, ricotta, prosciutto, eggs, parsley, salt, pepper and Tabasco; blend well. Spread each noodle with cheese-spinach mixture; roll up like a jelly roll.

Spoon 1 cup marinara sauce into bottom of baking dish. Set filled noodles upright in dish; top with 2 cups sauce. Sprinkle Parmesan on top; bake 35 minutes. Heat remaining sauce; serve with noodles. Rotolo can be prepared a day ahead and refrigerated. It freezes well. Thaw before baking. ***8 servings.***

Preparation Time: 45 Minutes   ***Cooking Time: 35 Minutes***

Sunset Beef Salad

Fresh spinach leaves
1 cup fresh mushrooms, sliced
½ cup celery, thinly sliced
2 small Italian plum tomatoes,
    seeded and chopped
¼ cup green pepper, chopped
3 tablespoons olive or vegetable oil,
    divided
¼ cup red wine vinegar, divided
½ cup red onion, sliced
1 teaspoon Worcestershire sauce
½ teaspoon dried parsley flakes
½ teaspoon dried basil, crushed
½ teaspoon dried oregano, crushed
¼ teaspoon salt
¼ teaspoon pepper
6 ounces cooked roast beef, cut into
    bite-size strips
⅔ cup canned garbanzo beans,
    drained
2 tablespoons bleu cheese,
    crumbled

Line three or four dinner plates with spinach leaves; set aside. In large bowl combine mushrooms, celery, tomatoes and green pepper. In large skillet heat 2 tablespoons oil and 2 tablespoons vinegar. Add onion; cook, covered, 2 minutes. Remove onion with slotted spoon; add to mushroom mixture.

Place remaining oil and vinegar in skillet; add Worcestershire, parsley, basil, oregano, salt and pepper. Add beef and beans; heat through. Add beef mixture to vegetables; toss to combine. Divide mixture among plates; sprinkle with cheese. Serve immediately.   *3 to 4 servings.*

Preparation Time: 20 Minutes   **Cooking Time: 10 Minutes**

Treasure Tip: *This tasty, colorful salad makes a good main dish for a hot summer night.*

Lamb and Vegetable Ragout

2 tablespoons vegetable oil
2 tablespoons butter or margarine
6 to 8 pounds lamb shoulder, cut
   in 1½-inch pieces
2 cups onion, chopped
¼ cup flour
1 teaspoon salt
¼ teaspoon pepper
2 cups dry white wine
2 cups tomato sauce
2 (13¾-ounce) cans chicken broth
½ cup fresh parsley leaves, chopped
   (reserve stems)
1 bay leaf
½ teaspoon thyme, crumbled
2 cups fresh or thawed frozen peas
4 cups (1 pound) small carrots,
   peeled and cooked, or 2 (16-
   ounce) cans small carrots,
   drained
2 (16-ounce) cans small white
   onions, drained

Heat oil and butter in skillet over medium heat; brown lamb in batches, adding more oil if needed. Remove lamb with slotted spoon; place in large, heavy pot or Dutch oven. Add onion to skillet; cook 2 to 3 minutes. Sprinkle with flour, salt and pepper; mix well. Add wine; bring to boil. Stir to loosen brown bits in pan. Add tomato sauce, chicken broth, parsley stems, bay leaf and thyme.

Pour sauce over lamb; cover pot. Simmer until meat is tender, about 1¼ hours. Discard parsley stems and bay leaf. Add peas, carrots and onions; simmer until heated through. Sprinkle with chopped parsley; serve. **12 servings.**

Preparation Time: 30 Minutes   *Cooking Time: 1 Hour*
                                        30 Minutes

Treasure Tip: For a more filling meal, serve this delicious lamb dish over white rice.

Spicy Szechwan Pork

6 green onions, sliced into 1-inch
   pieces, white pieces and green
   tops placed in separate bowls
1 tablespoon vegetable oil
2 pounds boneless pork shoulder,
   cut into 1-inch cubes
6 cloves garlic, minced
⅓ cup soy sauce
⅓ cup dry sherry
1½ teaspoons fresh ginger, grated
½ teaspoon crushed red pepper
½ teaspoon fennel seed, crushed
½ teaspoon Chinese 5-spice powder
6 medium carrots, peeled, cut into
   ½-inch pieces
3 tablespoons flour

Heat oil in 4-quart Dutch oven or heavy pot. Brown pork and garlic, one-half at a time. Drain fat; return pork mixture to pot. Add white onion pieces, 3 cups water, soy sauce, sherry, ginger, red pepper, fennel and 5-spice powder. Bring to a boil; reduce heat. Cover; simmer 20 minutes. Add carrots; cover; simmer 25 minutes more or until pork and carrots are tender. Skim fat. Blend flour with ¼ cup water; stir into pork mixture; add green onion tops. Cook, stirring, until thickened and bubbly; cook and stir 1 minute more. Serve over white rice, if desired.

6 to 8 servings.

Preparation Time: 20 Minutes   *Cooking Time: 1 Hour*

Treasure Tip: Chinese 5-spice powder can be made by combining 2 teaspoons each of crushed anise seeds, crushed fennel seeds, ground pepper, ground cloves, ground cinnamon and 1½ teaspoons ground ginger and ½ teaspoon allspice.

Fiery Turkey Chili

¼ cup olive oil
2 cups onion, chopped
4 cloves garlic, finely chopped
2 (28-ounce) cans plum tomatoes,
    including juice
1 (15-ounce) can tomato purée
¼ cup chili powder
1½ tablespoons ground cumin
1 tablespoon dried hot red pepper
    flakes (or to taste)
1 teaspoon dried oregano
½ teaspoon cinnamon
1 tablespoon salt
½ teaspoon black pepper
Drumsticks, thighs and wings
    from a cooked turkey
2 green bell peppers, coarsely
    chopped
2 (16-ounce) cans kidney beans,
    rinsed, drained well
Sour cream
Cheddar cheese, coarsely grated

3½ hours before serving: Heat oil in large kettle over moderate heat; cook onion and garlic, stirring until golden. Add tomatoes and juice, tomato purée, 2 cups water, chili powder, cumin, red pepper, oregano, cinnamon, salt and black pepper; combine well. Add turkey; reduce heat to low. Simmer uncovered for 2 hours, stirring occasionally. Using slotted spoon, transfer turkey to plate; let cool.

Remove turkey meat; discard skin and bones. Add meat, green bell peppers and beans to pot. Simmer, stirring occasionally, until peppers are tender, about 40 minutes. If made in advance, cool completely before covering and refrigerate. Serve topped with a dollop of sour cream and a sprinkling of cheddar.

8 servings.

Preparation Time: 30 Minutes　　　*Cooking Time: 3 Hours*

Treasure Tip: Chicken can be substituted for turkey in this dish.

Torte Milanaise

1 pound puff pastry
1 tablespoon vegetable oil
1 tablespoon butter
1 pound fresh or frozen spinach,
    blanched, chopped and squeezed
    dry
4 cloves garlic, minced
½ teaspoon nutmeg
Salt and pepper to taste
2 large red bell peppers, cut into
    1-inch pieces, blanched 2 to 3
    minutes
1 egg, beaten

Omelets

5 eggs
2 teaspoons chives, chopped
2 teaspoons fresh parsley, chopped
1 teaspoon fresh tarragon, chopped
Pinch salt
2 tablespoons butter, divided
8 ounces Gruyère or Swiss cheese,
    thinly sliced
8 ounces smoked turkey or ham,
    thinly sliced

Lightly grease 8-inch springform pan. Roll out pastry ¼-inch thick; use enough to line bottom and sides of pan. Refrigerate remaining pastry. In large skillet heat oil and butter; add spinach and garlic. Sauté 2 to 3 minutes over medium heat; add nutmeg, salt and pepper; set aside in bowl. In same pan sauté red peppers 3 to 4 minutes; place in another bowl.

Make omelets: Lightly beat eggs, chives, parsley, tarragon and salt together. Place 1 tablespoon butter in 8-inch skillet over medium heat; turn pan to coat with butter. Pour half of egg mixture into pan; stir until eggs start to set. Lift edges of omelet and tilt pan so the liquid can run underneath and cook. When set, slide omelet onto warm plate. Repeat procedure, making a second omelet.

Position rack in lower third of oven; preheat oven to 350° F. In pastry-lined pan layer, in order: one omelet, half of spinach, half of cheese, half of turkey, all the red pepper, half of turkey, half of cheese, half of spinach and second omelet.

Roll out remaining pastry ¼-inch thick; cut out 8-inch circle. Place circle over omelet; seal all around. Make slits in top of pastry; decorate with shapes cut from remaining pastry, if desired. Brush with beaten egg. Place on baking sheet; bake until golden brown 65 to 75 minutes. To serve, cool slightly. Remove sides of pan; slice torte with sharp, thin knife.

6 to 8 servings.

Preparation Time: 30 Minutes

*Cooking Time: 1 Hour
15 Minutes*

Treasure Tip: Gruyère is a cousin of Swiss cheese. It has smaller holes than regular Swiss cheese and a sharper flavor. Swiss cheese may be substituted when a less pungent flavor is desired.

Gulf Shrimp Newspaper Dinner

4 celery tops with leaves
1 to 2 green peppers, cut in chunks
2 lemons or limes, halved
Salt to taste
6 tablespoons Old Bay seasonings, divided
Lots of Tabasco (to taste)
16 new potatoes
12 small onions, peeled
12 chicken thighs
2 pounds Polish kielbasa, cut in chunks
12 ears corn, cut in half
2 ⅔ pounds fresh shrimp, unpeeled
3 clean brown grocery bags, placed 1 inside the other
1 stick melted butter or margarine (for corn)
Seafood cocktail sauce
4 lemons or limes, cut in wedges

Fill large stockpot with water. Add celery tops, green peppers, lemon or lime halves (squeeze juice into pot, add rinds), salt, 3 tablespoons Old Bay seasonings, Tabasco, potatoes, onions, chicken and sausage. Bring to boil; cook 20 minutes. Add 3 more tablespoons Old Bay seasonings and corn; cook 6 minutes. Add shrimp; cook until they turn pink, 2 to 3 minutes.

While dinner cooks, cover table with newspapers. When shrimp is done, use a colander to scoop everything out of stockpot; place food in grocery bags. Split bags down the middle; serve food from bags. Guests peel their own shrimp, butter their corn with pastry brushes and use lemon or lime wedges to season food and clean hands when dinner is over.

8 servings.

Preparation Time: 15 Minutes   ***Cooking Time: 35 Minutes***

Treasure Tip: *Fun meal for a casual party!*

Grilled Dill Salmon With Rice

¼ cup onion, finely chopped
1 carrot, peeled and finely chopped
1 stalk celery, finely chopped
1 cup basmati or long-grain rice
½ teaspoon lemon peel, finely shredded
3 tablespoons lemon juice
¼ teaspoon salt
1 bay leaf
8 ounces plain low-fat yogurt
¼ cup whole green onions, sliced
¼ cup fresh dill, snipped (or 1 teaspoon dried dill weed)
1 teaspoon capers
1 1-pound fresh salmon fillet, about 1 inch thick, skinned
1 tablespoon olive or vegetable oil
Lemon slices

Lightly grease a large skillet. Add onion, carrot and celery; cook 2 minutes over medium heat. Add water (1½ cups for basmati rice, 2 cups for long-grained rice), rice, lemon juice, salt and bay leaf. Bring to boil; reduce heat to low; cover skillet. Simmer until rice is tender about 20 minutes; keep warm. Grease rack of barbecue grill; heat grill to medium-high.

In small mixing bowl combine lemon peel, yogurt, green onions, dill and capers. Place half of mixture in food processor or blender; cover; blend until smooth. Stir into remaining mixture in bowl; set aside. Cut salmon into four portions; brush with oil. Grill salmon and lemon slices, turning once, just until fish flakes with fork about 7 minutes.

To serve, spoon about 2 tablespoons sauce onto center of each dinner plate; top with salmon. Serve with rice and lemon slices.

4 servings.

Preparation Time: 30 Minutes   ***Cooking Time: 7 Minutes***

Treasure Tip: *This dill sauce can be served with meat or as a salad dressing.*

Crabmeat-Spinach Casserole

2 tablespoons butter
1 pound fresh crabmeat, flaked and
   picked through
¼ cup sherry
2 (10-ounce) packages frozen
   chopped spinach, cooked and
   drained
2 teaspoons onion, grated
5 ounces sharp cheddar cheese,
   grated
1 (10¾-ounce) can tomato soup
1 cup sour cream

Preheat oven to 400° F. Melt butter in skillet; add crabmeat. Stir; add sherry; stir again. Cook just until heated through. Combine soup and sour cream. In casserole layer, in order, crabmeat, spinach, onion and cheese; top with soup mixture. Bake 25 to 30 minutes.

6 to 8 servings.

Preparation Time: 30 Minutes   *Cooking Time: 30 Minutes*

Spicy Shrimp and Rice

Rice

¼ cup olive oil
½ green bell pepper, chopped
½ red bell pepper, chopped
1½ cups rice
1 teaspoon salt

Shrimp

1 stick butter or margarine
2 tablespoons shallots, minced
1 sprig fresh rosemary (or ½
   teaspoon dried)
½ teaspoon dried oregano
1 bay leaf, crushed
½ teaspoon thyme
1 teaspoon cayenne pepper
Salt and pepper to taste
20 to 24 large shrimp, shelled and
   deveined
½ (8-ounce) bottle clam juice
¼ cup dry white wine

Make rice: Heat olive oil in large, nonstick skillet. Add peppers; cook until limp. Add rice; sauté until rice begins to brown. Add 3⅓ cups hot water and salt; stir until mixed. Cover; cook over low heat until done about 15 minutes.

Melt butter in large skillet. Add shallots, rosemary, oregano, bay leaf, thyme, cayenne, salt and pepper. Cook until well blended. Add shrimp, clam juice and wine; cook, shaking pan, until shrimp turn pink, about 3 minutes. Serve over rice.   *4 servings.*

Preparation Time: 10 Minutes   *Cooking Time: 20 Minutes*

Treasure Tip: Elephant garlic is a cross between a shallot and garlic. It has less moisture than garlic, so do not use for sautéing. Shallots, like fresh garlic, should be firm and not dry or sprouted.

Mango Shrimp with Jalapeño Rice

2 fresh jalapeño peppers, peeled
    and seeded
½ bunch fresh cilantro (leaves
    only)
¼ small white onion
1 jumbo clove garlic, peeled
1 cup long-grain rice
¾ cup fish or chicken stock
1 fresh jalapeño pepper, seeded and
    julienned
½ vanilla bean, cut in half
    lengthwise
1½ pounds fresh large shrimp,
    peeled
½ cup dark rum
Juice of 1 lime
1 small mango, peeled and thinly
    sliced*
1 lime, thinly sliced

*A peach or nectarine may be
substituted.

When working with jalapeños, always wear rubber gloves to protect hands. Char jalapeños: Place under hot broiler (or, using long-handled fork, hold over gas flame) until black, turning to char all sides. In food processor or blender purée charred jalapeños, most of cilantro (reserve a few leaves for garnish), onion, garlic and about ½ cup water.

Place 1¾ cups water in deep, heavy saucepan. Add jalapeño mixture and rice; bring to boil. Boil until level of liquid reaches level of rice, 2 to 3 minutes, skimming off any foam that comes to top of liquid. Turn heat to very low; cover tightly. Cook until all water is absorbed, 15 to 20 minutes.

In another deep saucepan place stock, julienned jalapeño and vanilla bean; bring to slow boil (don't let stock evaporate). Scrape tiny seeds from inside of vanilla bean; return seeds to saucepan; discard bean. Turn heat to high until stock evaporates to 2 to 3 tablespoons. Add shrimp; cook 4 to 5 minutes. Add rum; ignite mixture with match; let flame burn out. Add juice of lime; stir to glaze shrimp.

Remove shrimp from pan; add mango and lime slices. Toss to heat through. To serve, place rice on heated platter; top with shrimp. Arrange lime and mango slices decoratively around platter; garnish with fresh cilantro leaves.   **4 servings.**

Preparation Time: 1 Hour   **Cooking Time: 25 to 35 Minutes**

Treasure Tip: This is a spicy-hot and colorful dish for company!

Creamy Seafood Lasagna

Bechamel Sauce

½ stick butter
¼ cup flour
2 cups milk
Salt and white pepper to taste

Lasagna

*1 pound very thin fresh grouper,
    flounder or sole fillets, skinned*
1 tablespoon butter
*1 tablespoon shallots, finely
    chopped*
2 cloves garlic, chopped
*¾ pound medium fresh shrimp,
    peeled and deveined*
1 pound fresh scallops
*Salt, pepper and fresh lemon juice
    to taste*
½ cup dry white wine
*2 cups fresh mushrooms, thinly
    sliced*
1 cup fresh tomatoes, chopped
½ cup heavy cream
½ teaspoon red pepper flakes
*3 tablespoons fresh parsley, finely
    chopped*
9 lasagna noodles
*1 cup Gruyère or Swiss cheese,
    grated*

Up to several hours ahead, make bechamel sauce: Melt butter in saucepan. Add flour, stirring 2 minutes with wire whisk. Add milk, salt and pepper; whisk over medium heat until thickened and smooth. Reduce heat; cook 5 minutes. Makes 2 cups. (If making ahead, cover and refrigerate until needed.)

1 hour before serving: Poach fish in a little water until flaky; set aside. Cook noodles as package directs; drain. Melt butter in large skillet; add shallots, garlic, shrimp and scallops. Sprinkle with salt, pepper and lemon juice; sauté until shrimp start to turn pink. Add wine; heat just to boiling. With slotted spoon, remove shrimp, scallops and spices to large mixing bowl. Bring liquid in skillet to simmer; add mushrooms. Cook 5 minutes; add bechamel sauce, stirring. Add tomatoes; simmer 5 minutes. Add cream, red pepper flakes, parsley and any liquid from shrimp and scallops.

Preheat oven to 375° F. Lightly grease bottom and sides of 13½ x 9½ x 2-inch glass baking dish. Spoon layer of sauce over bottom of dish; add half of shrimp and scallops. Spoon additional sauce over seafood; cover with 3 noodles. Add layer of fish and thin layer of sauce; cover with 3 noodles. Add remaining shrimp and scallops; spoon on layer of sauce. Cover with 3 noodles; spoon on final layer of sauce. Sprinkle with cheese. Bake 30 minutes. Cool 10 to 15 minutes before serving.

8 servings.

Preparation Time: 40 Minutes   *Cooking Time: 30 Minutes*

Chili Ratatouille

1 eggplant (about 1 pound), cut into 1-inch chunks
5 tablespoons olive oil, divided
2 medium onions, chopped
3 cloves garlic, minced
2 medium zucchini, diced
2 large red bell peppers, diced
1 to 2 fresh jalapeño peppers, seeded and finely minced (wear rubber gloves)
1 (28-ounce) can Italian plum tomatoes, coarsely chopped, including juice
5 large fresh plum tomatoes, diced
½ cup dry red wine
2 tablespoons chili powder
1 tablespoon ground cumin
2 teaspoons oregano
1 teaspoon fennel seeds (optional)
1 cup white beans, cooked and drained
1 cup kidney beans, cooked and drained
Juice and peel of 1 large lemon, grated
⅓ cup fresh cilantro, chopped
Ground black pepper to taste
Sour cream (garnish)
Monterey Jack cheese, grated (garnish)
Green onions, chopped (garnish)

Preheat oven to 350° F. Place eggplant in small, shallow baking pan; toss with 2 tablespoons oil. Cover with foil; bake 30 minutes, stirring once. Set aside.

Heat 3 tablespoons oil over medium heat in large saucepan; add onions and garlic; cook 5 minutes. Add zucchini, red peppers and jalapeños; cook 5 more minutes, stirring once. Add canned tomatoes with juice, fresh tomatoes, wine, chili powder, cumin, oregano and fennel. Gently stir in eggplant; turn heat to low; simmer 20 minutes.

Add beans, lemon juice and peel, cilantro and pepper; stir; simmer 5 minutes. Serve with choice of garnishes.

8 to 10 servings.

Preparation Time: 45 Minutes   **Cooking Time: 35 Minutes**

Treasure Tip: *To preserve your fresh herbs, hang them upside down in a cool dry place until dry. The best herbs to preserve are bay, thyme and oregano. To freeze fresh herbs, wash, dry and discard the stems. Place herbs in freezer in a plastic bag.*

SOUPS, SALADS & DRESSINGS

Sports at Tampa Stadium

As bands play and cheerleaders lead the fans in rooting for their favorite teams, we need only follow the crowds to find our eighth treasure. Florida's sunny, bright blue sky frames another great day for sports in Tampa Stadium.

Tampa Stadium, built in 1967 for college football, was enlarged to more than 74,000 seats in 1976 for the arrival of the National Football League's Tampa Bay Buccaneers. Since the expansion, the bowl-shaped stadium, with an unobstructed view from any seat, has been the site of many NFL games, including the Super Bowl and the annual Hall of Fame Bowl. An important annual intrastate football rivalry is the Florida Classic, played here each year between Florida A & M University and Bethune-Cookman College. Tampa fans are often treated to games played by their alma maters: the Florida Gators, FSU Seminoles and Miami Hurricanes.

The Stadium is the setting for many other events and entertainment. Rock and country music played by internationally known artists fills the stadium, rising to the sky boxes and beyond during concerts. Other stadium events include everything from soccer to tractor-pulls. Grand Prix jumping brings magnificent horses and their riders to Tampa each spring for world-class competition.

Tampa's mild climate invites tailgating in many different styles. Elaborately served buffets can be found side by side with picnic-style cookouts. In this section you will find a variety of fresh, light salads, that can be artfully combined with thick, spicy soups or chilled, creamy ones for winning results with fans anywhere. A good choice for the hot weather is Gazpacho which is featured in the menu. Enjoy your soup! The Tampa Bay Buccaneers' game is about to begin!

The Stadium photograph was underwritten by
The Tampa Bay Buccaneers

SOUPS, SALADS & DRESSINGS

TAILGATE PARTY, TAMPA STYLE

Gazpacho

Shrimp and Rice Salad Florentine

Chicken Basil Salad

Garlic Herbed Potato Salad

Flaky Coconut Pound Cake

**The menu photograph was underwritten by
GTE Telephone Operations, South Area**

Gazpacho

1 (46-ounce) can tomato juice
1 medium onion, finely chopped
2 large ripe tomatoes, peeled and
   chopped
1 green bell pepper, finely chopped
1 cucumber, peeled, seeded and
   diced
2 whole green onions, minced
   (slice another for garnish)
1 whole green onion, sliced
   (garnish)
1 clove garlic, minced
¼ cup fresh parsley, chopped
2 tablespoons olive oil
2 tablespoons lime juice
2 tablespoons red wine vinegar
1½ tablespoons lemon juice
1 teaspoon dried whole tarragon
1 teaspoon dried whole basil
1 teaspoon honey
½ teaspoon salt
¼ teaspoon pepper
¼ teaspoon ground cumin
Dash Tabasco

At least 2 hours before serving: In large bowl combine all ingredients; stir to mix well. Chill at least 2 hours. Serve in soup bowls or mugs; garnish with sliced green onions.

10 to 12 servings.

Preparation Time: 45 Minutes

Treasure Tip: To make unusual individual bowls for chilled soups, slice the tops off of large green or yellow bell peppers. Carve out the seeds and inner membranes. Place on beds of colorful lettuce leaves; fill with soup. Use the pepper tops to cover your edible "soup tureens".

Shrimp and Rice Salad Florentine

1 cup long-grain rice
¾ pound fresh large shrimp,
   cooked, peeled, deveined and
   halved
1 (8-ounce) bottle wine-flavored
   vinaigrette dressing (or make
   your own)
1 tablespoon teriyaki sauce
1 teaspoon sugar
2 cups thin strips fresh spinach
½ cup celery, sliced
½ cup whole green onions, sliced
⅓ cup crisp-cooked bacon,
   crumbled
1 (8-ounce) can sliced water
   chestnuts, drained

Day before, or early in day: Cook rice as package directs . Place hot rice and shrimp in large bowl; cool slightly. Combine vinaigrette, teriyaki and sugar; stir into warm rice. Cover; chill.

Just before serving: Fold remaining ingredients into rice mixture; serve.

6 to 8 servings.

Preparation Time: 30 Minutes   *Cooking Time: 25 Minutes*

Treasure Tip: This beautiful salad makes a refreshing main dish for a summer supper or luncheon. For faster preparation, use pre-washed, packaged fresh spinach.

Chicken Basil Salad

⅓ cup red wine vinegar
2 tablespoons fresh basil, minced plus fresh leaves for garnish
1 tablespoon large capers, drained and chopped
½ teaspoon sugar
⅓ cup plus 3 tablespoons olive oil, divided
1¼ teaspoons salt, divided
4 small whole chicken breasts, skinned and boned
1 pound fresh green beans
2 medium ripe tomatoes, cut in wedges

At least 2 hours before serving: In large bowl mix vinegar, basil, capers, sugar, ⅓ cup olive oil and ¼ teaspoon salt; set aside. Cut each chicken breast in half, then cut each half lengthwise into 1-inch thick strips. In 12-inch skillet over medium-high heat, heat 3 tablespoons oil. Add half of chicken strips and ¼ teaspoon salt. Cook, stirring constantly, until chicken is tender and just loses its pink color, about 5 minutes. Remove chicken with slotted spoon; add to dressing in bowl. In skillet drippings, repeat with remaining chicken and ¼ teaspoon salt. Add to dressing; gently toss to coat well. Cover; refrigerate at least 1 hour to develop flavors.

Place 1 inch water and ½ teaspoon salt in 3-quart saucepan; bring to boil over high heat. Add whole green beans; heat to boiling. Reduce heat to low; cover; simmer until beans are tender-crisp, about 10 minutes. Drain; place in medium bowl; cover and refrigerate. To serve, toss beans and tomato wedges with chicken mixture; garnish with basil leaves.   *8 servings.*

Preparation and Cooking Time: 40 Minutes

Garlic Herbed Potato Salad

3 pounds new potatoes, unpeeled
3 large cloves garlic, finely mashed
½ cup fresh parsley, chopped
½ teaspoon oregano
¼ teaspoon dried thyme
½ cup vegetable oil
¼ cup red wine vinegar
⅓ cup whole green onions, chopped
1½ teaspoons salt, divided
¼ teaspoon pepper

Rinse potatoes well; cut in wedges; soak in cold water in sauce pan. Prepare dressing: Combine garlic, parsley, oregano, thyme, oil, vinegar, onions, ½ teaspoon salt and pepper in jar; shake well. Boil potatoes in water with 1 teaspoon salt until tender, about 10 minutes. Drain; place in bowl. Pour dressing over hot potatoes; mix gently to coat. Serve hot or cold.   *8 servings.*

Preparation Time: 10 Minutes   *Cooking Time: 10 Minutes*

Treasure Tip: For the best-tasting potato salad, always pour dressing over potatoes while they are hot. Hot potatoes absorb the flavors in the dressing.

Flaky Coconut Pound Cake

1 cup sugar
2 sticks butter or margarine,
   melted
5 eggs
3 cups flour
1 teaspoon baking powder
1 cup milk
1 teaspoon coconut flavoring
7 ounces flaked coconut

Glaze

1 cup sugar
1 stick butter or margarine
1 teaspoon coconut flavoring
1 teaspoon butter flavoring

In large bowl of electric mixer, cream sugar and melted butter until all sugar dissolves. Add eggs one at a time, beating at high speed 1 minute after each addition. Sift flour and baking powder together; add alternately with milk to sugar mixture. Add coconut flavoring; beat 2 minutes on low speed. Stir in coconut; pour into greased and floured tube pan. Place in cold oven; bake at 350° F. for 1 hour and 15 minutes.

Five minutes before end of baking time, make glaze: In saucepan combine all ingredients and ½ cup water; boil 3 minutes. Remove cake from oven; leave in pan. Spoon half of glaze over cake; let stand 1 minute. Stick holes in cake with toothpick or two-tined fork; spoon rest of glaze over cake. Cool completely in pan. If desired, bake batter in two loaf pans. Omit glaze; garnish with flaked coconut. **20 servings.**

Preparation Time: 20 Minutes   *Baking Time: 1 Hour 15 Minutes*

Treasure Tip: *To assure even heat distribution, always bake cakes in the middle of the oven. Resist the urge to peek. If you open the oven door during baking, your cake may not rise properly.*

Fresh Tomato-Mushroom Bisque

*³/₄ pound fresh, or 3 ounces dried,
   shitake mushrooms*
3 tablespoons olive oil, divided
*2 celery stalks, trimmed and
   chopped*
1 small onion, chopped
1 whole leek, chopped
1 large shallot, chopped
1 clove garlic, chopped
*2¹/₂ pounds fresh ripe tomatoes,
   peeled, seeded and chopped*
2 cups chicken stock or broth
³/₄ cup dry white wine
¹/₂ cup whipping cream
1 tablespoon fresh lemon juice
1 teaspoon dried thyme, crumbled
1 small bay leaf
Pinch saffron
Salt and white pepper to taste

One day before serving: Remove stems; then thinly slice fresh mushrooms. (If using dried, cover with hot water; soak 30 minutes; drain. Squeeze out water; cut out stems; slice.) Heat 2 tablespoons oil in large heavy saucepan over medium-high heat. Add celery, onion, leek, shallot and garlic. Cook, stirring occasionally, until vegetables are translucent, about 7 minutes. Add two-thirds of mushrooms (refrigerate the rest); sauté 5 minutes. Add tomatoes, stock, wine, cream, lemon juice, thyme, bay leaf and saffron. Bring to boil; reduce heat; simmer 30 minutes. Discard bay leaf; purée soup in food processor or blender until smooth. Season with salt and white pepper. Cover; refrigerate.

Just before serving: Heat 1 tablespoon oil in small, heavy skillet over medium-high heat. Add reserved mushrooms; sauté 5 minutes. Season to taste. Ladle bisque into serving bowls; garnish with sautéed mushrooms.

10 to 12 first-course servings.

Preparation Time: 20 Minutes   *Cooking Time: 50 Minutes*

Treasure Tip: A sprinkling of fresh herbs, a dollop of sour cream or a slice of lemon make a lovely, light garnish. Often, as in this recipe, you can reserve some of the soup ingredients for a garnish.

Rich 'n' Creamy Onion Soup

¹/₂ stick butter
¹/₂ cup flour
2 large onions, grated
*3 leeks, white part only, finely
   chopped*
1 small carrot, peeled and grated
*4 cups hot, homemade chicken
   stock**
Salt and pepper to taste
1 quart hot heavy cream
*1 bunch fresh parsley, finely
   chopped (garnish)*
*Parmesan cheese, freshly grated
   (garnish)*
Freshly made croutons (garnish)

Place chicken stock, onions, carrot and leeks in a large pot; boil 10 minutes. Melt butter in large, heavy saucepan; blend in flour; remove from heat. Slowly pour stock into butter mixture; whisk until well mixed. Bring to boil, stirring constantly. Add cream; season to taste. Serve in soup cups; garnish with parsley, Parmesan and croutons. ***6 to 8 first-course servings.***

Preparation Time: 10 Minutes   *Cooking Time: 25 Minutes*

Treasure Tip: To make fresh croutons, first cut bread into desired shapes. Add your choice of herbs to melted butter or olive oil; sauté bread shapes until browned; or place on cookie sheet, bake 8 to 10 minutes at 350° F. If desired, dust croutons with freshly grated Parmesan cheese; serve hot.

*See recipe on Page 186

Old World Minestrone Soup

2 to 3 tablespoons vegetable oil
2½ pounds beef stew meat, cut in
    ½-inch squares, seasoned with
    salt and pepper
5 carrots, peeled and sliced
4 small turnips, peeled, cut in
    matchsticks
½ pound fresh green beans,
    snapped
2 zucchini, sliced
1 large onion, diced
1 small head cabbage, diced
3 beef bouillon cubes
2 (16-ounce) cans stewed tomatoes
2 (28-ounce) cans whole peeled
    tomatoes
½ cup barley, or ½ pound thin
    spaghetti, or both
1 tablespoon seasoned salt
1 tablespoon seasoned pepper
Generous dash Tabasco
Generous dash Worcestershire
    sauce
1 bay leaf
1 teaspoon sugar
¼ cup fresh parsley, chopped
1 teaspoon oregano
1 (16-ounce) can white beans,
    drained
1 (16-ounce) can red kidney beans
Parmesan cheese, freshly grated

Heat oil in a heavy 8-quart pot; cook beef cubes until browned on all sides. Add 3 quarts water, carrots, turnips, green beans, zucchini, onion, cabbage, bouillon cubes, tomatoes, barley, salt, pepper, bay leaf, Tabasco, Worcestershire, sugar, parsley and oregano. Bring to boil; reduce heat; simmer 2 hours.

Remove bay leaf. Stir in white and kidney beans; heat. Ladle into bowls; sprinkle each serving generously with Parmesan cheese. Note: Use food processor to make preparing vegetables a snap. Adjust seasonings to your taste; add other vegetables if desired. Soup freezes well.

Makes 7 quarts (28 1-cup servings).

Preparation Time: 40 Minutes   **Cooking Time: 2 Hours
                                                      30 Minutes**

Treasure Tip: Bruschetta makes the perfect accompaniment to mine-strone. To make bruschetta, cut French, Italian or Cuban bread into thick slices. Toast the bread in your broiler or on the grill. Rub the warm bread with a halved clove of garlic; drizzle the top with extra virgin olive oil, and sprinkle with a little coarse salt.

Galicia's Soup

½ pound dried garbanzo beans
¼ pound lean salt pork, chopped
¼ pound cooked smoked ham, chopped
¼ pound chorizo, Spanish Sausage, sliced
1 ham bone
1½ teaspoons ground cumin
¼ teaspoon black pepper
1 (10-ounce) package frozen chopped spinach, thawed, squeezed dry
1 tablespoon butter or margarine
4 small potatoes, peeled and cubed

Night before: Cover beans with cold, salted water; soak overnight. Drain before cooking.

When ready to cook: Place salt pork in large stockpot; sauté until lightly browned. Add ham and chorizos; cook over medium heat until lightly browned. Add beans, 2 quarts water, ham bone, cumin and pepper. Cover; bring to boil. Reduce heat to simmer; cook until beans are tender, about 2 hours. While soup simmers, heat spinach with butter. Add potatoes to soup; cook 20 minutes. Add spinach; cook 5 minutes. Remove ham bone before serving. Flavor improves if refrigerated overnight.

6 servings.

Preparation Time: 30 Minutes

Cooking Time: 2 Hours 30 Minutes

Treasure Tip: Caldo Gallego, made with turnip or collard greens, is served in all of Tampa's Spanish restaurants. Galicia's Soup, from the Spanish province of Galicia, uses spinach instead of collard greens, which gives the soup a more delicate flavor.

Spanish Bean Soup

¾ pound dried garbanzo beans
4 ounces salt pork, or 4 slices bacon, chopped
4 to 8 ounces cooked ham, cut in chunks, or 1 small, meaty ham bone
2 to 3 cloves garlic
1 onion, chopped
1 medium tomato, cut in fourths
½ green pepper, cut in chunks
Pinch saffron
1 teaspoon salt
1 to 2 potatoes, peeled and cubed
2 chorizos, Spanish sausage, thinly sliced

2 days ahead: Cover beans with cold, salted water; soak overnight.

Next day: Partially fry salt pork; drain well. In large pot place salt pork, ham, garlic, onion, tomato, green pepper and enough water to rise 2 inches above ingredients. Bring to boil; cover; reduce heat. Cook 30 minutes. Meanwhile, dissolve saffron in ½ cup boiling water; set aside. Drain beans; add to pot with saffron-water mixture. Cook covered until garbanzos are tender, 1 to 1½ hours, stirring occasionally and adding water as needed. With slotted spoon, remove garlic cloves, tomato and green pepper. Add potatoes and chorizos; cover. Cook until potatoes are done, 30 to 40 minutes. Cover; refrigerate overnight.

30 minutes before serving: Skim fat from soup; heat soup and serve.

6 servings.

Preparation Time: 15 Minutes

Cooking Time: 2 Hours 30 Minutes

Springtime Soup

10 cups chicken broth
1 stick butter
2 cups onions, chopped
2 potatoes, peeled and thinly sliced
4 carrots, peeled and thinly sliced
½ cup long-grain rice
1 pound fresh asparagus, trimmed
    and chopped
1 pound fresh spinach, chopped
2 teaspoons salt
¼ teaspoon pepper
2 cups milk

Bring chicken broth to boil. Melt butter in large stockpot; sauté onions until golden. Add boiling broth; stir to blend. Add potatoes, carrots and rice; bring to boil. Cover; reduce heat; simmer 15 minutes. Add asparagus and spinach; simmer until tender, about 15 minutes. Season to taste. Add milk, stirring quickly to combine; serve.   **16 servings.**

Preparation Time: 20 Minutes   *Cooking Time: 40 Minutes*

Treasure Tip: When using canned chicken broth as a base for home-made soup, select the low-salt variety and remove any fat before adding to soup.

Lemony Chicken Soup

Chicken Stock

2 chickens (about 6 pounds total)
4 (10¾-ounce) cans chicken broth
1 chicken bouillon cube (optional)
Salt and pepper to taste

Soup

½ cup rice or orzo
3 carrots, peeled and chopped
3 stalks celery, chopped
2 teaspoons dill weed, divided
3 tablespoons cornstarch
4 eggs
¾ cup lemon juice

Day before, or early in day: Wash chickens; remove and discard giblets and necks. Place chickens in large stockpot; add chicken broth, enough water to cover and bouillon cube, if desired. Season to taste. Bring to boil; reduce heat to medium; simmer until tender, about 1 hour.

Remove chicken from broth; cool, remove meat from bones, cut into bit size pieces and return to broth. Add rice, carrots, celery and 1 teaspoon dill weed. Cook 20 minutes; remove from heat.

Make sauce: Dissolve cornstarch in ½ cup water. Place eggs and ½ cup water in food processor or blender; beat well. Add lemon juice, cornstarch mixture and 1 teaspoon dill weed; blend. Blend in some of hot stock from pot; add egg mixture to pot. Turn heat to high; bring soup to fast boil, stirring. Don't cover pot, or soup will curdle. Cook, stirring, until thickened; serve.

8 servings.

Preparation Time: 25 Minutes   *Cooking Time: 1 Hour*
30 Minutes

Chilled Curried Pea Soup

1 cup fresh or frozen green peas
1 medium onion, sliced
1 carrot, peeled and sliced
1 small potato, peeled and sliced
1 stalk celery with leaves, sliced
1 clove garlic, minced
1 teaspoon curry powder
1/2 teaspoon salt
1 (10 3/4-ounce) can chicken broth,
    undiluted, divided
1 cup milk
3/4 cup whipping cream

Day before, or early in day: In saucepan combine peas, onion, carrot, potato, celery, garlic, curry powder and salt. Add 1 cup broth; bring to boil. Cover; reduce heat; simmer until vegetables are tender, about 15 minutes. Cool slightly; place in blender. Add remaining broth; process until smooth. Add milk and cream; chill thoroughly before serving. *4 servings.*

Preparation Time: 10 Minutes   *Cooking Time: 20 Minutes*

Treasure Tip: This refreshing soup, topped with freshly made croutons, is an easy make-ahead for a hot summer day. For an interesting variation, substitute tarragon for curry powder; garnish with finely chopped fresh mint.

Velvety Beer Cheese Soup

1 stick margarine
3/4 cup celery, diced
3/4 cup yellow onion, diced
3/4 cup flour
5 ounces Ro-tel diced tomatoes
    with green chilies
2 pounds Velveeta cheese, diced
1 teaspoon white pepper
8 cups chicken stock, or 4 (14 1/2 -
    ounce) cans low-salt chicken
    broth
3/4 cup beer, room temperature
    (non-alcoholic or lite beer is
    fine)

In large saucepan melt margarine over medium heat; add celery and onion; sauté 3 minutes. Add flour; whisk to combine; cook 2 minutes. Add Ro-tel, Velveeta, pepper and chicken stock. Cook, stirring occasionally, until cheese melts and soup thickens. When ready to serve, slowly pour in beer; mix. *8 servings.*

Preparation Time: 10 Minutes   *Cooking Time: 45 to 50 Minutes*

Treasure Tip: This soup freezes beautifully. Cooked broccoli and cauliflower can be added for variety.

Yacht Club Seafood Gumbo

1 stick butter
1 cup flour
1/4 cup bacon drippings
2 medium onions, chopped
2 celery stalks, chopped
4 cloves garlic, crushed
1 pound fresh okra, chopped
1 ham bone
8 ounces smoked ham cubes,
    chipped
2 (28-ounce) cans Italian crushed
    tomatoes
1 (28-ounce) can Italian whole
    tomatoes
1/2 cup chopped raw chicken meat
    (1 breast)
1 tablespoon crushed red pepper
1 teaspoon salt
1 teaspoon pepper
1 teaspoon thyme leaves
4 bay leaves
4 shakes Tabasco
2 chicken bouillon cubes
2 beef bouillon cubes
1 tablespoon sugar
5 tablespoons Worcestershire sauce
2 pounds fresh grouper, skinned
    and chopped
1 pound fresh crabmeat, cartilage
    removed
1 pound fresh shrimp, peeled and
    deveined
Cooked rice (optional)
1/4 teaspoon grated fresh lemon or
    lime rind

Day before: In saucepan melt butter; add flour. Cook slowly, stirring until dark brown, making a roux. In skillet melt bacon drippings; sauté onion, celery, garlic and okra.

In large stockpot place roux, onion mixture, 4 cups water, ham bone, chipped ham, tomatoes, chicken, red pepper, salt, pepper, thyme, bay leaves, Tabasco, bouillon cubes, sugar, Worcestershire. Bring to boil; reduce heat; simmer 1½ hours.

Add shrimp, grouper and crabmeat; cook 10 to 15 minutes more. If desired, add cooked rice to thicken. The amount of rice depends on how thick you want the gumbo. Cover; refrigerate overnight. Remove from refrigerator; skim fat; reheat. Just before serving, sprinkle with grated rind.

12 generous servings.

Preparation Time: 1 Hour   *Cooking Time: 2 Hours*

Creamy Crab Stew

1 stick unsalted butter
³/₄ cup carrot, finely chopped
³/₄ cup celery, finely chopped
³/₄ cup onion, finely chopped
¹/₄ cup flour
4 cups milk
4 cups heavy cream or half-and-
    half
¹/₂ bay leaf
1 tablespoon freshly ground black
    pepper
1 teaspoon salt
¹/₈ teaspoon cayenne pepper
1 teaspoon Old Bay seasoning
1 tablespoon Worcestershire sauce
1 pound lump crabmeat, cartilage
    removed

In large saucepan melt butter; cook carrot, celery and onion over moderately low heat, stirring until softened, about 5 minutes. Add flour; cook, stirring, 3 minutes. Add milk, cream, bay leaf, pepper, salt, cayenne, Old Bay and Worcestershire. Bring to boil; reduce heat; simmer, stirring, until slightly thickened, 8 to 10 minutes. Add crabmeat; cook, stirring, 1 minute. Remove bay leaf before serving.   *8 to 10 servings.*

Preparation Time: 15 Minutes   *Cooking Time: 30 Minutes*

Treasure Tip: Thick stews and chowders can be served in bread bowls. Cut tops off of round loaves of bread; hollow out insides. Brush the bread shells with melted butter or olive oil; bake in a 350° F. oven for 8 to 10 minutes, until lightly crisp.

Bay Scallop Chowder

1 tablespoon butter
¹/₂ cup celery, chopped
1 carrot, peeled and grated
1 onion, chopped
1 cup peeled, chopped potatoes
1 pint half-and-half
Salt and pepper to taste
3 to 4 drops Tabasco
1 pound fresh bay scallops

In large saucepan heat butter and 1 or 2 tablespoons water; cook celery, carrot and onion over medium-low heat 10 minutes. Add potatoes; cook 10 minutes. Add half-and-half, salt, pepper and Tabasco; cook 20 to 25 minutes more. Add scallops; cook 5 to 10 minutes.   *4 to 6 servings.*

Preparation Time: 15 Minutes   *Cooking Time: 50 Minutes*

Chicken Melon Salad

1 envelope low-salt instant
  chicken bouillon
4 to 6 chicken breast halves,
  skinned and boned
1 small, ripe honeydew melon
  (about 1½ pounds), halved
1 small, ripe cantaloupe (about 1½
  pounds), halved, or 1 bunch
  seedless grapes
1 medium-size ripe papaya, halved
  and seeded
½ cup sour cream
2 tablespoons honey
1 tablespoon Dijon mustard
Salt and black pepper to taste
2 medium whole green onions, cut
  into 1-inch slices (½ cup)
1 head leaf lettuce

Place bouillon and 2 inches water in 2-quart saucepan; bring to boil over high heat. Add chicken; reduce heat to medium-low. Cover; simmer just until cooked through, about 20 minutes. Drain chicken. When cool enough to handle, cut into bite-size pieces; set aside in large bowl.

Using melon baller or small spoon, scoop small balls from half of honeydew and all of cantaloupe, about 3 cups; add to bowl with chicken. Cut remaining honeydew into ¼-inch slices; set aside. Peel papaya; cut into ¼-inch slices; set aside.

Prepare dressing: Place sour cream, honey, mustard, salt and pepper in small bowl. Beat with fork or whisk until blended and smooth; stir in green onions. Pour over chicken and melon; toss gently, but thoroughly, to coat. Arrange bed of lettuce leaves on large platter; place honeydew and papaya slices over lettuce around sides of platter; spoon chicken-melon mixture into center. ***4 to 6 servings.***

Preparation Time: 30 Minutes   ***Cooking Time: 20 Minutes***

Almond Ginger Chicken Salad

4 whole chicken breasts, boned and
  skinned
Juice of 1 fresh lemon
½ cup celery, chopped
¼ cup mayonnaise
1 (9-ounce) bottle Raffetto
  Chutney
2 tablespoons fresh ginger, grated
  (or more)
¼ cup slivered almonds

About 1 hour before serving: Poach chicken breasts in water with lemon juice until tender, about 20 minutes; cool; dice. Place chicken in bowl; add celery, mayonnaise and chutney; toss. Add ginger and almonds. Cover; refrigerate 30 minutes. ***4 to 6 servings.***

Preparation Time: 30 Minutes   ***Cooking Time: 20 Minutes***

Curry Chicken Apple Salad

2 large Granny Smith apples
2 tablespoons fresh lemon juice
3½ cups cooked chicken, cubed
1½ cup cooked brown or white rice
1 cup mayonnaise
½ cup pecans, chopped or slivered
    almonds, toasted
1 tablespoon green onion, chopped
3 teaspoons curry powder
1½ teaspoons salt
⅛ teaspoon pepper
Lettuce
Red grapes (optional)
Carrot curls (optional)
Orange slices (optional)
Paprika

Early in day: Core apples, leaving peel on; cube. In large bowl mix apples and lemon juice; add chicken, rice, mayonnaise, almonds, green onion, salt and pepper; chill. Serve on lettuce leaves; garnish with grapes, carrot curls or orange slices; sprinkle with paprika.   **6 to 8 servings.**

Preparation Time: 30 Minutes

Treasure Tip: This recipe also makes a tasty, unusual sandwich. Cut pita bread in half; stuff halves with chicken salad.

Chicken Fruit Salad Supreme

3 large whole chickens, or 6
    pounds boneless chicken breasts
¼ cup vegetable oil
¼ cup fresh orange juice
¼ cup wine vinegar
2 teaspoons salt
2½ cups raw rice
3 cups mandarin orange sections,
    drained
3 cups canned pineapple tidbits,
    drained
3 cups green grapes, halved
2 cups slivered almonds, toasted
3 cups celery, diced
2 cups mayonnaise (or to taste)
Mandarin orange sections
    (garnish)

Early in the day: Place chickens in saucepan; cover with water; bring to boil. Reduce heat to medium; cook until tender (about 1 hour for whole chickens, 20 minutes for breasts). Remove meat from bones; cube meat. In large bowl mix oil, orange juice, vinegar and salt. Add chicken; mix well. Cover; refrigerate.

Cook rice as package directs; drain; blanch with cold water. Add to chicken; add remaining ingredients. Mix well; refrigerate until serving time. Serve on lettuce; garnish with orange sections. Note: An 8-pound turkey may be substituted for chicken. Roast; proceed with recipe. Recipe halves easily.

20 servings.

Preparation Time: 30 Minutes   *Cooking Time: 50 Minutes to
1 Hour 30 Minutes*

Treasure Tip: Garnish fruit salad plates with frosted grapes. Combine 1 slightly beaten egg white and a little water; using pastry brush, glaze tops of grape clusters with mixture. Sprinkle with sugar; dry on a rack.

Tempting Turkey and Cracked Wheat Salad

2 tablespoons olive oil
4 cloves garlic, minced
5 teaspoons fresh ginger, minced
¼ to ½ teaspoon crushed red pepper
    flakes
1⅓ cups cracked wheat*
2⅔ cups chicken broth
1 pound cooked turkey, cut into
    bite-size pieces
½ cup whole green onions, chopped
10 cherry tomatoes, quartered and
    seeded
1 teaspoon sesame oil
5 teaspoons soy sauce
1½ tablespoons wine vinegar
Pepper to taste
¼ cup toasted almonds or pine
    nuts, chopped

*Available at gourmet shops
and health food stores

In medium saucepan heat oil over medium heat; sauté garlic, ginger and pepper flakes 2 to 3 minutes. Stir in cracked wheat and chicken broth. Bring to boil; reduce heat to low; cover. Simmer until wheat is tender and all liquid is absorbed, about 15 minutes.

Make dressing: Combine oil, soy sauce, vinegar and pepper; mix well. Spoon wheat into bowl; add turkey, green onions, tomatoes and dressing. Toss; allow flavors to blend about 10 minutes. Cover to keep warm, or serve at room temperature. Serve on bed of lettuce; top with nuts. *4 to 6 servings.*

Preparation Time: 25 Minutes   *Cooking Time: 20 Minutes*

Curry Chicken with Nectarine Salsa

2 whole chicken breasts (about
   1½ pounds total), halved
1 thick slice onion
1 leafy celery top
1 teaspoon salt
6 cups summer lettuce, torn
   (Boston, bibb, curly red leaf)
½ cup dry-roasted peanuts,
   coarsely chopped
1 nectarine, cut in thin wedges
   (garnish)
1 tablespoon green onion tops,
   sliced (garnish)

Curry Dressing

1½ teaspoons curry powder
2 tablespoons chicken broth
¼ cup mayonnaise
¼ cup plain yogurt
1 teaspoon fresh ginger, grated
Small clove garlic, crushed
Pinch ground hot red pepper

Nectarine Salsa

2 cups (about ¾ pound) unpeeled
   nectarines, diced
½ cup red onion, diced
⅓ cup red bell pepper, diced
⅓ cup olive oil
2 tablespoons fresh lime juice
¼ teaspoon salt
⅛ teaspoon pepper

Combine chicken, onion, celery top and salt in large skillet. Pour in just enough water to barely cover chicken. Bring to boil; lower heat; cover. Simmer, turning once, until meat is no longer pink near bone, 15 to 20 minutes. Take off heat; leave chicken in broth until cool. Remove and discard skin and bones from chicken. Cut chicken into wide strips; place in bowl; set aside. Strain broth; reserve 2 tablespoons broth; discard solids.

Make dressing: Heat curry powder, stirring constantly, in small skillet over low heat until fragrant. Add reserved broth; cook 30 seconds; remove from heat. Stir in mayonnaise, yogurt, ginger, garlic and hot red pepper.

Make salsa: In medium bowl stir together all ingredients. Add half of dressing to chicken; combine well. In another bowl put greens; toss with half of salsa. Divide greens equally among four serving plates. Mound chicken in center; sprinkle with peanuts. Garnish with nectarine wedges and sliced green onion. Pass remaining dressing and salsa. Do not make salsa too far ahead. Nectarines become soggy if left in salsa overnight.

4 servings.

Preparation Time: 30 Minutes *Cooking Time: 20 Minutes*

Treasure Tip: For crisper salad greens, wash thoroughly and pat dry with paper towels. Place in plastic bag; seal; refrigerate in your crisper compartment. Use Boston, bibb or leaf lettuce within a few days. Iceberg lettuce, endive, romaine and escarole will keep longer.

Turkey Salad with Cranberry Dressing

Cranberry Dressing

3/4 cup vegetable oil
1/4 cup vinegar
1 teaspoon salt
1 teaspoon sugar
1/4 teaspoon paprika
1/4 teaspoon dry mustard
1/2 cup jellied cranberry sauce

Turkey Salad

4 cups cooked turkey, diced
1 cup celery, chopped
1 cup green seedless grapes, halved
1/2 teaspoon salt
1/2 teaspoon pepper
3 hard-boiled eggs, chopped
4 ounces sliced water chestnuts
1 cup walnuts (optional)
2 tablespoons fresh lemon juice
Few drops Tabasco
1/3 cup mayonnaise
1/4 cup sour cream

Early in day, make dressing: Mix oil, vinegar, salt, sugar, paprika and mustard together in small bowl. Place cranberry sauce in food processor or blender; process until smooth. Add oil mixture; process until well blended; chill.

Just before serving: In large bowl combine turkey, celery, grapes, salt, pepper, eggs, water chestnuts and walnuts. Mix lemon juice, Tabasco, mayonnaise and sour cream together; stir into turkey mixture. Serve salad with Cranberry Dressing on the side. Dressing is also perfect for fruit or green salads.

8 servings.

Preparation Time: 1 Hour

Tangy Summer Salad

8 ounces thin fresh green beans

2 large ripe pears, halved and cored

1 tablespoon fresh lemon or lime
  juice

6 cups mixed curly red-leaf lettuce
  and romaine, torn

8 ounces honey-cured or wood-
  smoked ham, cut in 3 x $^1/_4$ x $^1/_4$-
  inch strips

3 ounce Saga bleu cheese, cut in
  $^1/_4$-inch cubes

$^1/_2$ cup walnut pieces, toasted

Honey-Mustard Dressing

$^1/_4$ cup red wine vinegar

$^1/_4$ cup honey

1 teaspoon grainy mustard

1 small clove garlic, chopped

1 (3 x 1-inch) strip orange peel,
  coarsely chopped, white part of
  peel removed

Pinch salt

$^1/_8$ teaspoon pepper

$^1/_2$ cup olive oil

Cook green beans in boiling water 5 minutes; drain; rinse with cold water. Cut each pear half into four wedges; sprinkle with lemon juice; gently toss to coat. Set aside.

Make dressing: In food processor or blender combine vinegar, honey, mustard, garlic, orange peel, salt and pepper; process until well mixed. With motor running, gradually pour in oil until smooth and well blended.

In large bowl combine lettuce and green beans; toss with ½ cup dressing until evenly coated. Divide evenly among four serving plates. Arrange pear wedges like spokes of wheel on each plate; place ham strips between pears. Sprinkle with cheese and walnuts; serve. *4 servings.*

Preparation Time: 20 Minutes

Treasure Tip: For perfect pear halves, slice in half, then core with melon ball cutter or teaspoon.

Tony's Salad

Classic Tampa salad from the former Tony's Restaurant

Garlic cloves
Olive oil
1 head lettuce, shredded
1 medium Bermuda onion, very
    thinly sliced
1 green bell pepper, chopped
2 stalks celery, chopped
1 ripe tomato, sliced
1 hard-boiled egg, chopped
$1/4$ pound Swiss cheese, cut into
    thin strips
$1/4$ pound baked ham or salami,
    chopped
8 Greek olives
8 green Spanish manzanilla olives
$1/2$ pound Parmesan cheese, coarsely
    grated
Salt and pepper to taste
2 tablespoons olive oil
1 tablespoon wine vinegar
Juice of 1 lime or lemon
2 teaspoons oregano

Several days before serving: Crush garlic into semi-purée; put in jar. Cover with olive oil. Cover jar; store in refrigerator.

When ready to serve: Rub wooden salad bowl with 1 tablespoon oil-garlic mixture. Place lettuce in bowl; place onion on top. Next add green pepper and celery; place tomato slices around edge of bowl. Add egg, cheese strips, ham, olives and grated cheese. Salt and pepper thoroughly. Drizzle oil, then wine vinegar over salad. Squeeze lime juice over all; add oregano. Using knife and fork, cut tomatoes into salad as last step, mixing down and up to get the right "shine" on the entire salad. Serve at once. *4 to 6 servings.*

Preparation Time: 30 Minutes

Treasure Tip: To peel garlic without using a knife, soak in lukewarm water. The thin skin will slip off easily between your fingers.

Terrific Tuna Salad

1 (6¹/₈-ounce) can solid-pack white
 tuna in water (chicken can be
 substituted)
1 (10-ounce) package frozen
 chopped broccoli, thawed,
 drained
4 carrots, peeled and grated
1 (8-ounce) can water chestnuts,
 chopped and drained
¹/₂ cup Parmesan cheese, freshly
 grated
1 tablespoon onion, chopped
1 fresh yellow or zucchini squash,
 trimmed and chopped
1 to 2 tablespoons celery, chopped
4 slices bacon, cooked crisp and
 crumbled
¹/₂ cup apple, chopped
¹/₂ cup raisins
1 tablespoon nuts, chopped
 (optional)
Seasoned salt, pepper and garlic
 powder to taste
Ranch or Italian salad dressing
 (just enough to blend)

Combine all ingredients. Chill thoroughly, then serve. Serve on bed of fresh lettuce or as sandwich.   **6 servings.**

Preparation Time: 15 Minutes

Treasure Tip: *For bright salad garnishes, make carrot curls or zigzags. Peel whole carrot; place on cutting board. With parer shave thin, wide lengthwise strips of carrot. For curls, roll up strips; secure with toothpicks. For zigzags, thread strips on toothpicks accordion-style. For both, crisp in ice water in refrigerator; remove picks before serving.*

Vegetable Mélange with Tarragon-Basil Dressing

Salad

1 cup fresh asparagus tips, cut in
    1-inch diagonal pieces, blanched
1 cup fresh snow peas, tips and
    strings removed, blanched
1 head fresh broccoli florets,
    blanched
1 head fresh cauliflower florets,
    blanched
1½ cups peas, fresh, blanched, or
    frozen
1½ cups fresh green beans, cut in
    1-inch pieces, blanched
1½ cups fresh baby carrots,
    blanched, halved
1 (16-ounce) can garbanzo beans,
    drained
1 (6-ounce dry weight) can small
    pitted ripe olives, cut in half
1 (7-ounce) jar baby corn, drained
1 (10-ounce) package frozen
    artichoke hearts, cooked, cut in
    chunks
1½ cups celery, sliced diagonally
    into ½-inch pieces
1 large red onion, diced
1 large red bell pepper, diced
1 large green bell pepper, diced
½ cup fresh parsley, chopped
¼ cup fresh basil, chopped
    (garnish)

Tarragon-Basil Dressing

½ cup tarragon vinegar
1 cup vegetable oil
1 tablespoon sugar
1 tablespoon salt
1 teaspoon Tabasco
4 tablespoons small, drained capers
2⅔ tablespoons fresh tarragon,
    chopped (or 2 teaspoons dried)
2⅔ tablespoons fresh basil, chopped
    (or 2 teaspoons dried)
2⅔ tablespoons fresh oregano,
    chopped (or 2 teaspoons dried)
¼ cup shallots, chopped (about 6
    large shallots)

At least 4 hours before serving: Drain all vegetables thoroughly. In very large bowl place all salad ingredients. In quart jar combine all dressing ingredients; shake well. Pour dressing over vegetables; toss to combine well. Cover; refrigerate, stirring occasionally. Toss and sprinkle with chopped basil before serving. Serve as salad course for buffet.

24 servings.

Preparation and Cooking Time: 1 Hour 30 Minutes to 2 Hours

Treasure Tip: *To blanch vegetables, plunge briefly into rapidly boiling water, then rinse with cold water. Blanch each vegetable separately. The process ensures bright color and crispness. Use fresh herbs in this recipe, they make a difference!*

Marinated Broccoli Salad

2 to 3 bunches fresh broccoli
1 cup cider vinegar
1½ cups vegetable oil
1 tablespoon sugar
1 tablespoon dill weed
1 teaspoon salt
1 teaspoon pepper
1 teaspoon garlic salt
Red lettuce leaves

24 hours before serving: Cut stems and leaves from broccoli; discard. Cut florets into 1 to 2-inch pieces. In large bowl mix together all remaining ingredients. Add broccoli; stir until well coated with dressing. Cover; refrigerate 24 hours. To serve, drain broccoli; place on plates lined with red lettuce.

10 to 12 servings.

Preparation Time: 15 Minutes

Bacon-Broccoli Salad

1 pound bacon
1 large bunch fresh broccoli
8 ounces Swiss cheese, chopped
1 large onion, chopped
¾ cup mayonnaise
2 tablespoons lemon juice
¼ cup sugar

24 hours before serving: Cook bacon in microwave or skillet; drain; crumble. Remove stems and leaves from broccoli; chop florets and tiny stems into bite-size pieces. In large bowl place bacon, broccoli, cheese, and onion. Mix mayonnaise, lemon juice and sugar; pour over broccoli; stir. Refrigerate 24 hours. Good side dish for picnic or barbecue.

6 to 8 servings.

Preparation Time: 30 Minutes   *Cooking Time: 20 Minutes*

Lobster and Avocado Salad

1½ cups fresh Florida lobster meat, cooked
1 cup iceberg lettuce, torn in pieces
1 cup romaine lettuce, torn in pieces
½ cup watercress leaves
1 cup celery, diced
¼ cup whole green onions, chopped
2 medium ripe tomatoes, diced
5 large pitted ripe olives, sliced
1 avocado, peeled, quartered and sliced
½ fresh grapefruit, sectioned
Spicy red-wine vinaigrette salad dressing*

*See recipe on Page 207

Place all ingredients in large salad bowl; toss well. Serve at once.

4 to 6 servings.

Preparation Time: 30 Minutes

Treasure Tip: When buying tomatoes, look for ones that are firm, smooth and ripe. If tomatoes are not quite ripe, keep them at room temperature. Do not refrigerate tomatoes, they lose their flavor.

Spiced Rice and Bean Salad

3 cloves garlic
¾ cup plus 2 tablespoons vegetable oil
¼ cup red wine vinegar
½ teaspoon salt
3 cups cold, cooked rice
1 (15-ounce) can pinto beans, rinsed and drained
1 (15-ounce) can black beans, rinsed and drained
1 (10-ounce) package frozen peas, thawed and drained
1 cup celery, sliced
1 medium red onion, chopped
2 (4-ounce) cans diced green chile peppers, drained
¼ cup snipped fresh cilantro or parsley
Pepper to taste

2 days before serving: Crush garlic; let stand overnight in oil.

Up to 24 hours before serving: Drain oil from garlic; discard garlic. Combine oil, vinegar and salt in jar; shake well to combine. Place rice, beans, peas, celery, onion, chile peppers and cilantro in 2½-quart container. Add dressing; season with pepper; toss gently to mix. Cover; chill up to 24 hours. Good choice for a covered-dish supper. **14 to 16 servings.**

Preparation Time: 20 Minutes

Layered Cabbage and Apple Salad

2 cups shredded cabbage
1 (17-ounce) can green peas, drained
1 (8-ounce) can water chestnuts, drained
¼ cup onion, chopped
¾ cup celery, chopped
1 large red apple, unpeeled, cored and chopped
¼ teaspoon salt
½ cup sour cream
½ cup mayonnaise or salad dressing
1 teaspoon sugar
1 cup (4 ounces) cheddar cheese, shredded
1 cup pecans, finely chopped

Early in day, or night before: In large bowl combine cabbage, peas, water chestnuts, onion, celery, apple and salt. Combine sour cream, mayonnaise and sugar; stir until blended. Spread sour cream mixture over cabbage mixture, sealing to edge of bowl. Layer cheese and pecans on top. Cover salad; chill 8 hours. Toss before serving. **8 servings.**

Preparation Time: 20 Minutes

Treasure Tip: For maximum effect, serve this pretty salad in a clear glass bowl to show off the colorful layers.

Crunchy Rice-Pea Salad

1 (6 ounce) package long grain and
    wild rice mix
1 (10 ounce) package frozen small
    peas, thawed and drained
½ cup walnuts, chopped
½ cup red bell pepper, chopped
¼ cup whole green onions, sliced
⅓ cup bottled buttermilk or creamy
    Italian salad dressing
Tomato wedges (garnish)
Green onions (garnish)

Cook rice as package directs. In serving bowl combine rice, peas, walnuts, pepper and onions. Add salad dressing; toss gently to coat. Chill several hours in refrigerator. Toss just before serving. Garnish with tomato wedges and green onions.

6 servings.

Preparation Time: 15 Minutes   *Cooking Time: 20 Minutes*

Bacon-Potato Salad

8 to 9 strips bacon
3 pounds small new potatoes
⅓ cup red onion, chopped
4 to 5 tablespoons fresh parsley,
    chopped
1½ tablespoons wine or herb
    vinegar
4½ tablespoons vegetable oil
¾ cups sour cream
Salt and pepper to taste
Fresh parsley (garnish)

Four hours before serving: Cook, drain and crumble bacon. Cover potatoes with cold, salted water; bring to boil; cook until tender but still firm, about 20 minutes. Drain; cool; peel if desired, but red skins are nutritious and make a prettier salad. Cut into ¼-inch slices. Add onion, parsley and half of bacon; toss. Combine vinegar, oil, sour cream, salt and pepper. Add to potatoes; toss. Chill 4 hours.

When ready to serve: Add a little more sour cream if potatoes seem dry. Garnish with parsley and remaining bacon.

8 servings.

Preparation Time: 45 Minutes   *Cooking Time: 20 Minutes*

Fresh Dill Potato Salad

2½ pounds Red Bliss new potatoes
1 tablespoon salt
1 teaspoon celery seed
¼ cup celery, chopped
3 hard-boiled eggs, coarsely
    chopped
½ cup whole green onions, sliced
1 tablespoon chives, chopped
2 tablespoons fresh dill, chopped
1¼ cups mayonnaise
1 tablespoon prepared mustard
½ teaspoon garlic powder
1 teaspoon seasoned salt
1 teaspoon ground pepper

Early in day, or night before: Wash potatoes; do not peel. Cut into bite-size pieces. Place in saucepan; cover with water; add salt and celery seed. Bring to boil; boil about 3 minutes. Remove from heat; leave in pan about 20 minutes. Drain; cool. Potatoes must cool before handling, or they will break up. In large bowl combine potatoes, celery, eggs, green onions, chives and dill; toss gently. Combine mayonnaise, mustard, garlic powder, seasoned salt and pepper; pour over potato mixture; stir to coat. Chill. ***6 to 8 servings.***

Preparation and Cooking Time: 30 Minutes

Treasure Tip: *Dressing is the bond that brings a salad together. A simple green salad should have the lightest of dressings. A robust salad needs a stronger dressing to bring out the full flavor.*

Napa Cabbage-Radicchio Salad

1 large, or 2 small, heads Napa
    cabbage
1 small head radicchio
5 whole green onions, chopped
2 (3-ounce) packages Ramen
    Noodle soup mix (any flavor)
½ cup butter or margarine
1 to 2 tablespoons sesame seeds
1 (2-ounce) package slivered
    almonds
½ cup vegetable oil
¾ cup brown sugar
½ cup tarragon vinegar
2 tablespoons soy sauce

Early in day: Tear cabbage and lettuce into small pieces; place in bowl, add green onions; refrigerate. Break noodles into small pieces; discard seasoning packets. Heat butter in medium skillet; sauté noodles, sesame seeds and almonds until golden brown; refrigerate. In jar mix oil, brown sugar, vinegar and soy sauce; shake well; refrigerate.

20 minutes before serving: Add dressing to noodle mixture.
Just before serving: Toss mixtures together. ***8 to 10 servings.***

Preparation Time: 30 Minutes   ***Cooking Time: 10 Minutes***

Treasure Tip: *Match your salad to the meal you are serving. A light salad goes best with a hearty dinner. A heavier salad complements a light entrée.*

Spinach-Apple Salad

1 green apple, cut in wedges
1 tablespoon fresh lemon juice
1 (10-ounce) package fresh spinach
½ pound fresh mushrooms, sliced
4 whole green onions, sliced
1 (6-ounce) can frozen orange juice
    concentrate, thawed, undiluted
¾ cup mayonnaise
Homemade croutons (see Treasure
    Tip on page 183)

Early in day: Place apple in large bowl; add lemon juice; toss. Add spinach, mushrooms and green onions; refrigerate. Mix orange juice and mayonnaise; refrigerate. Just before serving, pour dressing over salad; toss to mix well. Garnish with croutons; serve.   *4 to 6 servings.*

Preparation Time: 15 Minutes

Crispy Layered Spinach Salad

1 package fresh spinach
1 head lettuce, shredded
1 red onion, thinly sliced
1 (8-ounce) can sliced water
    chestnuts, drained
1 (10-ounce) package frozen green
    peas, thawed and drained
½ pound bacon, cooked, drained
    and crumbled
1½ cups sour cream
1½ cups mayonnaise
1 (1-ounce) package dry Hidden
    Valley Ranch original dressing
1 teaspoon sugar
Freshly grated Parmesan cheese

Night before: In large glass bowl layer, in order, spinach, lettuce, onion, water chestnuts, peas and bacon. Combine sour cream, mayonnaise, dressing mix and sugar; spread over top of vegetables, sealing to edge of bowl. Sprinkle generously with cheese. Cover tightly with plastic wrap; refrigerate 12 or more hours.   *10 to 12 servings.*

Preparation Time: 30 Minutes   *Cooking Time: 10 Minutes*

Treasure Tip: Serve this salad with Parmesan Crisps: Toast 6 slices of bread; trim crusts; cut each slice in five strips. Roll strips in 6 table-spoons melted butter or margarine; sprinkle one side of strips with 6 tablespoons freshly grated Parmesan cheese. Place on cookie sheet; bake at 400° F. degrees until crisp, 5 to 8 minutes.

Caesar Salad

1 egg
Pinch salt
2 large cloves garlic, minced
2 anchovies, minced
2 tablespoons red wine vinegar
1 teaspoon dry mustard
Juice of ½ large lemon
Pepper to taste
5 drops Worcestershire sauce
¼ cup olive oil
1 bunch romaine lettuce
Homemade croutons (see Treasure
   Tip on page 183)
Parmesan cheese, freshly grated

Coddle egg by lowering with spoon into small pan of boiling water. Turn off heat; cover pan; leave 3 minutes. Remove egg; plunge into cold water to stop cooking.

Sprinkle salt in large wooden salad bowl. Add garlic and anchovies; mince into paste with two forks. Blend in vinegar, mustard, lemon juice, pepper and Worcestershire. Whisk in olive oil; break coddled egg into bowl; whisk into dressing. Pour dressing into smaller bowl.

Wash and dry romaine; break into pieces into prepared salad bowl. Sprinkle with croutons and Parmesan; toss, gradually adding desired amount of dressing. For lower-cholesterol dressing, use just the egg white.

2 main-course, 4 side-dish servings.

Preparation Time: 30 Minutes

Henry Winkler's Mexican Salad

Henry Winkler contributed this recipe when he was in Tampa directing the movie, "Cop and a Half"

1½ cups mayonnaise
1 (7-ounce) can green chile salsa
⅓ cup catsup
½ teaspoon chili powder
1 to 2 heads romaine, broken into
   ½-inch pieces
2 (2¼-ounce) cans sliced black
   olives
2 to 3 large ripe tomatoes, diced
1 large red onion, diced
½ cup sharp cheddar cheese, grated
1 (4-ounce) can diced green chilies
1 to 2 (6½-ounce) bags tortilla
   chips, crumbled
2 avocados, diced

Early in day: Combine mayonnaise, salsa, catsup and chili powder; chill.

When ready to serve: Place romaine in large serving bowl; add olives, tomatoes, onion, cheese and chilies. Top with crumbled chips and avocados. Spread dressing on top; serve.

4 to 6 servings.

Preparation Time: 25 Minutes

Treasure Tip: *For an impressive presentation, serve this salad in flour tortilla shells. Brush both sides of 12- or 16-inch flour tortillas with melted butter. Press them into small ovenproof bowls; toast 5 to 8 minutes in a 375° oven. Unmold the tortillas; place them directly on the oven rack until they are crisp and toasted, 1 to 2 minutes.*

Mango-Tomato Salad With Basil Curry Dressing

4 ripe plum tomatoes
1 large ripe mango
1½ tablespoons extra-virgin olive
    oil
1 teaspoon white wine vinegar
Pinch curry powder
4 to 6 large fresh basil leaves
Salt and freshly ground pepper to
    taste

Core tomatoes; cut into ½-inch wedges. Cut mango from pit in ½-inch slices; remove skin with sharp knife. Alternate tomato and mango slices on serving plate. Pulverize basil with mortar and pestle or electric chopper. Combine oil, vinegar, curry powder, basil, salt and pepper. Drizzle dressing over tomatoes and mangoes; serve immediately. Dressing may be made 1 day ahead.

4 servings.

Preparation Time: 15 Minutes

Florida Orange and Avocado Salad

Orange Juice Dressing

½ teaspoon orange peel, grated
¼ cup fresh orange juice
½ cup vegetable oil
2 tablespoons sugar
2 tablespoons red wine vinegar
1 tablespoon fresh lemon juice
½ teaspoon salt

Avocado Salad

1 medium head iceberg lettuce
1 small cucumber, peeled and
    sliced thin
1 Florida avocado, peeled and
    sliced
1 (11-ounce) can mandarin
    oranges, chilled and drained
2 tablespoons whole green onion,
    sliced
¼ cup walnut pieces, broken
½ cup cheddar cheese, grated
Homemade croutons (see Treasure
    Tipe on page 183)

Make dressing: In jar combine all ingredients; shake well. Refrigerate just long enough to chill slightly. Tear lettuce into bite-size pieces in large bowl. Add remaining ingredients. Toss with dressing; serve.

6 servings.

Preparation Time: 20 Minutes

Treasure Tip: Look for cucumbers that are bright green, well-shaped and firm. The fat, heavily seeded kind are very watery, usually waxed and should be peeled before serving. The long, thinner cucumber, sometime called an English cucumber, is virtually seedless and does not need to be peeled.

Florida Citrus Salad

Grapefruit Salad Dressing

1 (³/₄-ounce) package Italian salad
    dressing mix
²/₃ cup vegetable oil, divided
½ cup fresh grapefruit juice

Citrus Salad

3 cups spinach leaves, torn
3 cups leaf lettuce leaves, torn
3 cups iceberg lettuce leaves, torn
1 Florida grapefruit, peeled and
    sectioned
2 Florida oranges, peeled and
    sectioned
1 Florida avocado, peeled and
    sliced
½ cup celery, sliced
½ cup green bell pepper, sliced
¼ cup toasted slivered almonds

Early in day, make dressing: In jar combine salad dressing mix with ⅓ cup oil; cover tightly; shake vigorously. Add remaining oil and grapefruit juice; shake vigorously. Refrigerate until serving time.

When ready to serve: Combine spinach and lettuces in large bowl; toss lightly. Arrange grapefruit and orange sections, avocado slices, celery, green pepper and almonds on top of greens. Shake dressing; pour over salad. Serve immediately.
6 to 8 servings.

Preparation Time: 30 Minutes

Treasure Tip: Citrus roses make an attractive garnish for fruit salads. Starting at the stem end of a lemon or lime, cut the peel off in a continuous spiral. With the stem end in the center, curl into a rose shape; secure with a toothpick. For a larger rose, curl several peels together. Squeeze the juice; use it within a day or two, or freeze it.

Fruit Salad with Apricot Nectar Dressing

Apricot Nectar Dressing

1 teaspoon cornstarch
⅛ teaspoon garlic powder
⅛ teaspoon ground ginger
²/₃ cup apricot nectar
¼ cup red wine vinegar
3 to 4 tablespoons honey
1 teaspoon sesame oil

Fruit Salad

3 cups Bibb lettuce leaves, torn
3 cups iceberg lettuce leaves, torn
1 pint fresh strawberries
3 Florida oranges, peeled and
    sectioned
3 Florida pink grapefruit, peeled
    and sectioned
1 banana, sliced
1 tablespoon toasted sesame seeds

At least 3 hours before serving, make Apricot Nectar Dressing: In small saucepan combine cornstarch, garlic powder and ginger; stir in apricot nectar, vinegar, honey and oil. Cook, stirring constantly, over medium heat until mixture thickens and bubbles. Remove from heat; cool. Cover; chill at least 2 hours. Makes 1 cup.

When ready to serve: Place lettuce leaves on large platter; arrange fruits in separate piles on top of lettuce. Sprinkle with sesame seeds; pass dressing separately.
6 servings.

Preparation Time: 15 Minutes   *Cooking Time: 10 Minutes*

Treasure Tip: To toast sesame seeds or almonds, spread in a thin layer on a cookie sheet; bake at 300° F. until golden, 3 to 5 minutes. Check often, stirring to prevent burning.

Fresh Vinaigrette Dressing

½ cup salad oil
⅓ white wine or red wine vinegar
1 tablespoon sugar
2 teaspoons snipped fresh (or ½ teaspoon dried) thyme, oregano or basil
½ teaspoon paprika
¼ teaspoon dry mustard or 1 teaspoon Dijon mustard (optional)
⅛ teaspoon pepper

Combine all ingredients in jar; cover tightly; shake vigorously. Store up to 2 weeks in refrigerator. **Makes ¾ cup.**

Oil-Free Dill Dressing

¼ cup white wine vinegar
3 tablespoons powdered fruit pectin
1⅓ tablespoons snipped fresh dill (or 1 teaspoon dried dill weed)
1 teaspoon sugar
¼ teaspoon garlic powder
¼ teaspoon dry mustard
⅛ teaspoon pepper

Up to 3 days before serving: Combine all ingredients with ⅔ cup water in jar; cover tightly; shake vigorously. Chill up to 3 days. Shake well before serving. **Makes 1¼ cups.**

French Roquefort Dressing

1 cup sugar
1 tablespoon salt
1 tablespoon paprika
¾ cup vinegar
1 cup vegetable oil
2 cloves garlic
¾ cup catsup
Juice of 1½ lemons
½ pound Roquefort or other blue cheese, crumbled

Place all ingredients except cheese in food processor or blender; process 5 to 10 seconds. Stir in cheese. Can be kept in refrigerator several weeks. Dressing makes an excellent dip for vegetables, shrimp or chicken wings. **Makes 1 quart.**

MEATS

Tampa Bay Performing Arts Center

Whether it is the theater, ballet or music that inspires you, a delightful performance awaits at the Tampa Bay Performing Arts Center (TBPAC). Renowned for its superior acoustics and three custom-sized auditoriums, the facility is often the first stop for touring productions leaving New York. Several production companies make TBPAC their home, nourishing a growing colony of local performing artists and providing year-round entertainment for patrons.

The waterfront setting affords a great view of the University of Tampa's rowing teams in action. Several Ivy League teams and Olympic contenders conduct winter practice here because of the fine weather and facilities. Area rivers and channels provide some of the country's longest and best rowing courses.

A short stroll along the river will bring us to the first of many museums to be found in the Bay area, the Tampa Museum of Art. Its extensive, permanent collection and children's art projects attract visitors of all ages. Directly across the river, the H.B. Plant Museum offers a glimpse of turn of the century Victorian elegance. Also in Tampa are the University of South Florida Art Museum and the Museum of Science and Industry (MOSI). MOSI houses permanent participation exhibits where you experience everything from the thrill of the Space Lab to the hair-raising electrical booth.

Whether it is a stroll through a museum or a gala performance this section will set the stage at home with recipes for a variety of entertainment. Here we feature many recipes for beef, lamb, pork, veal and venison. The Grilled Lamb in our menu is superbly elegant while others are for simpler, heartier fare that will please the most discriminating appetite.

**The Performing Arts Center photograph was underwritten by
H.L. and Betty Culbreath**

MEATS

AFTER-THEATRE DINNER

Marinated Asparagus Salad

Roast Lamb with Two Sauces

Coconut Orange Sweet Potatoes

Hyde Park Honey Rolls

**The menu photograph was underwritten by
Mac and Ruthanne McLean**

Marinated Asparagus Salad

24 fresh asparagus spears
½ cup olive oil
½ cup light vegetable oil
¼ cup fresh parsley, coarsely
   chopped
¼ cup fresh lime juice (1 to 2 large
   limes)
1 tablespoon sugar
2 tablespoons spicy brown mustard
⅓ cup yellow bell pepper, chopped
⅓ cup red bell pepper, chopped
½ small mild onion, sliced in rings
Red leaf lettuce

Night before, or 3 to 4 hours before serving: In steamer or large skillet, steam asparagus just until tender; drain. Refresh under cold water to stop cooking and retain color. Place in shallow 1½-quart serving dish. In medium bowl combine oils, parsley, lime juice, sugar and mustard; set aside. Layer bell peppers and onion slices on top of asparagus; pour marinade over vegetables. Cover with plastic wrap; refrigerate 3 to 4 hours or overnight.

When ready to serve: Line salad plates with lettuce, red edges to outside of plates. Place marinated vegetables diagonally in center of each plate.   *4 servings.*

Preparation Time: 20 Minutes   *Cooking Time: 10 Minutes*

Roast Lamb with Two Sauces

Red Wine Black Bean Sauce

1 cup dried black beans
2 tablespoons onion, chopped
2 tablespoons shallots, chopped
½ cup heavy cream
1 bay leaf
Pinch of thyme
Pinch of oregano
3 cups chicken stock
⅓ cup Madeira or port
2 tablespoons butter, softened

Lamb Filet

2 to 3 pounds lamb tenderloin
Salt
2 teaspoons crushed black and
 white peppers, combined
3 tablespoons vegetable oil

Basil Sauce

3 tablespoons butter
1 tablespoon flour
1 cup chicken stock
1 clove garlic, minced
1 bunch fresh basil

Night before, make Red Wine Black Bean sauce: Place black beans in medium pot; cover with water; soak overnight.

Next day: Drain beans; put back in pot; add onions, shallots, cream, bay leaf, thyme, oregano and add enough chicken stock to cover. Cover pot; bring to boil. Reduce heat; simmer until beans are very tender. Purée in blender or food processor, adding a little chicken stock if sauce is too thick. Strain through fine sieve. Pour wines into pot; bring to boil. Add bean purée; simmer 5 minutes; keep hot.

When ready to cook: Preheat oven to 375° F. Salt lamb on all sides; roll in crushed pepper to coat. Heat large, heavy skillet until very hot. Add oil; brown lamb on all sides. Place lamb in shallow baking pan; place in oven. Bake 8 minutes for rare, 12 to 15 minutes for well done. Remove from oven; cover to keep warm and seal in juices before slicing.

While lamb bakes, make Basil Sauce: In small saucepan over medium heat, melt butter; whisk in flour to combine well. Gradually add chicken stock; whisk until thickened. Remove from heat; add garlic and basil. Purée in blender or food processor. Strain through fine sieve; keep hot.

Just before serving: Whisk 2 tablespoons softened butter into hot black bean sauce; stir until butter melts. Carefully ladle sauce onto serving plate, just to cover bottom of plate. Slice lamb into medallions; arrange in fan shape on sauce. Make thin line of basil sauce around lamb. Using toothpick, swirl sauce decoratively.
 4 to 6 servings.

Preparation Time: 20 Minutes *Cooking Time: 1 Hour*

Treasure Tip: Buy a whole fresh leg of lamb. Have your butcher remove the tenderloin to use in recipes that call for this special cut. Freeze the remainder to cook another way. The tenderest, and most flavorful, legs of lamb are those weighing between 4 and 7 pounds.

Coconut Orange Sweet Potatoes

3 large Florida navel oranges, or 6
　smaller seedless oranges
2 large sweet potatoes
1/4 cup dark brown sugar
3 teaspoons sugar
1/2 stick butter, softened
1 egg
1/4 cup milk
1/4 teaspoon nutmeg
3/4 teaspoon cinnamon
About 1 cup shredded coconut

Preheat oven to 400° F. Bake sweet potatoes 1 hour or until soft. Cut oranges in half horizontally. Scoop out fruit, reserving for other use. Cut piece out of bottom of each half to lay flat; set orange shells aside. When potatoes are done, remove from oven; reduce oven to 325° F. Scoop out potato pulp; place in large bowl of electric mixer. Add brown sugar, sugar, butter, egg, milk, nutmeg and cinnamon; mix. Place sweet potato mixture in pastry tube; pipe into orange shells; top each with 1 1/2 teaspoons coconut. Bake 10 to 15 minutes. If coconut has not browned, increase heat to 350 ° F.; bake 5 more minutes. Serve hot.

6 servings.

Preparation Time: 20 Minutes

**Cooking Time: 1 Hour
15 Minutes**

Hyde Park Honey Rolls

1 package dry yeast
½ cup shortening
½ cup, plus 2 tablespoons, honey
2 teaspoons salt
2 cups milk
2 eggs
7½ to 8 cups flour
Melted butter

About 3 hours before serving: Dissolve yeast in ¼ cup warm water. Place shortening, honey and salt in large bowl of electric mixer. Heat milk almost to scalding; pour over mixture in bowl; cool. Add yeast and 3 cups flour; beat until smooth. Add eggs; beat. Add remaining flour to make stiff dough. Knead until satiny smooth, 10 minutes. Let rise until doubled, 1½ to 2 hours. Punch down; let rise again until doubled. Let stand 5 minutes. Divide into pieces (two for large loaf pans; three for small pans). Roll into loaves; place in greased loaf pans. Let rise until doubled.

When ready to bake: Preheat oven to 400° F. Bake 30 minutes or until golden brown. Remove loaves from oven; brush tops with butter. Remove from pans; cool on rack. Dough can be shaped into rolls, as in our picture. Allow dough and rolls to rise as directed; bake 20 minutes at 375° F. Rolls are done when faint hollow sound results when lightly tapped with finger. Makes 30 to 36 rolls. **2 large or 3 small loaves.**

Preparation Time: 20 Minutes   *Cooking Time: 30 Minutes*
(Plus Rising Time)

Treasure Tip: For twist rolls: Roll small pieces of dough into pencil-like strips about 9 inches long and ½ to ⅔ inches in diameter. Gently twist dough into loose knots; place on buttered cookie sheet. Let rise and bake according to recipe directions.

For crescent rolls: Roll dough out and cut into triangles. Brush with water; roll wide end of triangle to point end. Press tip in to seal roll. Bend rolls into semi-circles; brush with 1 beaten egg mixed with 1 teaspoon water. Let rise and bake according to recipe directions.

For cloverleaf rolls: Pinch off dough and form ¾-inch balls. Place in regular muffin cups, arranging 3 balls in each cup. Let rise and bake as directed.

For plain dinner rolls: Divide each portion of dough into 16 (1-inch) pieces and shape into balls. Arrange in greased pan; let rise and bake as directed in recipe.

Lemon Dijon Beef Pastry

4 frozen puff pastry shells, thawed
½ stick butter
4 beef filet steaks, 1-inch thick
1 clove garlic, minced
Pepper to taste
Juice of 1 lemon
12 fresh mushrooms, minced
1 teaspoon Dijon mustard
Salt and pepper to taste
1 egg white, slightly beaten

Melt butter in large skillet over medium-high heat; sear filets 1½ minutes per side. Remove from skillet; chill. Place garlic, pepper and lemon juice in medium saucepan; add mushrooms. Cover; cook over medium-high heat 15 minutes. Drain mushrooms; add mustard. Salt and pepper filets; spread with mushroom mixture.

Preheat oven to 450° F. Place filets on cookie sheet. Roll pastry shells out as thin as possible; cover top and sides, not bottom, of each filet with pastry. For attractive appearance, cut leaves or flowers from pastry; place on top of filets. Brush tops with egg white; bake 10 minutes. All steps except final baking may be done ahead. Refrigerate filets; bring to room temperature before baking. *4 servings.*

Preparation Time: 30 Minutes   *Cooking Time: 25 Minutes*

Garlic Ginger Tenderloin

1 whole (5 to 6-pound) beef
    tenderloin
1 cup Japanese soy sauce
3 garlic cloves, finely chopped
2 tablespoons fresh ginger, grated
½ cup dry sherry
¼ cup peanut oil

At least 3 hours before cooking: Trim all fat from tenderloin; place tenderloin in large bowl. In food processor or blender mix remaining ingredients until smooth; pour over meat. Turn meat to coat all sides. Cover; refrigerate 3 or more hours, turning meat occasionally.

When ready to cook: Preheat oven to 425° F. Drain meat; reserve marinade. Place meat in shallow baking dish; roast 25 to 30 minutes, basting occasionally with marinade. Test with meat thermometer to desired degree of doneness. Remove to heated platter; pour pan juices over; let stand 10 minutes before slicing. *6 to 8 servings.*

Preparation Time: 10 Minutes   *Cooking Time: 30 Minutes*

Marinated Sirloin Kabobs

Marinade I

³/₄ cup olive or salad oil
¹/₂ cup fresh lemon juice
¹/₄ cup fresh lime juice
1¹/₂ medium onions, cut in quarters
2 cloves garlic
1 tablespoon lemon pepper
seasoning
Salt to taste

Marinade II

2 cups tomato juice
1 stick butter
¹/₄ cup onion, finely chopped
¹/₂ cup catsup
1 teaspoon dry mustard
³/₄ teaspoon salt
3 tablespoons sugar
¹/₂ teaspoon paprika
¹/₂ teaspoon pepper
1 clove garlic, minced
1 tablespoon Worcestershire sauce
Dash Tabasco

Kabobs

2 pounds boneless sirloin steak, cut
into 1 ¹/₂-inch cubes
2 green bell peppers, seeded and
cut into eighths
1 large onion, cut into 16 pieces
4 tomatoes, cut into fourths, or 16
cherry tomatoes
4 to 8 large, fresh mushroom caps

Night before: Choose your marinade. For Marinade I, place ingredients in food processor or blender; purée. For Marinade II, place ingredients in medium saucepan; bring to boil. Simmer, uncovered, 30 minutes. Cool. Place steak cubes in large bowl; pour marinade over. Cover; refrigerate overnight.

When ready to cook: Remove meat from marinade; reserve marinade. Alternate meat with remaining kabob ingredients on four long or eight average skewers. Grill over hot coals, turning and basting frequently with reserved marinade, 5 to 7 minutes for rare, 12 minutes for well done. Serve over rice.   ***4 servings.***

Preparation Time: 15 Minutes   ***Cooking Time: 5 to 12 Minutes***

Treasure Tip: *Marinades are especially good for tenderizing, moistening and adding flavor. The acids in marinades serve to tenderize, the oils to moisten and the herbs to add flavor.*

Filete Steak Salteado ⛵

From the Columbia Restaurant

2 potatoes, peeled and diced
Vegetable oil
1 pound beef tenderloin
½ cup virgin olive oil
2 garlic cloves, chopped
1 Spanish onion, chopped
1 green bell pepper, chopped
2 Spanish chorizos
15 fresh mushrooms, stems
   removed
Salt to taste
Pinch white pepper
½ cup dry red wine

In deep fryer or deep, heavy pot, heat vegetable oil to 350 ° F. Fry potatoes in hot oil until brown, about 10 minutes; drain on paper towels. Cut meat into cubes. In large skillet heat olive oil; brown meat on all sides. Add remaining ingredients except wine; heat thoroughly. Add wine just before serving. Serve over white or yellow rice.   *2 to 4 servings.*

Preparation Time: 15 Minutes   *Cooking Time: 10 Minutes*

Grilled Marinated Flank Steak

2 pounds flank steak

Marinade I

1 medium yellow onion, thinly
   sliced
2 bay leaves, crushed
10 whole black peppercorns
1 cup red wine
1 small bunch Italian parsley,
   leaves only
3 to 4 sprigs fresh thyme
Salt and freshly ground black
   pepper to taste

Marinade II

½ cup wine vinegar
½ cup olive oil
¼ cup bleu cheese salad dressing
1 (5-ounce) bottle soy sauce
1 teaspoon ground ginger
1 teaspoon meat tenderizer
1 teaspoon garlic salt
1 teaspoon oregano

Night before: Choose your marinade. Mix all ingredients well. Place flank steak in baking dish; pierce meat several times with fork. Pour marinade over meat; refrigerate overnight.

When ready to cook: Grill over hot coals, or broil in oven, 7 to 10 minutes per side; slice thinly on diagonal to serve.
                    4 to 6 servings.

Preparation Time: 5 to 10 Minutes   *Cooking Time: 20 Minutes*

Treasure Tip: Italian parsley has larger, flatter leaves and a stronger flavor than regular parsley.

Catalan Pot Roast

¼ teaspoon marjoram
¼ teaspoon pepper
¼ teaspoon ground cloves
1 large clove garlic, crushed
¾ teaspoon salt
1 teaspoon cinnamon
1 tablespoon fresh parsley, minced
¼ cup olive oil, divided
1 (4 to 5 pound) beef rump or
    bottom round roast
1 medium green bell pepper,
    minced
¾ cup onion, chopped
1 cup dry red wine
1 (16-ounce) can crushed tomatoes
½ cup fresh orange juice
1 tablespoon cornstarch

5 to 6 hours before serving: In small bowl blend marjoram, pepper, cloves, garlic, salt, cinnamon and parsley with 2 tablespoons olive oil. Place roast on plate; rub herb mixture into meat on all sides. Let stand 30 minutes at room temperature before cooking.

When ready to cook: Heat remaining olive oil in Dutch oven. Over medium heat, brown meat on all sides. Remove meat; add green bell pepper and onion to pot; sauté until tender. Return meat to pot; add tomatoes, wine and orange juice. Simmer slowly 3 to 4 hours, basting and turning meat occasionally. Remove roast; let stand 20 minutes before slicing. Blend cornstarch with ¼ cup water; stir into liquid in pot; simmer 1 minute. Serve liquid with roast.   *8 to 10 servings.*

Preparation Time: 15 Minutes   *Cooking Time: 3 to 4 Hours*

Boliche

3 to 4 pounds eye of the round
    roast
1 Spanish chorizo, chopped
1 medium slice (about ½ pound)
    cured ham, chopped
1 clove garlic, minced
1 medium Spanish onion, chopped
½ green bell pepper, chopped
2 tablespoons olive oil
⅔ cup red wine
Salt and pepper to taste

Ask butcher to cut lengthwise pocket in center of roast, leaving opposite end closed. In medium bowl mix chorizo, ham, garlic, onion and green pepper. Stuff meat pocket with mixture, packing well, but not too tightly. Secure open end with skewers or wire. Salt and pepper meat. Heat olive oil in electric skillet or Dutch oven; brown meat on all sides. Combine wine and ⅓ cup water; pour over meat. Simmer, basting occasionally, until tender, 4 to 5 hours. Serve with yellow or white rice and pan juices. This traditional Spanish roast makes excellent sandwiches. Serve on Cuban, French or other hard-crusted bread.   *12 to 16 servings.*

Preparation Time: 30 Minutes   *Cooking Time: 4 to 5 Hours*

Stir Fry Beef and Tomatoes

1-3 pound center cut beef
    tenderloin
Freshly ground pepper
¼ cup olive oil
4 bunches scallions, sliced
    diagonally
1 yellow bell pepper, coarsely sliced
8 to 10 plum tomatoes, sliced
1 bottle Lawry's Stir Fry Sauce

About 1 hour before serving: Rub tenderloin with freshly ground pepper and cook for 20 minutes in 450° F. oven. Let stand for 30 minutes before slicing to ¼" thickness. In large skillet, heat olive oil. Add onions and yellow bell pepper and stir until tender. Add sliced beef, stir fry sauce and tomatoes. Heat through until tomatoes are limp.   *6 to 8 servings.*

Preparation time: 1 hour   *Cooking time: 25 minutes*

Pot Roast in Red Wine

1 (3½ to 4 pound) boneless beef
    roast
1 to 2 tablespoons olive or
    vegetable oil
¼ cup red wine vinegar
Salt and pepper to taste
1 cup red wine
2 tablespoons sugar
¼ cup catsup
2 medium onions, sliced
3 carrots, peeled and sliced
4 to 5 medium potatoes, peeled and
    quartered

About 4 hours before serving: In large, oven-safe pot or Dutch oven, brown meat on all sides in hot oil. Pour vinegar over roast; sprinkle with salt and pepper. Cover; simmer 20 minutes over low heat. Preheat oven to 350° F. In small bowl mix wine, sugar and catsup; pour over roast; add onions and carrots. Cover; bake until meat is tender, 2 to 2½ hours, adding potatoes the last 45 minutes. Remove roast from pot; place on platter to rest 10 minutes. Keep carrots and potatoes warm. Slice roast; serve with pan juices.   *6 to 8 servings.*

Preparation Time: 30 Minutes   *Cooking Time: 3 Hours*

Picadillo

1 to 2 tablespoons olive oil
2 medium onions, chopped very
  fine
1 large green bell pepper, chopped
  very fine
6 small tomatoes, chopped, or 1
  cup canned tomatoes
Salt and pepper to taste
1 teaspoon garlic powder
1 pound ground beef
1 pound ground pork
1 tablespoon brown sugar
1/4 cup vinegar
1/4 cup stuffed green olives, chopped
1/2 cup raisins
1 tablespoon drained capers
1/2 cup red wine or tomato juice

Heat olive oil in large skillet over medium heat; brown onions and pepper; drain. Add tomatoes, salt, garlic powder, pepper, beef and pork, stirring to break meat into small bits. Add remaining ingredients; simmer 1 hour. Serve over mashed potatoes, white rice or split buttered and toasted sandwich buns. Tastes best if prepared a day ahead and refrigerated.

8 to 10 servings.

Preparation Time: 15 Minutes   *Cooking Time: 1 Hour*

Treasure Tip: Picadillo is a traditional Latin American dish. The name, from the Spanish word "picar" which means to chop, is appropriate for this delicious blend of chopped meats and vegetables.

Creamy Garlic Meatloaf

3/4 cup fresh bread crumbs
1/2 cup light cream
2 pounds lean beef, ground twice
1 pound boneless pork shoulder,
  ground twice
1 pound boneless veal shoulder,
  ground twice
1 large onion, grated
2 carrots, peeled and finely
  shredded
4 to 6 cloves garlic, finely chopped
2 teaspoons salt
2 teaspoons Dijon mustard
1 teaspoon freshly ground black
  pepper
1 teaspoon crushed rosemary
1/4 teaspoon nutmeg
1/2 teaspoon Tabasco
3 eggs, slightly beaten
12 slices bacon

In small bowl place bread crumbs to soak in cream. In large bowl combine remaining ingredients except eggs and bacon; blend well. Mix in eggs and soaked bread crumbs, combining thoroughly.

Preheat oven to 350° F. Cover the bottom of a shallow baking pan with 8 bacon slices. Form meat mixture into firm loaf; place on top of bacon. Place 4 bacon slices across top. Bake 1½ to 2 hours, depending on thickness of loaf. Baste often with pan juices. Remove from oven; let stand 10 minutes before slicing.

8 to 12 servings.

Preparation Time: 30 Minutes   *Cooking Time: 1 Hour 30
                                        Minutes to 2 Hours*

Treasure Tip: Meatloaf should not be baked in a loaf pan, because it becomes too moist and often falls apart. For best results, bake in an oversized pan.

Garden Variety Meatloaf

1½ tablespoons unsalted butter

4½ tablespoons white onion, minced

4½ tablespoons whole green onions, minced

¼ cup celery, minced

¼ cup peeled carrot, minced

2 tablespoons green bell pepper, minced

2 tablespoons red bell pepper, minced

1 teaspoon garlic, minced

½ teaspoon salt

⅛ teaspoon cayenne pepper

½ teaspoon freshly ground black pepper

¼ teaspoon white pepper

¼ teaspoon ground cumin

¼ teaspoon ground nutmeg

¼ cup half-and-half

¼ cup catsup

¾ pound lean ground beef

¼ pound lean ground pork

2 eggs, beaten

4½ tablespoons dry toasted bread crumbs

Preheat oven to 350° F. In large skillet melt butter; sauté onions, celery, carrot, bell peppers and garlic until softened. Cool to room temperature. In small bowl combine salt, cayenne, black and white peppers, cumin and nutmeg; stir into cooled vegetables. Add remaining ingredients. Lightly form into loaf shape; place in ovenproof skillet or shallow baking pan. Bake 1 hour 15 minutes; cool 5 minutes before slicing.   *3 to 4 servings.*

Preparation Time: 20 Minutes   *Cooking Time: 1 Hour 15 Minutes*

Basil Sour Cream Meatballs

3 slices bread, crumbled
¼ cup milk
1 egg, beaten
5 tablespoons butter or margarine,
    divided
½ cup onion, chopped
1 pound ground beef
1 pound ground pork
1 teaspoon salt
½ teaspoon pepper
½ teaspoon nutmeg
1 clove garlic, crushed
¼ cup flour
2 cups beef broth
1 teaspoon tomato paste
1 teaspoon dried whole basil
8 ounces sour cream

Preheat oven to 350° F. Place bread in small bowl; combine with milk and egg to soak up moisture. In small saucepan melt 2 tablespoons butter; sauté onion until tender. Combine bread mixture with onion, beef, pork, salt, pepper and nutmeg, mixing well; shape into 1½-inch meatballs. Place on lightly greased broiler pan rack; bake until done, about 25 minutes. In large saucepan melt 3 tablespoons butter; sauté garlic; add flour, stirring well. Cook 1 minute. Gradually add broth, stirring until smooth; stir in tomato paste and basil. Remove from heat; add sour cream and meatballs. Cook over medium heat, stirring constantly, just until heated. Serve over buttered pasta or in chafing dish as appetizer. **_8 servings._**

Preparation Time: 1 Hour   **_Cooking Time: 25 Minutes_**

Treasure Tip: _Baking is a reduced fat alternative to the traditional way of cooking meatballs by pan-frying. When baked, the meatballs tend to retain their shapes better. If you are serving meatballs as an appetizer, make them smaller than dinner-sized meatballs._

Lamb Chops with Fresh Vegetables

6 (¾-inch thick) lamb shoulder
    blade chops
¼ teaspoon pepper
1 teaspoon salt, divided
3 tablespoons flour
¼ cup vegetable oil
3 medium carrots, peeled and
    sliced
1 large onion, diced
1 large celery stalk, sliced
1 garlic clove, minced
½ cup dry red wine
2 tomatoes, peeled, seeded and
    diced
1 beef-flavored bouillon cube
1 bay leaf
½ teaspoon thyme leaves
¼ teaspoon ground allspice

Sprinkle chops with pepper and ½ teaspoon salt; coat well with flour. Heat oil in large skillet over medium-high heat. Cook chops, three at a time, until browned on both sides. Remove to platter as they brown; leave drippings in skillet. Add carrots, onion, celery and garlic to skillet; cook 5 minutes, stirring occasionally. Add wine, tomatoes, bouillon cube, bay leaf, thyme, allspice and ½ teaspoon salt. Add chops; heat to boiling. Reduce heat to low; cover; simmer 50 minutes or until chops are tender, turning once. Transfer chops to heated platter. Discard bay leaf and any bones; spoon remaining mixture from skillet into food processor or blender; skim fat from top. Cover; blend until mixture is very smooth. Pour sauce into skillet; heat to boiling over medium heat. Spoon sauce over chops; serve.
4 to 6 servings.

Preparation Time: 40 Minutes   **_Cooking Time: 1 Hour_**

Treasure Tip: _Use leftover roast lamb for a Shepherd's Pie. To serve, grind lamb with onion and a little green pepper, season to taste, top with mashed potatoes and bake at 350° F. until heated through, about 30 minutes. If you have some leftover gravy, mix it with the ground lamb._

Rosemary Chutney Leg of Lamb

1 (6 to 8 pound) leg of lamb
Juice of 1 lemon
Seasoned salt
Powdered rosemary
2 garlic cloves, minced, divided
1 stick butter
1½ cups chutney, puréed
¼ cup soy sauce
½ teaspoon rosemary

Night before: Season meat with lemon, seasoned salt, rosemary and 1 clove garlic; refrigerate overnight.

2½ hours before serving: Preheat oven to 325° F. In medium saucepan combine butter, chutney, soy sauce, rosemary and half of garlic; bring to boil; simmer 3 minutes. Place lamb in baking dish; brush with sauce. Roast 1 hour 50 minutes. Increase temperature to 400° F. Brush lamb with sauce; roast 10 minutes more for medium, longer for well-done, meat. Remove from oven; let lamb stand 10 minutes before carving. Heat remaining sauce; serve with lamb.   *6 to 8 servings.*

Preparation Time: 15 Minutes   *Cooking Time: 2 Hours*

Royal Rack of Lamb

¼ cup olive oil
3 tablespoons Dijon mustard
1 clove garlic, crushed
½ teaspoon salt
1½ teaspoons dried whole thyme, divided
1½ teaspoons dried rosemary, divided
2 (8-rib) lamb rib roasts, about 2¼ pounds each
1 cup soft bread crumbs
½ stick butter or margarine, melted
29 ounces beef broth (undiluted if canned)
¼ cup, plus 2 tablespoons onion, minced
¼ cup, plus 2 tablespoons carrot, minced
2 tablespoons celery, minced
4 sprigs parsley
2 large bay leaves
2 tablespoons tomato paste
1 cup dry vermouth
2 tablespoons arrowroot

Preheat oven to 375° F. In small bowl combine olive oil, mustard, garlic, salt, ½ teaspoon thyme and ½ teaspoon rosemary; mix with wire whisk. Trim fat from lamb, leaving a ¼-inch layer; spread lamb with mustard mixture. Combine bread crumbs and butter; pat over mustard mixture. Place roasts, fat side up, on rack in roasting pan; insert meat thermometer in thickest part, away from fat or bone. Roast, uncovered, 45 minutes or until thermometer registers desired degree of doneness, 140° for rare, 160° for medium.

While lamb roasts, prepare sauce: In large saucepan combine broth, onion, carrot, celery, parsley, bay leaves, 1 teaspoon rosemary and 1 teaspoon thyme; bring to boil over medium heat. Reduce heat to low; simmer, uncovered, 20 minutes. Strain broth; discard vegetables. Return broth to saucepan; add tomato paste and vermouth. Combine arrowroot and 2 tablespoons water, stirring until smooth; add to broth, stirring well. Cook over medium heat, stirring constantly, until thickened and bubbly. Serve sauce with lamb.   *6 to 8 servings.*

Preparation Time: 40 Minutes   *Cooking Time: 1 Hour*

Treasure Tip: When buying rack of lamb, ask the butcher to cut almost through the chine bone for easy carving at the table.

Festive Stuffed Lamb

1 (6-pound) leg of lamb, boned and
  butterflied
3 cloves garlic, minced
3/4 teaspoon salt
1/2 teaspoon pepper
1 teaspoon dried rosemary leaves
3 tablespoons butter or margarine
1/2 cup onion, chopped
1/2 cup celery, chopped
3 tablespoons green bell pepper,
  chopped
1/2 cup canned mushrooms, chopped
1/4 cup walnuts, chopped
1 1/2 tablespoons parsley, chopped
1/8 teaspoon each salt and pepper
1/4 cup ripe olives, chopped
2 cups fresh white bread cubes
1/2 teaspoon poultry seasoning

Lay lamb out flat; season with garlic, salt, pepper and rosemary. In hot butter in large skillet, sauté onion, celery, green pepper and mushrooms until tender, 5 minutes. Remove from heat; add remaining ingredients; mix well. Place mixture on top of lamb; roll up. Tie with string to keep stuffing from falling out. Preheat oven to 325° F. Place roast on rack in shallow roasting pan; roast 2 hours for rare, 3 hours for well-done.   *8 to 10 servings.*

Preparation Time: 35 Minutes   **Cooking Time: 2 to 3 Hours**

Treasure Tip: Mint sauce, traditionally served with roast lamb, can be made quickly by combining 1/2 cup mint jelly and 2 teaspoons fresh lemon juice in a small saucepan. Heat slowly, stirring occasionally, until jelly melts. For a spicier version, increase lemon juice to 1 tablespoon and add 2 tablespoons butter or margarine, 2 tablespoons wine vinegar and 1/2 teaspoon dry mustard; bring to boil over medium heat.

Bobotjie (Colonial Dutch Meatloaf)

From the province of Zeeland, The Netherlands

1 slice coarse bread
1 cup milk
1 teaspoon vegetable oil
1 large onion, coarsely chopped
3 cloves garlic, minced
2 tablespoons curry powder
1 teaspoon ground ginger
1 tablespoon turmeric
1 teaspoon salt
1 tablespoon freshly ground black
   pepper
1 tablespoon brown sugar
1½ pounds very lean ground lamb
1 tablespoon spicy prepared
   mustard
1 tablespoon lemon juice
½ cup raisins
1 tablespoon Worcestershire sauce
¼ cup chutney
½ cup almonds, chopped
1 large tomato, chopped
1 Granny Smith apple, chopped
1 egg

Preheat oven to 325° F. In small bowl soak bread in milk; set aside. Heat oil in small skillet; add onion and garlic; sauté. Add curry powder, ginger, turmeric, salt, pepper and brown sugar; mix; cook 5 minutes over low heat. Squeeze bread dry; reserve milk. In large bowl place bread, lamb, mustard, lemon juice, raisins, Worcestershire, chutney, almonds, tomato and apple; mix well. Turn into 8 x 12-inch casserole dish. Beat egg; combine with reserved milk; pour over lamb mixture. Bake 40 minutes or until golden. Serve, if desired, with Spiced Red Cabbage. ***8 to 10 servings.***

Preparation Time: 30 Minutes   ***Cooking Time: 40 Minutes***

Treasure Tip: *To make Spiced Red Cabbage, thinly shred 1 small red cabbage. Place 1 tablespoon butter and 1 cup water in saucepan; add cabbage, 3 whole cloves and 2 cooking apples, peeled, cored and sliced. Cover; simmer 45 minutes. Add 2 more tablespoons butter, 1 tablespoon sugar, 1 tablespoon white or cider vinegar and a pinch of salt; simmer 5 more minutes. Serve as a condiment with Bobotjie, or make a larger batch and serve as a side dish.*

Grilled Lemon Rosemary Lamb

1 (5-pound) leg of lamb, boned and
   butterflied
2 teaspoons lemon pepper
   seasoning
¼ cup, plus 2 tablespoons,
   Worcestershire sauce
Salt and freshly ground black
   pepper to taste
¼ cup, plus 2 tablespoons, lemon
   juice (about 4 lemons)
2 tablespoons olive oil
1 tablespoon fresh rosemary,
   crumbled
2 cloves garlic, minced
1 stick butter

Night before, or at least 8 hours before cooking: Remove skin and excess fat from lamb; spread out flat. Combine all remaining ingredients except butter; pour over meat; marinate at least 8 hours.

When ready to cook: Drain meat; reserve marinade. Melt butter; add to marinade. Grill meat, basting with marinade, over medium-hot coals at least 15 minutes per side for rare. ***8 to 10 servings.***

Preparation Time: 10 Minutes   ***Cooking Time: 30 Minutes***

Cucumber Mint Loin of Lamb

*½ cucumber, peeled, seeded and
    chopped*
1 small onion, minced
1 tablespoon fresh mint, minced
1 tablespoon butter
*1 (3½-pound) boneless lamb loin,
    trimmed of all fat*
1 cup fresh white bread crumbs
Salt and pepper to taste
1 egg, beaten

In small skillet sauté cucumber, onion and mint in butter until onion is transparent. Place in bowl; add bread crumbs, salt, pepper and egg. Stir well. Preheat oven to 375° F. Place stuffing down center of lamb; roll; tie with string every ½ inch. Roast until pink, moist and tender, about 1¼ hours.   ***6 to 8 servings.***

Preparation Time: 25 Minutes

***Cooking Time: 1 Hour
15 Minutes***

Grilled Lamb with Creamy Cumin Marinade

2 tablespoons ground cumin
¼ cup fresh lemon juice
¼ cup vegetable oil
16 ounces plain yogurt
*1 (6 to 7 pound) leg of lamb,
    trimmed, boned and butterflied*
Fresh mint sprigs (garnish)

Night before: In large, shallow dish whisk together cumin, lemon juice, oil and yogurt. Arrange lamb, fat side down, on cutting board. With sharp knife, make ½-inch deep slashes every 1½ to 2 inches down length of thicker parts of meat. Transfer lamb to dish containing marinade, turning to coat. Marinate, fat side up and covered, overnight in refrigerator.

When ready to cook: Start grill. Bring lamb to room temperature. Place lamb flat into oiled grill basket; close top of basket. Grill, fat side down, 5 to 6 inches above glowing coals for 15 minutes. Turn; grill 10 to 12 minutes more, until meat thermometer inserted into thickest part registers 140° F. for medium rare. (Or cook in preheated broiler 4 inches from heat, 10 to 12 minutes on each side.) Transfer to carving board; let stand 10 minutes. Slice across grain to serve.   ***8 servings.***

Preparation Time: 10 Minutes

Cooking Time: 25 Minutes

South-of-the-Border Pork Chops

2 cups salsa, divided
4 boneless pork chops
2 large onions, cut into rings and
    separated
2 tablespoons butter
½ cup sliced, pitted ripe olives
    (optional)
½ cup sour cream

Night before, or early in day: Spread salsa on both sides of pork chops. Marinate in refrigerator, turning once, 6 to 8 hours or overnight.

When ready to cook: Scrape salsa from chops. Grill chops over hot coals 20 to 25 minutes, turning once. Meanwhile, pan-fry onion rings in butter. Add remaining 1 cup of salsa and olives; heat to boiling. Turn down heat; mix in sour cream; serve on chops. Serve with cornbread and salad of chopped lettuce, tomatoes and shredded cheese.   ***3 to 4 servings.***

Preparation Time: 10 Minutes   Cooking Time: 20 to 25 Minutes

Davis Islands Pork Tenderloin

3 pounds pork tenderloin
½ cup soy sauce
½ cup whole green onions, cut in
    ½-inch pieces
½ cup fresh parsley, minced
1 teaspoon salt
1 teaspoon white pepper
1 teaspoon garlic powder
½ teaspoon cinnamon
½ teaspoon allspice
⅛ teaspoon cayenne pepper
Meat stock or red wine

Night before: Place pork in shallow container; coat with soy sauce. In food processor chop onions and parsley together; add salt, white pepper, garlic powder, cinnamon, allspice and cayenne; whirl to combine well. Cover meat on all sides with onion-spice mixture. Cover; refrigerate overnight.

When ready to cook: Bring pork to room temperature, no longer than 30 minutes. Preheat oven to 325° F. Place meat on wire rack in roasting pan; insert meat thermometer into thickest part. Bake until meat thermometer registers 145° F. Increase heat to 350° F.; cook until thermometer registers 165° F., 10 to 15 minutes more. Remove meat from pan; slice; keep warm. Deglaze pan with a little stock or wine; strain if necessary. Serve over pork slices.   ***6 servings.***

Preparation Time: 15 Minutes   Cooking Time: 25 to 30 Minutes

Treasure Tip: The more marbling pork has, the more tender the meat. Always use a meat thermometer when roasting pork. For juicy, tender pork, cook to 160 to 165° F. Pork will be over-done if the temperature reaches 170° F.

Apple Cider Pork Loin

2 teaspoons salt
1 teaspoon freshly ground pepper
1 teaspoon dried sage, crumbled
1 teaspoon dried thyme, crumbled
1 (3-pound) rib-end boneless pork
    loin, rolled and tied
2 tablespoons vegetable oil
2 cups onion, chopped
4 large cloves garlic, minced
½ cup apple cider
1 large Granny Smith apple
1 large Red Delicious apple
2 tablespoons unsalted butter
Salt and pepper to taste

Night before, or at least 3½ hours before serving: In small bowl combine salt, pepper, sage and thyme. Place pork on large sheet of waxed paper; rub spice mixture over pork, coating well. Wrap pork in waxed paper; chill at least 2 hours or overnight.

When ready to cook: Preheat oven to 325° F. In heavy, flameproof casserole, heat oil over moderately high heat until hot but not smoking; brown pork on all sides. Transfer pork to plate; pour off all fat except 2 tablespoons. In fat remaining in casserole cook onion and garlic over moderate heat, stirring, 1 minute. Return pork to casserole; add cider; bring liquid to boil. Cover casserole; bake until meat thermometer registers 155° F., about 50 minutes to 1 hour for juicy, barely pink meat.

About 15 minutes before serving: Core apples; cut each into 12 wedges. In large skillet, over moderately low heat, melt butter with ¼ cup water. Add one layer of apples, if necessary, cook in batches; cover; cook until apples are barely tender, 2 to 4 minutes. Season apples with salt and pepper. Increase heat to moderate; cook and turn apples, uncovered, until tender and lightly golden. When pork is done, transfer it to heated platter; discard string; let stand 10 minutes. In food processor or blender, purée pan juices; season with salt and pepper. Arrange sautéed apples around pork. Serve. **6 servings.**

Preparation Time: 20 Minutes   *Cooking Time: 50 to 60 minutes*

Curried Pork-and-Onion Kabobs

¼ cup soy sauce
2 tablespoons chili sauce
2 tablespoons honey
1 tablespoon vegetable oil
1 tablespoon green onion, minced
1 teaspoon curry powder
2 pounds boneless pork shoulder
    blade roast, fat trimmed, cut
    into 1-inch cubes
3 medium onions, quartered

At least 8 hours before serving: In medium bowl combine all ingredients except pork and onions; add pork; stir to coat. Cover; refrigerate at least 8 hours, stirring occasionally.

When ready to cook: Start grill. Thread pork cubes alternately with onion chunks on metal skewers; reserve marinade. Grill over medium coals, turning occasionally and basting frequently with marinade until pork is tender, about 20 minutes.

4 servings.

Preparation Time: 15 Minutes   *Cooking Time: 20 Minutes*

Sensational Spareribs

2 tablespoons butter or margarine
1 onion, diced
2 teaspoons pepper
2 tablespoons sugar
4 teaspoons dry mustard
4 teaspoons paprika
¼ cup Worcestershire sauce
1 teaspoon Tabasco
½ cup catsup
½ cup vinegar
2 teaspoons salt
3 to 4 pounds meaty pork spareribs

In medium saucepan melt butter; cook onion slowly until transparent. Add pepper, sugar, mustard, paprika, Worcestershire, Tabasco, catsup, ½ cup water, vinegar and salt; bring to boil. Reduce heat; simmer 30 minutes. Preheat oven to 325° F. Place ribs in baking pan; cover with sauce. Bake until tender, about 1½ hours. To brown ribs, broil in oven, or place ribs on barbecue grill over hot coals. *4 servings.*

Preparation Time: 10 Minutes   *Cooking Time: 2 Hours*

Treasure Tip: Give your ribs a head start by cooking in the oven or on the stove first. Just 30 minutes on the grill will give your dinner that barbecued flavor.

Grilled Pork Medallions

2 pork tenderloins (about 3 pounds total)
6 bacon slices
1 large lemon
Garlic salt
Lemon pepper seasoning

About 1 hour before cooking: Cut pork into 1½-to-2-inch thick slices; remove fat. Place 2 to 3 slices together; wrap bacon slice around each pork "filet"; secure with toothpicks. Place in pan; squeeze lemon juice over pork; season to taste with garlic salt and lemon pepper. Start grill. Marinate at room temperature 30 minutes. Grill over hot coals 15 to 20 minutes, turning once. *6 servings.*

Preparation Time: 10 Minutes   Cooking Time: 15 to 20 Minutes

Orange Ginger Glazed Ham

1 (7 to 8 pound) smoked, fully cooked ham
1 cup fresh orange juice
1 cup ginger ale
½ cup brown sugar, firmly packed
2 tablespoons vegetable oil
1 tablespoon white vinegar
2 teaspoons dry mustard
½ teaspoon ground ginger
¼ teaspoon ground cloves

Early in day: Trim skin from ham, leaving no more than a ¼-inch layer of fat. Place ham in large plastic bag. Combine remaining ingredients; pour over ham. Tie bag tightly; place in bowl; refrigerate 8 hours.

When ready to cook: Preheat oven to 325° F. Remove ham from marinade; reserve marinade. Place ham on rack in shallow roasting pan; bake 1½ hours, basting with reserved marinade every 20 minutes. *14 servings.*

Preparation Time: 15 Minutes   *Cooking Time: 1 Hour 30 Minutes*

Pork Chops with Cranberry Orange Stuffing

6 cups cubed white bread
6 (1 to 1½-inch thick) loin pork
   chops
¾ stick butter or margarine
1 large onion, chopped
1 cup celery, thinly sliced
¼ cup, plus 2 tablespoons, fresh
   mushrooms, chopped
1 chicken bouillon cube
½ cup cranberry-orange relish
½ teaspoon salt
½ teaspoon leaf thyme, crumbled
½ teaspoon leaf sage, crumbled
¼ teaspoon pepper

Preheat oven to 350° F. Place bread cubes in shallow pan; toast in oven 20 minutes or until golden. Meanwhile, trim all fat from pork chops. Sauté a few fat trimmings in large skillet; discard fat. Place chops in pan drippings; sauté slowly, turning once, until richly browned. Remove from pan; keep warm.

In same pan melt butter; sauté onion, celery and mushrooms until soft. Add bouillon cube, 1 cup water, relish, salt, thyme, sage and pepper; stir; heat to boiling. Place toasted bread cubes in large bowl; pour butter-bouillon mixture over cubes; toss until bread is evenly moist. Spoon stuffing into lightly greased 13 x 9 x 2-inch baking pan. Arrange browned chops in single layer on top; cover. Bake 1½ hours, or until chops are tender. Turn chops after 45 minutes.   **6 servings.**

Preparation Time: 30 Minutes

**Cooking Time: 1 Hour
30 Minutes**

Champion Veal Piccata

18 slices veal round (about 2
   pounds total)
Flour
Vegetable oil
2 tablespoons butter or margarine
Juice of 2 lemons
½ cup dry white wine
Fresh parsley, chopped
Salt and pepper to taste
Lemon wedges

Pound veal paper-thin between two sheets of waxed paper; dip each slice in flour. In large skillet sauté veal, a few slices at a time, in small amount of oil adding more as needed. Cook until browned, turning once, about 30 seconds per side. Keep warm after removing from pan. Drain pan; add butter and lemon juice. Add wine; cook to reduce by one-third. Add parsley, salt and pepper. Return veal to pan; heat through. Serve with lemon wedges.   **6 to 8 servings.**

Total Preparation and Cooking Time: 45 Minutes

Braised Veal with Grand Marnier

2 pounds veal cutlets
Flour
Salt and pepper
5 tablespoons vegetable oil, divided
1 cup onion, minced
1/2 cup celery, minced
1/2 cup carrots, minced
3 garlic cloves, minced
1 cup dry white wine
1/4 cup, plus 2 tablespoons, Grand
    Marnier, divided
1 1/2 cups beef broth
1 1/2 cups canned crushed tomatoes
1/2 teaspoon dried thyme
1/2 teaspoon basil
1/2 teaspoon rosemary
1 bay leaf
2 (3-inch) slices orange peel
2 tablespoons cornstarch

Garnish
1 tablespoon orange peel, grated
1 tablespoon lemon peel, grated
1/4 cup fresh parsley, minced
1 teaspoon garlic, finely minced

Dredge veal in flour seasoned with salt and pepper. In large casserole, over moderate heat, cook veal in 3 tablespoons oil until browned on both sides. Transfer veal to plate. Pour off fat from casserole; add remaining oil. Cook onion, celery, carrot and garlic over moderate heat, stirring, until onion is golden. Add wine and 1/4 cup Grand Marnier; boil 2 minutes.

Preheat oven to 350° F. Add broth, tomatoes, thyme, basil, rosemary, bay leaf and orange peel to casserole; bring to simmer. Add veal. Bake, covered, until veal is tender, 30 to 40 minutes. Transfer veal to heated platter; skim fat from cooking liquid.

In small bowl combine cornstarch with 2 tablespoons Grand Marnier. In another small bowl combine garnish ingredients; set aside. Bring liquid in casserole to boil; stir in cornstarch mixture; simmer 2 to 3 minutes or until sauce thickens slightly. Spoon sauce over veal; sprinkle with garnish.   *4 servings.*

Preparation Time: 45 Minutes   Cooking Time: 30 to 40 Minutes

Treasure Tip: This garnish of citrus peels, parsley and garlic called "gremolada" in Italian, may be used to enhance the flavor of many veal dishes.

Elegant Stuffed Veal Bundles

3 slices bread, crusts removed
Milk
1½ sticks butter, divided
½ cup shallots, coarsely chopped
¼ cup fresh parsley, minced
2 hard-boiled eggs, finely chopped
Salt and pepper to taste
Pinch nutmeg
Pinch thyme
6 thin slices veal
6 thin slices ham
6 carrots, peeled and sliced
1 cup fresh mushrooms, sliced
1 large onion, sliced
2 to 4 tablespoons flour
1½ cups beef stock
¼ cup port or Madeira
1 bay leaf

Make stuffing: Place bread slices in bowl; cover with milk; let stand until bread absorbs milk. In large skillet melt ½ stick butter; sauté shallots; add parsley. In medium bowl combine eggs, bread, salt, pepper, nutmeg, thyme and shallots; mix well.

Assemble veal: Take one veal slice; sprinkle lightly with salt and pepper; place ham slice on top. Cover with one-sixth of stuffing. Roll tightly; secure with string or toothpicks. Repeat process for remaining veal slices. In same pan used for shallots, melt 1 stick butter. Brown veal roll-ups on all sides. Remove from pan; arrange in baking dish. Add carrots, mushrooms and onions to skillet; sauté. Remove vegetables to baking dish with veal.

Preheat oven to 350° F. To remaining butter in skillet, add enough flour to make paste. Gradually add ½ cup water, beef stock and wine, whisking to make smooth gravy. Pour gravy over veal and vegetables; add bay leaf. Cover; bake 1 hour, basting with gravy if necessary. Serve on white or wild rice.

6 servings.

Preparation Time: 1 hour 10 Minutes   *Cooking Time: 1 Hour*

Treasure Tip: For the best veal, look for a pale pink flesh color. If veal is cooked too long, or at too high a temperature, it will become tough.

Veal with Prosciutto and Fontina

16 slices veal cutlets (about 2
    pounds), cut ¼ inch thick
16 thin slices prosciutto
⅓ cup flour
7 to 9 tablespoons butter, divided
8 slices Fontina cheese (about ½
    pound), cut in half
¾ cup dry sherry or Marsala
1¼ cups chicken broth
¼ cup fresh parsley, chopped

At least 1 hour before cooking: Place veal slices in single layer on flat surface; top each with slice of prosciutto. Place meat between two pieces of waxed paper; pound with mallet to flatten slightly and make prosciutto adhere to veal. Refrigerate at least 1 hour.

When ready to cook: Dust both sides of meat combinations lightly with flour, patting to remove excess. In large skillet melt 6 to 8 tablespoons butter over medium heat; increase heat to medium-high. Add meat, veal side down, a few pieces at a time; sauté until brown, 5 to 7 minutes. Turn; sauté until prosciutto side browns, 3 to 4 minutes. Transfer, prosciutto side up, to large baking dish. Top each prosciutto slice with ½ slice cheese. Cover dish with waxed paper; set aside.

Pour off drippings from skillet. Stir in sherry; cook over medium-high heat 30 seconds, scraping up crusty bits in pan. Stir in broth; bring to boil over high heat. Continue to boil until mixture is reduced by half, about 5 minutes. Stir in 1 tablespoon butter and parsley; cook just until butter melts. Remove from heat; cover; keep warm while broiling veal. Preheat broiler. Broil veal until cheese melts and meat is heated, about 2 minutes. Arrange veal on platter; pour sauce over meat.

8 servings.

Preparation Time: 20 Minutes   *Cooking Time: 1 Hour*

Venison with Dijon-Chutney Sauce

Sauce
3 tablespoons grainy mustard
1½ tablespoons Dijon mustard
2 tablespoons chutney

¼ cup flour
¼ teaspoon salt
¼ teaspoon pepper
¼ teaspoon paprika
¼ teaspoon garlic powder
Pinch ground red pepper
1 pound venison tenderloin, cut
    into ½ x ½-inch strips
2 to 3 tablespoons butter or
    margarine

At least 2 hours before serving: In small bowl combine mustards and chutney; stir well. Refrigerate sauce at least 2 hours.

When ready to cook: In large plastic bag combine flour, salt, pepper, paprika, garlic powder and red pepper; add venison strips. Close bag securely; shake vigorously. Melt 2 tablespoons butter in large skillet; cook half of venison strips until golden; turning once. Drain on paper towels. Repeat procedure with remaining venison, adding butter if necessary. Serve with sauce.

4 servings.

Preparation Time: 5 Minutes   *Cooking Time: 40 Minutes*

Venison Stroganoff

3¹/₂ tablespoons flour
¹/₂ teaspoon salt
¹/₂ teaspoon pepper
1¹/₂ pounds venison steak, cut into
   long, thin strips
2 tablespoons vegetable oil
1 medium onion, sliced thin
1 cup tomato juice
1 teaspoon sugar
³/₄ cup sour cream
¹/₂ cup canned sliced mushrooms

Mix salt, pepper and flour in paper bag. Add venison, a few strips at a time; shake bag to coat all with flour mixture. Heat oil in large skillet; lightly brown venison and onion. Add tomato juice, 1½ cups water and sugar; simmer until venison is tender. Ten minutes before serving, add sour cream and mushrooms; heat. Serve over white rice. **6 servings.**

Preparation Time: 15 Minutes   *Cooking Time: 20 Minutes*

Outback Meat Dipping Sauce

From the popular Outback Steakhouse restaurants

4 cups sour cream
1 cup prepared horseradish
1 tablespoon dill weed

Combine all ingredients in mixing bowl; blend with wire whisk until texture is smooth. Store in refrigerator; use as meat sauce or dip for fondued meat.   **5 cups.**

Preparation Time: 5 Minutes

Special Spiced Barbecue Sauce

1 tablespoon vegetable oil
¹/₄ cup onion, chopped
1 (12-ounce) bottle chili sauce
¹/₄ cup fresh lemon juice
2 tablespoons brown sugar
2 tablespoons vinegar
1 tablespoon Worcestershire sauce
1 teaspoon prepared mustard
¹/₂ teaspoon salt
¹/₄ teaspoon each pepper and
   paprika

Heat oil in medium saucepan; sauté onion until soft. Add ½ cup water and remaining ingredients; bring to boil. Reduce heat; simmer 20 minutes. Use to baste meat while grilling, or serve as side sauce with grilled meats.   **Makes about 2 cups.**

Preparation Time: 10 Minutes   *Cooking Time: 20 Minutes*

International Barbecue

11 pounds beef brisket or Boston
    butt pork roast

Sauce

2 sticks margarine
4 to 5 large onions, chopped
16 ounces catsup
1/4 cup vinegar
1 1/2 cups tomato paste
1 tablespoon dry mustard
1 tablespoon paprika
3 1/2 tablespoons chili powder
2 tablespoons sugar
1/4 cup fresh lemon juice
5 ounces bottle Worcestershire
    sauce
1 tablespoon liquid smoke
Tabasco sauce to taste
1 clove garlic, crushed
Dash ginger (optional)
Dash nutmeg (optional)
Dash ground cloves (optional)
Dash thyme (optional)

Cook meat; preheat oven to 225° F. Place meat in large roasting pan; sprinkle with salt and pepper. Cover pan; roast about 30 minutes per pound, uncovering pan during the last 45 minutes. Cool before shredding or slicing.

Make sauce: In large skillet or deep medium saucepan, melt margarine; sauté onions until very soft. Add 1 cup water and all remaining ingredients except meat. Mix well; bring to boil. Reduce heat; simmer, stirring occasionally, until sauce is thickened.

Shred meat or slice it very thin; add to sauce; continue simmering until meat is hot. Serve alone or on sandwich buns. Sauce can be made ahead and frozen, with or without meat.

25 servings.

Preparation Time: 15 Minutes   *Cooking Time: 2 Hours*

BREADS & SANDWICHES

Festival in Ybor City

The past lives on in Tampa's next treasure, Ybor City. Wonderful arts and crafts festivals are held in Ybor Square, an 1886 brick cigar factory built by Vincente M. Ybor. The factory, which once produced cigars, has been restored to house restaurants, specialty and antique shops. In its heyday, from the late 19th century until World War II, Ybor City was home to many factories that made handrolled Cuban cigars. It was the neighborhood of choice for immigrant Cubans, Spaniards and Italians who built fine club buildings, restaurants and commercial establishments. In 1991 the oldest part of Ybor City was named a National Landmark Historic District.

Festive crowds come to Ybor City every October for Guavaween, a colorful Ybor-style Halloween celebration and parade named for the guava trees that once graced the city's backyards. During Gasparilla, crowds fill the streets for Fiesta Day, the Night Parade and the avant garde Artists and Writers Ball. Throughout the year vibrant music sounds within the solid brick walls of the old clubs and theaters, as jazz and reggae echoes in the courtyards.

For many years, tourists and residents have visited Ybor City for the best in Cuban-Spanish food, including Trout Russian Style, Flan de Leche and other treasured recipes found in this book. The following bread section has recipes for Italian biscotti and other sweet rolls that taste marvelous with Ybor's favorite beverage, Cafe con Leche. Cafe con leche is strong Cuban coffee laced with cream. This menu begins with Ybor's trademark recipe, the Cuban sandwich created from yard-long loaves that are baked wrapped in palm leaves. Filled with ham, pork, salami and cheese these sandwiches are annually the subject of contests and can be found on the menu of many Tampa cafes and delicatessens.

The Ybor City photograph was underwritten by
J. Andrew Bever

BREADS & SANDWICHES

AN ETHNIC BUFFET

Cuban Sandwich

Fried Plantains

Louis Pappas' Famous Greek Salad

Coconut-Pineapple Muffins

Walnut Roll Bread

Orange Cranberry Nut Bread

Glazed Lemon Bread

Spanish Sangria

Biscotti

**The menu photograph was underwritten by
Harris and Kay Mullen**

Cuban Sandwich

Classic recipe for Tampa's favorite sandwich from the Silver Ring Café

1½ loaves Cuban bread
Plain prepared mustard
Mayonnaise
¼ pound baked ham, thinly sliced
½ pound barbecued or roast pork
¼ pound Swiss cheese, thinly
    sliced
¼ pound Italian salami, thinly
    sliced
Dill pickles, sliced lengthwise

Cut Cuban bread into six pieces, 8 inches long. Split bread lengthwise. Spread mustard on six slices of bread, mayonnaise on the other six. Divide ham, pork, Swiss cheese, salami and pickle slices among the sandwiches, arranging in layers on the bread. Secure with toothpick. Note: Flavor is improved by warming in a 350° F. oven 10 minutes before serving.   **Makes 6.**

Preparation Time: 10 Minutes   ***Cooking Time: 10 Minutes***

Fried Plantains

4 large green plantains
Vegetable oil
Salt to taste

Peel plantains; slice very thin. In large skillet, over medium-high heat, heat enough oil to cover plantains. Add plantains; fry, stirring occasionally, until crisp and golden, 5 to 7 minutes. Drain thoroughly on paper towels; salt to taste. Serve warm.
6 servings.

Preparation Time: 10 Minutes   ***Cooking Time: 5 to 7 Minutes***

Louis Pappas' Famous Greek Salad

Potato Salad

6 boiling potatoes
4 whole green onions, finely
 chopped
¹/₄ cup fresh parsley, finely chopped
¹/₂ cup whole green onions, thinly
 sliced
¹/₂ cup mayonnaise
1 to 2 tablespoons red wine vinegar
Salt to taste

Greek Salad

1 medium head iceberg lettuce
3 cups potato salad
12 roka (Greek vegetable) leaves or
 12 sprigs watercress
2 ripe tomatoes, cut into 6 wedges
 each
1 cucumber, peeled and cut
 lengthwise into 8 fingers
1 avocado, peeled and cut in
 wedges
Juice from ¹/₂ lemon
4 (3-inch-square) portions feta
 cheese
1 green bell pepper, cut into 8
 rings each
4 canned beet slices
4 large shrimp, cooked and peeled
4 anchovy filets
12 Greek olives
12 Greek Salonika peppers (from a
 jar)
4 to 8 radishes, cut into flowers
4 to 8 whole green onions
¹/₂ cup distilled white vinegar
¹/₂ cup olive oil
Oregano

Make potato salad: Cook unpeeled potatoes in unsalted water until tender, about 20 minutes; cool until you can handle them. Peel potatoes; cut into chunks in large bowl. Sprinkle with vinegar and salt; add chopped green onions; toss. In small bowl combine parsley, sliced green onions, mayonnaise and salt. Add to potatoes; mix well. **Makes 3 cups.**

Line large platter with outside lettuce leaves; mound potato salad in center. Shred remaining lettuce; place on top of potato salad; top with roka or watercress. Place tomatoes around the outer edge, with a few on top. Place cucumber wedges between tomatoes. Sprinkle lemon juice on avocado to prevent browning. Add avocado. Arrange feta on top of salad; place green pepper rings, beets, shrimp and anchovies on top of feta. Place olives, Salonika peppers, radishes and green onions around the edge. Sprinkle with vinegar, then oil. Sprinkle oregano on top; serve at once. Serve with toasted garlic bread. **4 main-dish servings.**

Preparation and Cooking Time: 1 Hour 30 Minutes

Treasure Tip: *This recipe comes from Louis Pappas Restaurant, family-owned and operated on Tarpon Springs' sponge docks since 1925. It's worth the time and trouble to make this festive salad for guests in your home. Serve it with bread as a complete lunch, or as a side salad with meat or seafood at dinner. This salad was featured on the cover of The Gasparilla Cookbook.*

Coconut-Pineapple Muffins

1¼ cups sugar
2¼ cups flour
1 tablespoon cinnamon
2 teaspoons baking soda
½ teaspoon salt
½ cup shredded coconut
½ cup raisins
2 cups carrots, peeled and grated
   (4 large carrots)
1 apple, shredded
8 ounces canned crushed
   pineapple, drained
½ cup pecans or walnuts, chopped
3 eggs
1 cup vegetable oil
1 teaspoon vanilla extract

Preheat oven to 350° F. In large bowl sift together sugar, flour, cinnamon, baking soda and salt. Add coconut, raisins, carrots, apple, pineapple and nuts; stir to combine. In small bowl whisk eggs with oil and vanilla; add to dry ingredients; blend well. Spoon batter into two muffin tins lined with paper baking cups, filling each cup to brim.

Bake 35 minutes, or until toothpick inserted in center comes out clean. Cool in pan 10 minutes; remove from pans; finish cooling on a rack. Serve with cream cheese or butter. For a full flavor, bake 24 hours ahead. Muffins freeze well. **Makes 24.**

Preparation Time: 40 Minutes   **Cooking Time: 35 Minutes**

Treasure Tip: *Mix muffin batter only until the ingredients are combined. Over-mixing results in tough, chewy muffins. When adding fruit or nuts as a topping, press them into the batter firmly, or they will pop out during baking.*

Walnut Roll Bread

2 packages dry yeast
6½ cups flour
3 tablespoons sugar
1 teaspoon salt
2 sticks butter or margarine,
   melted
3 eggs, slightly beaten
1 cup sour cream
5 cups walnuts, ground
1 stick butter or margarine,
   softened
1 cup sugar
3 tablespoons vanilla extract

Grease two large cookie sheets. Pour ½ cup warm water into small bowl; sprinkle in yeast; stir to dissolve. In large bowl mix flour, sugar and salt; stir in melted butter, eggs and sour cream. Add dissolved yeast; mix well. Let dough stand 10 minutes. In large bowl mix walnuts, butter, sugar and vanilla to make a paste.

On well-floured board, divide dough into four equal parts. Roll out each piece into a rectangle, approximately 14 inches by 12 inches. Spread each rectangle with one-fourth filling mixture. Roll up like a jelly roll; seal edges. Cover with cloth; let rise until doubled in size, about 1 hour. Preheat oven to 350° F. Bake 35 to 40 minutes. **4 loaves.**

Preparation Time: 50 Minutes   **Cooking Time: 40 Minutes**
(Plus rising time)

Orange Cranberry Nut Bread

4 cups flour
2 cups sugar
1 teaspoon baking powder
2 teaspoons baking soda
1 teaspoon salt
2 eggs, beaten
½ stick butter, softened
1 cup fresh orange juice
Grated rind of 2 oranges
3 cups fresh cranberries, chopped
1 cup pecans, coarsely chopped

Preheat oven to 350° F. In large bowl of electric mixer combine flour, sugar, baking powder, baking soda and salt. Add eggs, ½ stick butter, ¼ cup hot water, orange juice and rind; mix well. Blend in cranberries and pecans. Pour into greased loaf pans (two large or four small). Bake 1 hour and 10 minutes for large pans, less time for small pans. Remove from pans immediately; rub loaves with 2 tablespoons softened butter. Wrap tightly in wax paper; refrigerate 1 hour. Rewrap in plastic wrap; refrigerate at least 4 hours before using. Store in refrigerator or freezer. **Makes 2 large or 4 small loaves.**

Preparation Time: 15 Minutes   **Cooking Time: 1 Hour**

Treasure Tip: *When baking just one loaf of bread, place it in the center of the oven to ensure that it receives even heat and does not rise more on one side than the other. When baking more than one loaf, make sure loaves are evenly spaced to allow good air circulation and even heat distribution.*

Glazed Lemon Bread

⅓ cup melted butter
1¼ cups sugar, divided
2 eggs
¼ teaspoon almond extract
1½ cups flour, sifted
1 teaspoon baking powder
1 teaspoon salt
½ cup milk
1 tablespoon lemon peel, grated
½ cup nuts, finely chopped
3 tablespoons fresh lemon juice

Day before serving: Preheat oven, 325° F. for glass loaf pan, 350° F. for metal pan. In large bowl of electric mixer, blend butter and 1 cup sugar well. Beat in eggs, one at a time; add almond extract. In medium bowl sift together flour, baking powder and salt; add to first mixture alternately with milk. Blend just to mix; fold in lemon peel and nuts. Turn mixture into greased 8½ x 4½ x 2¾-inch loaf pan. Bake about 1 hour 10 minutes, or until toothpick inserted in center comes out clean.

In small bowl mix lemon juice and ¼ cup sugar; immediately spoon over hot loaf. Cool 10 minutes. Remove from pan; cool on rack. Wait 24 hours before slicing. **Makes 1 loaf.**

Preparation Time: 20 Minutes   **Cooking Time: 1 Hour
10 Minutes**

Spanish Sangria

Juice of 1 large orange
Juice of 2 large lemons
Juice of 2 large limes
½ cup sugar
1 (750 ml) bottle burgundy or dry
   red wine
⅓ cup Cognac

In small saucepan combine orange, lemon and lime juices and sugar. Cook over medium heat until sugar dissolves, stirring constantly; cool. Add wine and Cognac; chill thoroughly.

4 to 6 servings.

Preparation Time: 20 Minutes   *Cooking Time: 5 Minutes*

Biscotti

6 eggs, beaten
1½ cups sugar
1½ cups vegetable oil
1 tablespoon baking powder
1 teaspoon vanilla extract
1 tablespoon almond extract
3½ cups flour
½ cup almonds, chopped, toasted
   (optional)

Preheat oven to 400° F. In large bowl of electric mixer, combine eggs, sugar, oil, baking powder, vanilla and almond extracts. Gradually add flour, mixing until flour disappears. Do not overbeat. Add almonds, if desired. Pour onto greased and floured jelly roll pan; spread mixture evenly in pan. Bake 20 minutes. Slice into 1-inch slices; toast on each side before serving. Serve like a shortcake with sliced, sugared fresh fruit; with sherbet or ice cream; or with Café con Leche. Can be made ahead and frozen.

6 to 8 servings.

Preparation Time: 15 Minutes   *Cooking Time: 20 Minutes*

Treasure Tip: Always store packages of yeast in the refrigerator and use them before the expiration date. When you are baking bread and want a chewy, crisp crust like that on Italian or French bread, place a pan with water on the bottom rack of your oven. Place the bread on the rack directly above and the rising steam will create this effect. For a tender crust, brush loaves with melted butter or margarine before baking or as soon as you take them out of the oven.

Applesauce Muffins

2 sticks butter or margarine, softened
3 to 3½ cups sugar, divided
2 eggs
1 teaspoon vanilla extract
4 cups flour
1 teaspoon ground cloves
1 teaspoon salt (optional)
2 teaspoons ground allspice
3 teaspoons cinnamon
2 teaspoons baking soda
2 cups applesauce
1 cup raisins (optional)
1 cup nuts, chopped (optional)
1 stick butter or margarine, melted

Preheat oven to 375° F. In large bowl of electric mixer, cream softened butter and 2 cups sugar together. Beat in eggs; add vanilla. In large bowl sift together flour, cloves, salt, allspice, cinnamon and baking soda. Add to butter and egg mixture. Add applesauce, raisins and/or nuts. Do not overmix.

Spoon batter into greased or paper-lined muffin tins, filling cups half full. Bake 12 to 15 minutes. Remove from pan; cool on rack. Melt 1 stick butter in saucepan on top of stove or in microwave oven. Brush tops of cooled muffins with butter; roll muffin tops in 1 to 1½ cups sugar to coat tops completely.

Makes 38 to 48 muffins.

Preparation Time: 15 Minutes   *Cooking Time: 15 Minutes*

Treasure Tip: *After baking muffins, remove them from pans immediately to cool. If you leave them in pans, they will begin to steam and become soggy.*

Cream Cheese Orange Muffins

3 ounces cream cheese, softened
¼ cup sugar
1 egg, beaten
½ cup fresh orange juice
1¾ cups buttermilk biscuit mix
¼ cup pecans, chopped (optional)
6 teaspoons orange marmalade

In medium bowl of electric mixer, beat cream cheese and sugar. Add egg and orange juice; beat well. Stir in biscuit mix just until dry ingredients are moistened. Fold in pecans, if desired. Preheat oven to 400° F. Generously grease six jumbo muffin pans.

Spoon ¼ cup batter into each muffin cup. Spoon 1 teaspoon marmalade into center of each muffin; divide remaining batter over marmalade. Bake until golden brown, about 20 minutes. Let stand 5 minutes before removing from pans to cooling rack. You may use regular or mini muffin tins, adjusting amount of batter and marmalade in each cup and adjusting cooking time.

Makes 6 jumbo muffins.

Preparation Time: 10 Minutes   *Cooking Time: 20 Minutes*

Cinnamon-Nut Swirls

2 loaves frozen white bread dough
1½ sticks butter or margarine,
    melted, divided
Cinnamon
Sugar
1 cup pecans or walnuts, chopped
Powdered sugar
About ¼ cup milk

Thaw bread dough, but do not let rise. On well-floured board, roll dough out flat until loaf is rectangular in shape. Spread ½ stick melted butter on each rectangle; sprinkle generously with cinnamon and sugar. Distribute nuts on top. Starting at wide end, roll dough tightly so that filling stays inside. Cut crosswise into ½ to 1-inch thick cinnamon swirls.

Place in greased 9 x 13 baking dish, allowing a little room between each roll. Lay dampened cloth over rolls; set aside in warm place; let rise until tops are almost even with top of pan.

Preheat oven to 350° F. Bake until golden brown, about 15 minutes. While rolls are baking, melt ½ stick butter; add powdered sugar to make a thick mixture. Gradually add milk until thin enough to make a glaze. Pour over warm cinnamon rolls.   ***Makes 24.***

Preparation Time: 20 Minutes   ***Cooking Time: 15 Minutes***
(Plus rising time)

Treasure Tip: *Do not glaze rolls if they are to be frozen. Wrap in plastic wrap. Seal, label and freeze up to 3 months. To reheat, remove plastic wrap, place frozen rolls in foil. Place in a 350° F. oven until warm, 20 to 25 minutes. Drizzle with glaze while warm.*

Whole Wheat Carrot Bread

1 cup raw carrots, peeled, finely
    grated
1 cup brown sugar
1 teaspoon baking soda
1 tablespoon butter or margarine,
    melted
2 eggs
2½ teaspoons baking powder
1 teaspoon salt
1½ cups flour, sifted
1 cup whole wheat flour
1 cup walnuts, chopped

Night before: In large bowl combine carrots, brown sugar, soda and butter. Add 1 cup boiling water; stir just enough to mix. Set aside until cool.

Preheat oven to 350° F. Beat eggs with fork; add to cooled carrot mixture. Sift baking powder, salt and all-purpose flour into mixture. Stir in whole wheat flour; fold in nuts. Place in greased 8½ x 4½ x 2½-inch loaf pan; let stand 5 minutes. Bake 1 hour. Remove from pan; cool on wire rack. A loaf of bread slices better if wrapped in foil or plastic wrap and allowed to stand overnight in a cool place.   ***12 servings.***

Preparation Time: 20 Minutes   ***Cooking Time: 1 Hour***

Pumpkin Coffee Bread

1 stick butter or margarine,
  softened
1/2 cup vegetable oil
2 2/3 cups sugar
4 eggs
1 (16-ounce) can pumpkin
3 1/2 cups flour, sifted
1 teaspoon salt
1 teaspoon cinnamon
1/2 teaspoon nutmeg
2 teaspoons baking soda
1 cup walnuts, chopped (optional)
2/3 cup cold, strong black coffee

Preheat oven to 375° F. In large bowl of electric mixer, cream together butter, oil and sugar. Add eggs one at a time, mixing well after each addition. Blend in pumpkin. Sift together flour, salt, cinnamon, nutmeg and soda; add walnuts. Stir flour mixture into pumpkin mixture alternately with coffee.

Pour batter into two greased 9 x 5 x 3-inch loaf pans and greased muffin tin (or one loaf pan and 18 muffin cups). Bake 50 to 55 minutes for loaves and 15 to 20 minutes for muffins, or until toothpick inserted in center comes out clean. Cool 10 minutes; remove from pans; cool completely on rack.
Makes 2 loaves and 8 muffins, or 1 loaf and 18 muffins.

Preparation Time: 25 Minutes   Cooking Time: 50 to 55 Minutes

Country Yam Tea Bread

3 cups flour, sifted
1 cup brown sugar, packed
2 teaspoons baking powder
1 teaspoon salt
1 teaspoon baking soda
1 teaspoon ground ginger
1 teaspoon cinnamon
1/2 teaspoon nutmeg
2 eggs, beaten
3/4 cup fresh orange juice
2 tablespoons vegetable oil
1 cup cold, cooked yams, mashed
1 cup nuts, chopped

Preheat oven to 300° F. Sift flour, brown sugar, baking powder, salt, soda, ginger, cinnamon and nutmeg into large bowl. Combine eggs, orange juice and oil in small bowl; beat until well mixed. Add egg mixture, yams and nuts to dry ingredients; mix until well blended. Turn into greased 9 x 5 x 3-inch loaf pan. Bake until toothpick inserted in center comes out clean, about 1 hour 10 minutes. Cool in pan 10 minutes. Remove from pan; cool completely. ***10 servings.***

Preparation Time: 20 Minutes   ***Cooking Time: 1 Hour
10 Minutes***

Treasure Tip: *Fruit and nut breads usually are best if baked the day before serving. After baking, cool loaves completely; wrap tightly, and store at room temperature. This will develop the flavors and keep the bread from crumbling when it is sliced.*

Cinnamon Marmalade Ring

½ cup marmalade
2 tablespoons nuts, chopped
1 teaspoon cinnamon
1 cup brown sugar
2 (10-count) packages refrigerated
   biscuits
1 stick butter or margarine, melted

Preheat oven to 350° F. Grease bundt pan; place marmalade in bottom of pan, then nuts. In small bowl mix cinnamon and brown sugar. Dip biscuits, one at a time, into melted butter, then into sugar mixture. Stand biscuits on end to form ring in pan. Sprinkle any remaining butter and sugar over top. Bake until brown, 25 to 30 minutes. **12 servings.**

Preparation Time: 15 Minutes   Cooking Time: 25 to 30 Minutes

Sour Cream Cinnamon Roll-ups

2 large loaves thinly sliced white
   bread
8 ounces cream cheese, softened
2 cups sour cream
1 teaspoon vanilla extract
4 sticks butter or margarine,
   melted
¼ cup cinnamon
1 cup sugar

Several days before: Trim crusts from bread; roll each slice flat with rolling pin. In medium bowl mix cream cheese, sour cream and vanilla. Spread about 1 tablespoon mixture on each bread slice. Roll up like small jelly rolls; chill 20 to 30 minutes. In small bowl mix cinnamon and sugar. Slice each bread roll in half; dip into melted butter, then roll in cinnamon-sugar mixture. Place on foil-lined cookie sheets; cover tightly with foil; freeze.

When ready to serve: Preheat oven to 350 ° F. Bake frozen rolls covered, 15 minutes; remove cover; watch carefully until lightly browned, 15 to 25 more minutes. **Makes 80.**

Preparation Time: 45 Minutes   Cooking Time: 30 to 40 Minutes

Orange-Bran Nut Bread

1 cup dried figs, finely chopped
2 tablespoons butter or margarine
¾ cup all-purpose flour, sifted
¾ cup whole wheat flour
½ cup sugar
1 teaspoon salt
3 teaspoons baking powder
1 teaspoon vanilla extract
1 egg, beaten
4 teaspoons orange peel, grated
⅓ cup fresh orange juice
¾ cup whole-bran cereal
½ cup walnuts, chopped

Preheat oven to 350° F. In large bowl of electric mixer, pour ¾ cup boiling water over figs and butter; let stand 10 minutes. Sift together flours, sugar, salt and baking powder. Add vanilla, egg, orange peel and juice to figs; beat well. Add dry ingredients and cereal; beat well; fold in chopped nuts.

Pour batter into greased 8½ x 4½ x 2½-inch loaf pan; spread batter into corners. Bake until toothpick inserted in center comes out clean, about 45 to 50 minutes. Leave in pan 10 minutes; loosen sides with knife; turn onto wire rack to cool. Wrap in foil or plastic wrap; store in cool place or freeze. Let stand overnight before slicing, or bread will crumble

12 servings.

Preparation Time: 20 Minutes   Cooking Time: 45 to 50 Minutes

Cinnamon Orange Oat Bread

1½ cups fresh orange juice
1 cup regular oats
1 stick butter or margarine, softened
1 cup sugar
½ cup brown sugar, packed
2 eggs
1 teaspoon vanilla extract
1¾ cup flour, sifted
1 teaspoon baking powder
1 teaspoon baking soda
½ teaspoon salt
½ teaspoon cinnamon
½ cup walnuts, chopped
1 tablespoon orange peel, grated

Topping (optional)
½ cup brown sugar, packed
½ stick butter or margarine
Grated rind of 1 orange
1 tablespoon fresh orange juice
1 cup flaked coconut
½ cup walnuts, chopped

To make bread: Preheat oven to 350° F. Heat orange juice to boiling; pour over oats in medium bowl; set aside. In large bowl of electric mixer, cream butter, sugar and brown sugar until light and fluffy. Beat in eggs, one at a time; add vanilla. Sift together flour, baking powder, soda, salt and cinnamon; blend into creamed mixture. Add orange juice and oats; mix until moistened. Add walnuts and orange peel. Pour into two greased 9 x 5 x 3-inch loaf pans. Bake 45 to 50 minutes.

Make topping: In medium saucepan combine brown sugar, butter, orange rind and juice; bring to boil. Cook, stirring constantly, 1 minute. Add coconut and walnuts; spread on top of warm bread loaves. If topping seems too thick, add a little more butter.   **Makes 2 loaves.**

Preparation Time: 30 Minutes   Cooking Time: 45 to 50 Minutes

Treasure Tip: Be careful not to over-mix quick breads. If over-mixed, they will be coarse textured or tough and will not rise to their full volume while baking.

Traditional Southern Cornbread

½ stick butter
2 tablespoons shortening
2 cups water-ground cornmeal
2 tablespoons self-rising flour
2 teaspoons baking powder
1 heaping teaspoon salt
4 eggs, beaten
1 cup buttermilk

Preheat oven to 450° F. Put butter and shortening in 12-inch cast-iron skillet; place in oven. In large bowl thoroughly mix remaining ingredients. Pour batter over melted butter in heated pan; bake about 15 minutes. **8 to 12 servings.**

Preparation Time: 10 Minutes   *Cooking Time: 15 Minutes*

Golden Parmesan Popovers

¼ cup Parmesan cheese, freshly grated
1 cup milk
1 cup flour
1 tablespoon butter or margarine, melted
¼ teaspoon salt
2 large eggs

Place rack on next-to-lowest oven shelf. Preheat oven to 450 ° F. Thoroughly grease eight deep muffin or custard cups; sprinkle with cheese. In medium bowl combine milk, flour, butter and salt. Beat in eggs; mix just until blended. Fill cups one-fourth full; bake 15 minutes. Reduce heat to 350° F., but do not open oven door. Bake 20 minutes more; serve at once. **Makes 8.**

Preparation Time: 15 Minutes   *Cooking Time: 35 Minutes*

Buttery Biscuit Drops

2 sticks butter or margarine, softened
2 cups self-rising flour
8 ounces sour cream

Preheat oven to 350° F. In large bowl mix sour cream and flour; add butter. Drop mixture by teaspoon into lightly greased mini-muffin tins. Bake until lightly browned, about 20 minutes. To freeze, bake only 15 minutes; freeze. Reheat at 350° F, 5 to 10 minutes. **Makes 36.**

Preparation Time: 10 Minutes   *Cooking Time: 20 Minutes*

York Family Dinner Rolls

1 package dry yeast
¼ cup sugar
¾ cup milk, scalded and cooled
1 teaspoon salt
1 egg
¼ cup shortening
3½ cups flour

In large bowl of electric mixer, stir yeast into ¼ cup warm water. Add sugar, milk, salt, egg, shortening and 2 cups flour. Beat until smooth. Beat in enough additional flour about 1½ cups to make dough handle easily. Knead until smooth, about 5 minutes. Place in large, greased bowl, turning to grease top of dough. Cover with cloth; let rise until doubled. Punch down; shape into favorite roll shapes. Let rise. Preheat oven to 400° F. Bake 12 to 15 minutes.

Makes 12.

Preparation Time: 20 Minutes (Plus rising time)   ***Cooking Time: 15 minutes***

Treasure Tip: *Sugar provides food for yeast to grow, adds flavor and aids in browning. Salt adds flavor and helps control growth of yeast.*

Savory Beer Bread

3 cups self-rising flour
3 tablespoons sugar
1 (12-ounce) can beer, room
    temperature
Melted butter

Preheat oven to 350° F. In large bowl combine flour, sugar and beer until well mixed. Pour dough into greased and floured 9 x 5 x 3 loaf pan; allow to rise 10 minutes. Bake until knife inserted in center comes out clean, about 45 minutes. Five minutes before bread is done, brush top with melted butter.

Makes 1 loaf.

Preparation Time: 10 Minutes   ***Cooking Time: 45 Minutes***

Wheat Biscuit Bread

2 regular size shredded wheat
  biscuits, crushed
1 teaspoon salt
1/3 cup sugar
1/3 cup molasses
3 tablespoons shortening
1 package dry yeast
7 to 8 cups flour

In large bowl of electric mixer, mix shredded wheat, salt, sugar, molasses and shortening with 2 cups boiling water. Dissolve yeast in 1/2 cup lukewarm water; add to shredded wheat mixture. Add 6 1/2 cups flour; mix. Add enough additional flour, 1/2 cup at a time, to make dough handle easily.

On floured board, knead dough until elastic and not sticky. Place in large greased bowl, turning to grease top of dough. Cover with cloth; Let rise until doubled, about 2 hours in warm place. Punch down dough; form into two loaves. Place in greased 9 x 5 x 3-inch loaf pans; let rise. Preheat oven to 350° F. Bake 30 to 35 minutes. **Makes 2 loaves.**

Preparation Time: 20 Minutes
(Plus rising time)

Cooking Time: 35 Minutes

Amaretto Cinnamon Rolls

1 package dry yeast
3/4 cup lukewarm milk
1/4 cup sugar
1 teaspoon salt
1 egg
1/4 cup shortening, softened
3 1/2 cups flour
1/2 stick butter, softened
3/4 cup brown sugar
1/2 cup pecans, chopped
1 tablespoon cinnamon
Powdered sugar
1 tablespoon Amaretto

In large bowl, dissolve yeast in 1/4 cup warm water. Add milk, sugar, salt, egg, shortening and half of flour; stir until smooth. Add remaining flour; knead until smooth. Transfer dough to large, greased bowl, turning dough to grease top. Cover; let rise until doubled in size. Punch down.

Roll dough into 15 x 9-inch rectangle. Spread with butter; sprinkle with brown sugar, pecans and cinnamon. Starting at wide end, roll up dough; cut into 1-inch slices. Place in greased 13 x 9-inch pan; let rise. Preheat oven to 375 ° F. Bake 25 minutes. Make glaze of powdered sugar, water and Amaretto; drizzle over rolls. **Makes 15.**

Preparation Time: 25 Minutes
(Plus rising time)

Cooking Time: 25 Minutes

Treasure Tip: Water to dissolve yeast should be about 110 °. A hotter temperature will kill the yeast. If the water is cooler, the yeast will take longer to activate. It is best to test water with a candy thermometer.

Toasted Pecan Garlic Bread

1 stick butter, softened
1/2 cup parsley, very finely minced
1/2 cup pecans, finely chopped
1 small clove garlic, finely minced
Pinch salt
2 medium-size loaves French bread

Preheat oven to 350° F. In medium bowl cream together until light and fluffy all ingredients except bread. Cut bread into slices, almost to (but not through) bottom crust; spread with butter mixture. Bake 10 minutes.   **20 to 24 slices.**

Preparation Time: 10 Minutes   *Cooking Time: 10 Minutes*

The Willie Moore

Much-requested sandwich recipe from Mise en Place in Hyde Park

Curry Chicken Salad

1/4 cup onion, chopped
1/4 cup celery, diced
2 cups chicken, cooked, diced
2 tablespoons curry powder
2 tablespoons slivered almonds, toasted
2 tablespoons raisins
1 cup mayonnaise
Salt and pepper to taste

Sandwich

Softened butter
4 slices pumpernickel bread
4 slices provolone cheese
2 tablespoons mango chutney
1 small ripe tomato, sliced

Make Curry Chicken Salad: In medium bowl toss all ingredients; mix well. Butter both sides of each slice of bread; place in nonstick sauté pan; sauté on both sides over medium-high heat until crisp. Top each bread slice with a slice of provolone; heat until cheese melts. Assemble sandwiches: Top 1 bread slice with half of chicken salad, 1 tablespoon chutney, 1 or 2 slices tomato and another bread slice; repeat. Serve immediately.   **Makes 2.**

Preparation Time: 15 Minutes

Curried Tuna Sandwiches

1 (9-ounce) can water-packed
   white tuna
1 tablespoon lemon juice
1 stalk celery, chopped
1 cup slivered almonds, chopped
1 cup flaked coconut
½ cup mayonnaise (or to taste)
¾ teaspoon curry powder
Dash pepper
Sliced apples

At least 1 hour before serving: Drain and rinse tuna. Place tuna in bowl; break up with fork. Pour lemon juice over tuna; add celery, almonds, coconut, mayonnaise, curry powder and pepper; mix well. Chill 1 hour to blend flavors. Spread on your choice of bread; serve with sliced apples. **Makes 4.**

Preparation Time: 10 Minutes

Pork Souvlaki

5 pounds lean pork, cut into 1-inch
   cubes
1 cup imported olive oil
Juice of 2 lemons
¼ cup dry white wine
¾ tablespoon oregano
½ tablespoon black pepper
5 garlic cloves, crushed
6 to 8 large pita bread rounds,
   warmed
2 tomatoes, chopped
1 medium onion, chopped
½ cup iceberg lettuce, shredded

Tzatziki (Greek Dressing)
4 cups plain low-fat yogurt
2 medium cucumbers, peeled,
   seeded and diced
2 cloves garlic, finely minced
3 tablespoons finely chopped fresh
   dill

Night before serving: Place pork cubes in large bowl. In small bowl thoroughly mix olive oil, lemon juice, wine, oregano, pepper and garlic. Pour marinade over meat; toss. Cover; refrigerate overnight.

Several hours before serving, make Tzatziki: In medium bowl, thoroughly mix yogurt, cucumbers, garlic and dill; cover; chill several hours.

When ready to cook: Start grill. Thread meat on skewers; reserve marinade. Grill over hot coals (or 6 inches below broiler). Turn frequently, brushing with marinade, until cubes are cooked through, 10 to 15 minutes. Remove meat from skewers; place on warm pita rounds. Garnish with tomato, onions and lettuce. Serve Tzatziki on side. **6 to 8 servings.**

Preparation Time: 10 Minutes   Cooking Time: 10 to 15 Minutes

Treasure Tip: For a more authentic pita bread than that sold in supermarkets, buy it from a Greek restaurant or a Middle Eastern specialty food store.

Spicy White Barbecue

3¼ pounds lean beef stew meat
1¾ pounds boneless pork, cubed
4 large onions, chopped
½ stick butter
1 teaspoon ground dried red pepper
1 tablespoon salt
½ cup vinegar
1 tablespoon black pepper
1 teaspoon oregano
2 teaspoons ground cumin
Rolls or sandwich buns

Night before: In large saucepan place beef, pork and onions; cover with water. Bring to boil; reduce heat to simmer; cook, covered, until meat is soft, about 3 hours. Drain meat, saving liquid. Allow meat to cool; shred meat and return to liquid. Add butter, red pepper, salt, vinegar, black pepper, oregano and cumin. Bring to boil; reduce heat to simmer. Cook, uncovered, until no juice remains. Refrigerate overnight before serving or freezing. Serve on rolls or sandwich buns or as appetizer.

10 to 12 servings.

Preparation Time: 15 Minutes   *Cooking Time: 4 to 5 Hours*

Spinach-Cheese Stuffed Bread

1 loaf frozen bread dough
18 slices ham
¾ pound Italian sausage, crumbled
1 (10-ounce) package frozen
    chopped spinach
1½ teaspoons garlic, minced
¼ teaspoon crushed red pepper
8 ounces cheddar cheese, grated
8 ounces mozzarella cheese, grated

Thaw bread dough; let rise as package directs. While dough rises, brown sausage in large skillet; drain excess grease; set sausage aside. In same skillet sauté spinach, garlic and red pepper until spinach is tender, about 5 minutes. Add sausage; toss to blend. Roll out dough into large rectangle. On the dough layer, in order, 9 slices ham, sausage mixture, cheddar, mozzarella and remaining ham. Preheat oven to 425° F. Starting with wide side of dough, roll up like a jelly roll. Bake 20 minutes. Cool; slice; serve.

5 to 6 servings.

Preparation Time: 25 Minutes   *Cooking Time: 20 Minutes*
(Plus rising time)

Treasure Tip: To test whether yeast dough has risen enough, make an indentation in it with two fingers. If the dough does not spring back, it is ready.

CONDIMENTS & CONFECTIONS

A Day at Our Parks

Bird-watching takes on a new dimension at Lowry Park Zoological Gardens and at Tampa's Busch Gardens. The pink flamingo elegantly poised against a background of tropical foliage have become a Florida trademark, illustrating the best of living in the tropics. These parks are treasure troves of entertainment and family fun.

The Lowry Park Zoo, one of the finest in the Southeast, features animals living in authentic settings and a walk-through aviary that dazzles the eye with tropical birds. Native and exotic animals are featured in natural habitats including Florida's most unique mammal, the gentle manatee.

Tampa is home to the original Busch Gardens theme park. Busch Gardens has more than 3,000 exotic mammals, birds and reptiles roaming on its 300 acres. The park offers photo safaris, thrilling rides, the famed Anheuser-Busch Clydesdales and live entertainment for millions of annual visitors.

True treasures for our children are the many hands-on conservation programs offered by both parks. Children assist zoo personnel with the care, feeding and habitat maintenance of some of the animals. Both facilities are active participants in worldwide species survival and sanctuary efforts.

A glimpse of old Florida can be found in the five vast wilderness parks that offer city dwellers camping, horseback riding, canoeing and hiking. Indigenous alligators can be seen basking in the sun along the sandy banks of black-bottomed rivers, that meander through stands of pine and lacy cypress trees. Wherever your destination may be, there is a snack or treat in this section for you. You'll discover portable goodies for backpacks, tackle boxes and coolers. Also included in this section are sauces and condiments for a dessert extravaganza as well as delectable, edible gifts guaranteed to brighten anyone's day.

The Parks photograph was underwritten by
Terry Hentschel Pepin
Cynthia S. Lewis

CONDIMENTS & CONFECTIONS

NOT JUST FOR KIDS

State Fair Taffy Apples

Caramel Popcorn

Pretzels in White Chocolate

Refreshing Apple Lemonade

Rich Vanilla Ice Cream

with

Yesterday's Chocolate Sauce

and

Creamy Caramel Sauce

**The menu photograph was underwritten by
Joan Steinbrenner
Jenny Swindal**

State Fair Taffy Apples

12 large tart apples
12 Popsicle sticks
1 cup plus 3 tablespoons firmly
    packed dark brown sugar
1 (14-ounce) can sweetened
    condensed milk
½ cup light corn syrup
1 tablespoon butter
½ teaspoon vanilla extract

Up to 2 days ahead: Line large cookie sheet with well-greased waxed paper. Wash apples with soap to remove wax; rinse well. Wax may make the caramel coating slide off. Remove stems; insert Popsicle stick into stem end of each apple. Combine brown sugar, milk and corn syrup in heavy, medium-size saucepan over medium heat. Cook, stirring occasionally, until candy thermometer registers 240° F., firm ball stage, about 20 minutes.

Remove pan from heat; add butter and vanilla; stir until butter melts. Dip apples, one at a time, into caramel, coating completely and allowing excess to drip back into pan. Stand apples on lightly greased cookie sheet. If prepared ahead, cool; wrap in waxed paper; refrigerate. Serve at room temperature. While apples are warm, you can add various toppings; small chocolate candies, white chocolate chips, chopped nuts, etc.

Makes 12.

Preparation Time: 10 Minutes   Cooking Time: 20 to 25 Minutes

Caramel Popcorn

2 cups light brown sugar
2 sticks butter
½ cup white corn syrup
½ teaspoon salt
½ teaspoon baking soda
20 to 25 cups popped corn, plain
    unsalted

Preheat oven to 250° F. Mix brown sugar, butter, corn syrup and salt in medium saucepan. Cook 5 minutes over medium heat; add soda. Pour warm mixture over popped corn in large bowl, stirring well. Pour into large roasting pan; bake 1 hour, stirring every 15 minutes. If you want to make popcorn balls, test a scoop after 30 minutes to see if mixture will stick together; stop cooking when it will. Remove from oven; break apart. If desired, add candies or nuts after baking. Serve warm or cold.

20 to 25 servings.

Preparation Time: 10 to 30 Minutes   Cooking Time: 1 Hour

Pretzels in White Chocolate

1 tablespoon shortening
1 (1-pound) bag white chocolate
  wafers for baking*
1 (12-ounce) can Spanish peanuts,
  chopped, or 2 cups chopped
  almonds
2 cups pretzel sticks, or large
  pretzel twists

*available at candy-making
shops and some bakeries

Melt shortening and chocolate together; add nuts and pretzels to coat. Lightly grease cookie sheet. Spread pretzel mixture on sheet; refrigerate 30 minutes; break apart to serve. As alternative, cover cookie sheet with waxed paper. Dip large pretzels in chocolate, then coat with peanuts; place on cookie sheet until set. Chocolate mixture, without nuts, can be used to coat strawberries or other fruits.   **16 to 20 servings.**

Preparation Time: 10 Minutes

Refreshing Apple Lemonade

¼ to ½ cup sugar
2 cups apple juice
½ cup fresh lemon juice

Combine sugar and ½ cup water in saucepan; cook, stirring, over medium heat until sugar dissolves. Combine sugar mixture and juices; stir well. Serve hot, with cinnamon stick for stirring, or chill and serve over ice.   **4 servings.**

Preparation Time: 5 Minutes   *Cooking Time: 1 to 2 Minutes*

Rich Vanilla Ice Cream

2 to 3 (14-ounce) cans sweetened
  condensed milk
1½ to 2 pints whipping cream
¾ to 1 cup sugar
1½ to 2 teaspoons vanilla extract
Pinch salt
Milk

Mix all ingredients except milk; add enough milk to fill container of ice cream maker. Freeze according to manufacturer's instructions. (Variations: For cinnamon ice cream, add 2 to 3 teaspoons cinnamon and a dash of allspice. For peach ice cream, add 6 to 8 fresh peaches, peeled, mashed and sweetened to taste.)   **Makes 1 gallon.**

Preparation Time: Varies, depending on machine used

Yesterday's Chocolate Sauce

From Yesterday's Restaurant in Cashiers, North Carolina

½ stick butter
1 square bitter chocolate
1 cup powdered sugar
1 egg, beaten
1 teaspoon vanilla extract
¼ cup cream

Melt butter and chocolate together; add remaining ingredients. Cook 5 minutes, stirring until smooth, but do not allow mixture to boil. Serve warm over ice cream or ice cream-filled cream puffs. Note: May be refrigerated and reheated before serving.

Makes 1½ cups.

Preparation Time: 5 Minutes   **Cooking Time: 5 Minutes**

Creamy Caramel Sauce

1 (14-ounce) bag caramels
⅔ cup light cream
½ cup miniature marshmallows
1 tablespoon rum flavoring

Unwrap caramels; place with cream in glass bowl. Microwave at 50% power, stirring often until melted. Add marshmallows and rum flavoring; stir until melted. If too thick, add more cream to thin to desired consistency. Serve over ice cream or in chafing dish with apple slices, angel food cake cubes, regular-size marshmallows, banana slices and/or pecan halves as dippers for dessert fondue.

10 to 12 servings.

Preparation Time: 20 Minutes   **Cooking Time: 5 Minutes**

Treasure Tip: *Recipes for condiments and confections range from fresh salsas, relishes and pickles to sweet mixtures you can make for children's parties or to take to school. Many of these recipes make excellent gifts for Christmas or to welcome a new neighbor. Homemade gifts from your kitchen are always welcome!*

Spicy Black Bean Salsa

1 cup fresh corn kernels
1/4 cup red bell pepper, diced
1 1/4 teaspoons fresh chile peppers,
    diced
Pinch sugar
1 1/2 cups cooked or canned black
    beans, well drained
1/4 cup chicken broth
2 tablespoons fresh tomato, diced
2 tablespoons vinegar
1 teaspoon olive oil
2 tablespoons fresh basil, chopped
Juice of 1/2 lime

Combine corn, red pepper, chile peppers and sugar in medium saucepan; add 1/3 cup water; bring to boil. Reduce heat; cover; simmer 3 minutes. Add beans, broth and tomatoes; cook just until warmed through. Add vinegar and oil; cook over low heat 2 minutes. Transfer to serving bowl; stir in basil and lime juice just before serving. Serve warm or at room temperature.

Makes 3 cups.

Preparation Time: 10 Minutes   ***Cooking Time: 10 Minutes***

Treasure Tip: *Salsas make perfect accompaniments to many foods. They are interesting condiments to serve with meatloaf, grilled meat or fish.*

Pepper-Parsley Salsa

1/4 cup white vinegar
2 tablespoons vegetable oil
2 teaspoons sugar
1/4 teaspoon salt
1/4 teaspoon black pepper
1 medium red bell pepper, diced
1 medium yellow bell pepper, diced
1 medium green bell pepper, diced
2 tablespoons fresh parsley,
    chopped

Combine vinegar, oil, sugar, salt and black pepper in small saucepan; bring to boil, stirring until sugar dissolves. Remove from heat. Combine bell peppers and parsley in glass bowl; add hot mixture; stir gently; cool. Cover; chill. Serve with chicken, pork or ham.

Makes 1 2/3 cups.

Preparation Time: 5 Minutes   ***Cooking Time: 5 Minutes***

Treasure Tip: *For a fresh and colorful spring salad, place thick slices of ripe tomato over a bed of lettuce; cover with Pepper-Parsley Salsa.*

Ruskin Tomato Salsa

5 medium ripe tomatoes, diced
⅓ cup tomato sauce
¼ cup purple onion, finely chopped
3 cloves garlic, minced
1 to 2 small fresh jalapeño peppers,
   minced and seeded
2 tablespoons fresh cilantro or
   parsley, minced
1⅓ tablespoons fresh oregano,
   minced (or 1 teaspoon dried)
2 tablespoons fresh lime juice
1 teaspoon salt

Combine all ingredients, stirring gently; cover; chill. Serve with tortilla chips or as sauce for chicken or fish.   ***Makes 3⅓ cups.***

Preparation Time: 15 Minutes

Treasure Tip: *Use this sauce to make instant Huevos Rancheros: serve fried eggs over hot corn tortillas; top with Ruskin Tomato Salsa. A great brunch dish!*

Patchwork Relish

3 cantaloupes, peeled and chopped
3 cucumbers, peeled and chopped
3 red bell peppers, chopped
3 onions, chopped
Salt (to taste)
4 to 6 cups cider or white vinegar
4 cups sugar
1 tablespoon dry mustard
1 tablespoon celery seed
1 teaspoon turmeric

Night before making: Combine cantaloupes, cucumbers, peppers and onions in large crock or glass bowl; sprinkle with salt. Cover; let stand at room temperature overnight.

Next day: Drain; place in large saucepan; cover with vinegar. Add sugar, mustard and celery seed; boil 1 hour. Remove from heat; stir in turmeric. Ladle into sterilized pint jars, leaving ½-inch head space. Seal jars; process in boiling water bath 10 minutes   ***Makes about 12 pints.***

Preparation Time: 30 Minutes   *Cooking Time: 1 Hour*

Treasure Tip: *Turmeric, the root of a plant related to ginger, adds bright color to this relish. It is brilliant yellow and has a peppery aroma and musty flavor.*

Holiday Cranberry Relish

1 pound fresh cranberries
2 Florida navel (or other seedless)
   oranges, with peel, quartered
4 red apples, with peel, cored,
   seeded and quartered
2 cups sugar

Grind cranberries, oranges and apples in food processor; mix in sugar; refrigerate. Serve with your holiday turkey.
12 to 16 servings.

Preparation Time: 15 Minutes

Home-style Mustard Pickles

12 large cucumbers, peeled
12 large onions
1 cup salt
3 cups sugar
½ cup flour
1 quart bottle white vinegar
1 heaping teaspoon dry mustard
1 heaping teaspoon white mustard
    seed
1 heaping teaspoon turmeric

Night before making: Slice cucumbers and onions very thin; place in large bowl. Pour salt over them; let stand overnight.

The next morning: Pour cucumbers and onions into colander; drain; mash with large spoon to remove all juice, vegetables must be as dry as possible. Combine cucumbers, onions and remaining ingredients in large saucepan; bring to boil; cook 5 minutes. Place in sterilized pint jars; seal. Fabulous with baked ham!
                                                        Makes 8 pints.

Preparation Time: 45 Minutes   *Cooking Time: 10 Minutes*

Spicy Garlic Pickles

1 quart jar whole dill pickles
1½ cups sugar
1 handful mixed pickling spices
½ cup white vinegar
Tabasco to taste (optional)
Garlic cloves, peeled

Early in morning: Slice pickles; wash, drain and dry on paper towels. Place layers of towels over and under pickle slices 2 or 3 times, until thoroughly dry. In large bowl place layer of sugar and layer of pickles; repeat layers until all are used. Pour spices, vinegar and Tabasco (if desired) over top. Stir mixture frequently throughout the day.

That night: Fill sterilized pint or quart jars with pickles and juice; add 4 to 6 garlic cloves to each jar. Seal; refrigerate. Wonderful served with turkey or on turkey sandwiches.
                                                        Makes 2 quarts.

Preparation Time: 1 Hour

Green Tomato Crisps

Traditional Southern recipe

7 pounds small green tomatoes
3 cups pickling lime
5 pounds sugar
3 pints cider vinegar
1 teaspoon ground cloves
1 teaspoon ground ginger
1 teaspoon celery seed
1 teaspoon mace
1 teaspoon cinnamon

48 hours ahead: Slice green tomatoes into slices small enough to fit into canning jars, smaller are preferred. Mix lime and 2 gallons water; soak tomatoes in mixture 24 hours. Use a big crockery bowl, if possible. After soaking, drain tomatoes. Soak 4 hours in fresh water, draining and changing water every hour. Drain the last time on a kitchen towel to remove all water. Place tomatoes in crockery bowl. Place sugar and remaining ingredients in large, heavy pot; bring to boil. Pour over tomatoes; let stand overnight.

Next morning: Place tomatoes and syrup in large, heavy pot; bring to boil. Boil 1 hour; seal in sterilized wide-mouth jars. Process in boiling water bath about 10 minutes.

Makes 10 to 12 pints.

Preparation Time: 4 Hours 30 Minutes   Cooking Time: 1 Hour

Treasure Tip: Pickling lime can be found at most large supermarkets.

Festive Hot Pepper Jelly

10 to 12 fresh jalapeño peppers (to make 1 cup ground)
3 sweet bell peppers, green or red (to make ¾ cup ground)
1½ cups apple cider vinegar
6 cups sugar
6 ounces liquid pectin

Wash and dry peppers; cut in chunks. Grind jalapeños in food processor; measure to make 1 cup. Remove ribs and seeds from green peppers but not from jalapeños, unless you want a milder product. Grind bell peppers in food processor; drain well; measure to make ¾ cup. Place peppers, vinegar and sugar in large, heavy pot; bring to rolling boil. Remove from heat; skim; add liquid pectin. Reheat; boil hard 1 minute.

Remove from heat; pour into sterilized jars, ½ pint or smaller. Fabulous with pot roast, as a glaze for cooking poultry or with cream cheese and crackers as appetizer. Use rubber gloves when handling fresh jalapeños, they will burn your hands.

Makes 8 half-pints.

Preparation Time: 30 Minutes   Cooking Time: 15 Minutes

Sweet 'n' Spicy Mustard

½ cup granulated sugar
½ cup brown sugar
1 cup white wine vinegar
2 (2-ounce) cans Coleman's dry
    mustard*
3 eggs

*For a milder taste, use 1½ cans
dry mustard

Place all ingredients in food processor or blender; blend well. Cook in double boiler over hot, not boiling water, stirring occasionally until thick and smooth, about 30 minutes. If sauce curdles, strain before placing in jars. Keeps well in refrigerator; makes great Christmas present. Serve with egg rolls, turkey or ham, or use on sandwiches. **Makes 2½ cups.**

Preparation Time: 3 Minutes   **Cooking Time: 30 Minutes**

Cranberry Chutney

1 (12-ounce) package fresh
    cranberries
2 cups sugar
1 cup fresh orange juice, divided
1 cup raisins
1 cup walnuts, chopped
1 cup celery, chopped
1 cup apples, chopped
2 tablespoons orange peel, freshly
    grated
Half a fresh orange, peeled and cut
    up
1 teaspoon ground ginger

Wash cranberries and remove any stems. Combine cranberries, sugar, ½ cup water and ½ cup orange juice in large pot. Bring to boil; reduce heat to low; cook about 20 minutes. Stir frequently, pressing spoon against side of pot to break up cranberries.

Remove from heat; stir in ½ cup orange juice and remaining ingredients. Cover; refrigerate. When cool, spoon into sterilized jars; keep refrigerated. **Makes 3 to 4 pints.**

Preparation Time: 30 Minutes   **Cooking Time: 25 Minutes**

Treasure Tip: This chutney, served with your holiday turkey, is a delightful alternative to canned cranberry sauce.

Ginger Peach Chutney

3 pounds peaches, peeled and
    chopped (4 cups)
½ cup cider vinegar
1 teaspoon allspice
¼ cup candied ginger, minced
1 to 3 fresh jalapeño peppers,
    minced
1 teaspoon garlic, minced
1 cup golden raisins
⅓ cup onion, chopped
½ teaspoon ground ginger
1 tablespoon salt
½ teaspoon cinnamon
½ teaspoon ground cloves
¼ cup fresh lemon juice
6 ounces liquid pectin
¾ cup light brown sugar, packed
4½ cups granulated sugar
Paraffin

In large pot mix peaches and all ingredients except pectin, sugars and paraffin. Blend in pectin; bring to rolling boil, stirring constantly. Add brown and granulated sugars; boil 5 more minutes, stirring constantly.

Remove from heat; skim foam; stir for 10 minutes. Ladle into sterilized ½ pint jars; top with hot, melted paraffin; seal with metal lids. Keeps well in cool place up to 1 year. Serve with meats, or use with cream cheese and crackers for cocktail party.
Makes 12 half-pints.

Preparation Time: 45 Minutes   *Cooking Time: 30 Minutes*

Treasure Tip: To melt paraffin, place it in a small, clean metal can and set in a saucepan with about 1 inch of water. Heat, uncovered, over medium heat until paraffin melts; keep hot so it won't congeal. Caution: Never put paraffin directly on heat, it is extremely flammable!

Curried Mango Chutney

2¼ cups dark brown sugar
1 pint cider vinegar
4 large green mangoes, peeled and
    cut in 1-inch strips
1 pound currants
1 tablespoon salt
¼ pound slivered almonds, toasted
1 (2-inch) piece ginger root, peeled
    and diced small
½ teaspoon cayenne pepper
1 to 2 tablespoons curry powder
1 tablespoon green peppercorns

In large pot bring sugar and vinegar to boil; add remaining ingredients. Cover pot; reduce heat to medium; boil slowly 30 minutes, stirring occasionally. Pack in sterilized canning jars; seal.
Makes 6 pints.

Preparation Time: 35 Minutes   *Cooking Time: 30 Minutes*

Treasure Tip: Green, rather than ripe, mangoes are best for chutney. Ripe mangoes are hard to cut into strips and will not hold their shapes as well.

Fresh Lime Jelly

¾ cup fresh lime juice
Grated rind of 5 limes
4 cups sugar
6 drops green food coloring
Half of a 3-ounce package liquid
    pectin (just less than ¼ cup)

Add juice to rind; let stand 10 minutes; strain. Place strained juice, sugar and 1¾ cups water in heavy pot; bring to boil; add food coloring. Stir in pectin; boil ½ minute. Pour into sterilized jelly jars.

Makes 5 small jars.

Preparation Time: 15 Minutes   ***Cooking Time: 5 Minutes***

Plant City Strawberry Preserves

This Plant City Strawberry Festival Prize Winning Recipe is more than 100 years old.

1 heaping quart fresh strawberries
3 cups sugar, divided

24 hours ahead: Remove caps from strawberries; wash twice; drain well. Place berries and 1½ cups sugar in large, heavy saucepan; slowly bring to boil; boil 5 minutes. Add remaining sugar; boil 10 to 15 minutes, or until fruit is thickened. Pour into large mixing bowl; let stand 24 hours, stirring occasionally.

Next day: Pour fruit into sterilized ½ pint canning jars; screw on tops; process in boiling water bath 15 minutes to seal. Wonderful on hot biscuits! You can prepare as many strawberries as your mixing bowl will hold, but cook only 1 quart at a time.

Makes 3 to 4 half-pints.

Preparation Time: 35 Minutes   ***Cooking Time: 20 Minutes***

Treasure Tip: *To process jars in a boiling water bath, place a rack in the bottom of a canner or large pot. Fill the canner half full of water; heat to boiling. Carefully place the filled jars in the canner far enough apart to allow water to circulate. Add additional boiling water to cover the jars by 1 or 2 inches. Bring back to a boil; start timing when the water boils. If necessary, add boiling water to keep the jars covered. Remove jars with tongs; seal caps as manufacturer directs.*

Low Sugar Strawberry Preserves

1/3 cup sugar
1 quart strawberries, cleaned and
  sliced
1 tablespoon freshly squeezed
  lemon juice

Mix sugar and berries in heavy saucepan; bring to boil; boil gently 15 minutes. Strain, reserving fruit. Put liquid back in pan; add lemon juice; boil 5 minutes. Return fruit to pan; stir well; pack in sterilized 1/2-pint jars.   *Makes 1 to 2 half-pints.*

Preparation Time: 20 Minutes   *Cooking Time: 20 Minutes*

Cream Cheese Mint Patties

3 ounces cream cheese, softened
1/2 teaspoon peppermint extract
2 to 2 1/2 cups powdered sugar
Food coloring
Granulated sugar

Mix cream cheese and peppermint. Gradually add powdered sugar; stir until mixture is no longer sticky. Divide into four portions; mix in food coloring of your choice until desired shade is reached. Shape into 1/4 to 1/2 inch balls; roll in granulated sugar. Flatten balls with fork; let dry at room temperature. Store, loosely covered, in refrigerator.
Makes 4 to 6 dozen.

Preparation Time: 15 Minutes

Fruity White Fudge

1/4 cup pecans, finely ground
1/4 cup walnuts, finely ground
1/4 cup almonds, finely ground
2 tablespoons flaked coconut, finely
  ground
1/4 cup candied red cherries,
  chopped
1/4 cup candied green cherries,
  chopped
2 cups superfine sugar
2 tablespoons white corn syrup
1/2 cup milk
2 tablespoons butter or margarine
1 teaspoon vanilla extract
1/2 teaspoon pure almond extract

Mix nuts and coconut together; add candied cherries; mix well. Combine sugar, syrup, milk and butter in large saucepan; boil gently until syrup forms soft ball when tested in cold water or use candy thermometer to test for soft-ball stage. Remove from heat; add nut-fruit mixture, vanilla and almond flavoring. Set pan in larger pan of cold water; beat until creamy and thick. Do not overbeat, or fudge will be grainy. Pour into buttered 8 x 8-inch pan; cool. Cut into 1-inch squares when cool.
Makes 64 small pieces.

Preparation Time: 5 Minutes   *Cooking Time: 8 Minutes*

Treasure Tip: To make your own superfine sugar, whirl granulated sugar in your food processor.

Coconut Pecan Rum Balls

1 (12-ounce) box vanilla wafers,
  crushed
1 cup pecans, finely chopped
1 (3 ½-ounce) can flaked coconut
1 (14-ounce) can sweetened
  condensed milk
¼ cup rum
Powdered sugar

Night before: Combine all ingredients in large bowl; mix well. Chill overnight.

Next day: Using teaspoon as guide, shape mixture into 1-inch balls; roll in powdered sugar.　　**Makes 5 to 6 dozen.**

Preparation Time: 15 Minutes

Peanut Butter Coconut Balls

1 (12-ounce) jar creamy peanut
  butter
1 cup flaked coconut
½ cup graham cracker crumbs
1 cup nuts, chopped
1 (1-pound) box powdered sugar
2 sticks margarine, softened
¼ to ⅓ of a block of household
  paraffin
1 (6-ounce) package chocolate
  chips

Mix peanut butter, coconut, crumbs, nuts, sugar and margarine; form 1-inch balls. Melt paraffin and chocolate chips in top of double boiler over hot water. Using toothpick, dip balls in chocolate mixture; cool on waxed paper.　　**Makes 6 dozen.**

Preparation Time: 30 Minutes

Peanut Butter Chocolate Bites

1 stick margarine
1 cup creamy peanut butter
1 (12-ounce) package chocolate
  chips
1 (12¾-ounce) box Crispix cereal
3 cups powdered sugar

Melt together margarine, peanut butter and chocolate chips; add Crispix; mix until cereal is coated. Place powdered sugar in plastic bag; add cereal mixture; shake well. Place on cookie sheet until dry.　　**Makes about 7 cups.**

Preparation Time: 20 Minutes

Honey-Roasted Nuts

4 cups unsalted nuts (mixture of
   pecans, walnuts, almonds),
   lightly toasted
2 tablespoons unsalted butter,
   melted
½ cup honey
½ teaspoon orange peel, freshly
   grated
½ teaspoon cinnamon

In large microwave-safe baking dish stir all ingredients together. Microwave on high for 7 minutes, stirring once. Pour onto sheet of foil; let cool. Break up nuts; store in cool place.

Makes about 4 cups.

Preparation Time: 5 Minutes **Cooking Time: 7 Minutes**

Brown Sugared Pecans

1 egg white
1 cup brown sugar
1 teaspoon vanilla extract
2 cups pecan halves (1 pound
   unshelled)

Preheat oven to 225° F. Beat egg white until stiff; gradually add brown sugar, beating. Stir in vanilla and pecan halves. Drop by teaspoon, one at a time, onto well-greased cookie sheet. Bake until light brown, about 1 hour. Remove from oven; cool. Store in cookie tin.

Makes about 2 cups.

Preparation Time: 10 Minutes **Cooking Time: 1 Hour**

DESSERTS

Plant Hall

Moorish minarets, gleaming silver in the sunshine, rise above the trees and add the signature touch to Tampa's skyline. Atop the architectural masterpiece known as Plant Hall, these distinctive features mark the end of the journey through Tampa's treasures and give another glimpse of life in our community.

This national historic landmark, built by railroad magnate Henry B. Plant, opened in 1891 as the Tampa Bay Hotel. It now serves the community as the central building on the campus of the University of Tampa. Opulent salons and wide terraces framed in Victorian gingerbread trellises overlook the river and provide a historic backdrop for students. In the spring, the sweeping lawns and spreading oak trees are the setting for the Florida Orchestra's ever popular Symphony in the Park.

During the holidays, the University of Tampa and the University of South Florida (USF) invite the community to take part in their festivities. The Henry B. Plant Museum is the site of the annual Victorian Christmas Stroll highlighting the museum's collection of late Victorian furniture and artifacts alive with the sparkle and glow of magnificent holiday decorations. USF's College of Fine Arts School of Music stages Madrigal Dinners with all the majesty and merriment of true Renaissance holiday feasts.

As we reach the end of our culinary treasure hunt, we offer a collection of tempting desserts for a fabulous finale. Chocolate, butterscotch and fruits of all kinds flavor delectable cakes, cookies, pies, mousses, and ice creams. From the Classic Banana Pudding to the dazzling Chocolate Pecan Toffee Mousse, these desserts are the creative culmination of *Tampa Treasures*.

We hope you have enjoyed exploring the treasures we have chosen knowing many more await, should you venture this way. It has been our pleasure to share with you those features of our city and coastal living that provide the color, ambience and texture to the fabric of community life here. Tampa's rich cuisine is the inseparable thread that binds us as we enjoy these events and places with family members and friends.

**The University of Tampa photograph was underwritten by
The Bank of Tampa**

DESSERTS

HOLIDAY DESSERT PARTY

Fudge Truffle with Raspberry Sauce

Date-Pecan Bars

Florida Key Lime Tarts with Coconut Crust

Café Ybor

Bavarian Cream with Raspberries

Cinnamon Baked Pears in Cointreau

The menu photograph was underwritten by
Mary Lee Nunnally Farrior
Lera Finley Farrior

Fudge Truffle with Raspberry Sauce

8 ounces semi-sweet chocolate
1 cup sugar
2 sticks unsalted butter
1/4 cup brewed coffee, cooled
4 eggs, beaten
1 (10-ounce) package frozen
    raspberries, thawed
2 tablespoons powdered sugar
Fresh raspberries or strawberries
    (garnish)

Night before: Preheat oven to 350° F. Melt chocolate, sugar and butter in top of double boiler; cool. Add coffee and eggs, beating well. Lightly grease a 8½-inch springform pan; line with foil. Pour batter into prepared pan; bake until top forms a crust, 30 to 40 minutes. Cool; refrigerate overnight. Cake can be frozen at this point.

Before serving: Purée raspberries in food processor; strain to remove seeds; stir in powdered sugar. To serve, slice cake in pie-shaped wedges; spoon sauce over each piece. Garnish, if desired, with fresh berries. **8 to 10 servings.**

Preparation Time: 15 Minutes   Cooking Time: 30 to 40 Minutes

Date-Pecan Bars

2 sticks butter
1 (1-pound) box dark brown sugar
3 large eggs
2 teaspoons vanilla
3 cups flour
2 teaspoons baking powder
1 teaspoon salt
1 pound dates, chopped
2 cups pecans, chopped
Powdered sugar

Preheat oven to 325° F. In large bowl of electric mixer, cream butter and brown sugar until fluffy. Add eggs, one at a time, beating after each addition; add vanilla. Sift flour, baking powder and salt together in a separate bowl. Place dates and nuts in a third bowl. Add half of flour mixture to butter mixture; mix well. Sift remaining flour mixture over dates and nuts; mix well. Add dates and nuts to butter mixture; mix well.

Spread in greased and floured 9 x 13-inch baking pan; bake about 45 minutes. Do not overbake. Like brownies, mixture may appear gooey while hot. After cooling, cake-like texture will develop. Cut with sharp knife immediately after baking; allow to cool until warm, but not hot; sift powdered sugar over top. **Makes 12 bars.**

Preparation Time: 25 Minutes   Cooking Time: 45 Minutes

Florida Key Lime Tarts with Coconut Crust

Crust

1 cup flaked coconut
½ cup gingersnap crumbs
½ cup graham cracker crumbs
½ stick butter or margarine, melted
2 tablespoons flour

Filling

8 ounces cream cheese, softened
1 (14-ounce) can sweetened
　condensed milk
½ cup fresh or bottled key lime
　juice
1 cup sour cream

Topping

½ cup whipping cream
2 tablespoons granulated or
　powdered sugar
Grated Persian lime rind
　(optional)

At least 3½ hours before serving, make crust: Preheat oven to 350° F. Combine all ingredients, mixing well. Firmly press mixture evenly over bottoms and ¾ inch up sides of eight individual tart pans or one 9-inch springform pan or pie plate. Bake 5 minutes; chill.

At least 2½ hours before serving, make filling: Blend cream cheese and condensed milk. Add juice; stir in sour cream. Pour filling into chilled crusts. Refrigerate at least 2 hours.

Just before serving, make topping: Whip cream with sugar until stiff peaks form; spread over tarts; sprinkle with grated rind, if desired. *8 servings.*

Preparation Time: 30 Minutes　　　　*Cooking Time: 5 Minutes*

Treasure Tip: Key limes are smaller than Persian limes and, when mature, have yellow skin. The abundant juice is yellow and, unless food coloring is used, pies made with key limes will not be green.

Café Ybor

½ cup strong, hot brewed coffee
2 tablespoons "43 Liqueur"
2 tablespoons half-and-half or light
　cream, warmed
Dollop of whipped cream (garnish)

Combine coffee, liqueur and warm cream in coffee cup; top with whipped cream, if desired. *1 serving.*

Preparation Time: 5 Minutes

Bavarian Cream with Raspberries

1 envelope unflavored gelatin
4 egg yolks
½ cup sugar
1 cup milk
2 tablespoons candied ginger, very
    finely chopped
5 tablespoons rum, divided
½ cup whipping cream
1 (10-ounce) package fresh
    raspberries
¾ cup slivered almonds, toasted

Early in day: Soften gelatin in 2 tablespoons water. Mix egg yolks and sugar until smooth and creamy. Scald milk; pour gradually over yolk mixture, stirring constantly. Place in top of double boiler over boiling water; cook until smooth and thick. Remove from heat; add gelatin; stir until gelatin dissolves. Add ginger and 3 tablespoons rum. Place plastic wrap over mixture to prevent formation of skin; chill until mixture begins to set. Whip cream; fold into partially set mixture. Spoon mixture into eight lightly greased small molds or custard cups; refrigerate until set.

Before serving: Purée raspberries in food processor or blender; strain to remove seeds, if desired. Stir in 2 tablespoons rum.

To serve: Pour some sauce onto each serving plate; unmold Bavarians on top of sauce. Sprinkle with almonds. If desired, decorate with mint leaves and candied violets.   *8 servings.*

Preparation Time: 15 Minutes   Cooking Time: 8 to 10 Minutes

Cinnamon Baked Pears in Cointreau

Juice of 1 lemon
8 fresh Bosc pears (leave stems on)
1½ cups dry white wine
1¼ cups sugar
Peel of 2 Florida oranges, removed
    with vegetable peeler
2 (3-inch) cinnamon sticks
⅓ cup Cointreau or other orange-
    flavored liqueur

Night before: Preheat oven to 375° F. Squeeze lemon juice into bowl of cold water large enough to hold pears. Carefully peel pears, retaining stems; place into bowl of water. In saucepan combine wine, 2 cups water and remaining ingredients. Bring to boil, stirring until sugar dissolves. Reduce heat; simmer 5 minutes. Drain pears; arrange them on their sides in baking dish just large enough to hold them in one layer. Pour syrup over pears. Cover tightly with foil; bake 30 minutes.

Remove foil; gently turn pears over; replace foil. Bake until tender, 20 to 30 minutes more. Let cool; carefully transfer to deep serving dish; ladle cooking syrup over pears. Chill, covered, overnight. Serve with some of syrup.   *8 servings.*

Preparation Time: 20 Minutes   Cooking Time: 50 to 60 Minutes

Mocha Macadamia Cake

Cake

1½ teaspoons instant coffee powder
¾ cup sour cream
1 cup flour
½ cup sugar
1 stick butter or margarine,
    softened
¼ cup unsweetened cocoa powder
½ teaspoon baking soda
½ teaspoon baking powder
½ teaspoon vanilla extract
¼ teaspoon salt
1 egg

Topping

1 cup heavy cream
½ cup sugar
2 tablespoons butter
1 tablespoon corn syrup
4 squares semi-sweet chocolate
1 teaspoon vanilla extract
1 (3½-ounce) jar macadamia nuts,
    chopped

Make cake: Preheat oven to 350° F. Grease 9-inch cake pan; line with waxed paper; grease again. In large bowl of electric mixer dissolve instant coffee powder in sour cream; add all other ingredients. Mix well, scraping bowl occasionally. Pour batter into prepared pan. Bake until toothpick in center comes out clean, 30 to 35 minutes; cool.

About 45 minutes before serving, make topping: Place cream, sugar, butter, corn syrup and chocolate in 2-quart saucepan over medium heat. Bring to boil, stirring constantly. Reduce heat to medium-low; cook 5 minutes. Remove from heat; stir in vanilla. Cool slightly, about 10 minutes. Stir in nuts. Refrigerate until thickened but not stiff, 20 to 30 minutes. Pour over cake; serve.

8 to 10 servings.

Preparation Time: 20 Minutes   Cooking Time: 45 to 50 Minutes

Treasure Tip: When baking a cake always follow the recipe exactly, use pans of the correct size and a well-regulated oven. To prevent excess browning, use solid vegetable shortening, not butter or oil, to grease baking sheets, aluminum foil or waxed paper.

Deep Dark Chocolate Cake

Filling

1 cup heavy cream, chilled
¼ cup powdered sugar
1 teaspoon vanilla extract

Cake Layers

1 cup unsweetened cocoa
2¾ cups cake flour
2 teaspoons baking soda
½ teaspoon salt
½ teaspoon baking powder
2 sticks butter, or 1 stick butter
    and 1 stick margarine
2½ cups sugar
4 eggs
1½ teaspoons vanilla extract

Frosting

1 (6-ounce) package chocolate
    chips
½ cup light cream
1 cup butter or margarine
2½ cups powdered sugar

At least 3 hours before serving, make filling: Combine all ingredients in small bowl of electric mixer; whip until stiff peaks form; refrigerate.

Make cake: Preheat oven to 350 ° F. In medium bowl, combine cocoa and 2 cups boiling water; mix with wire whisk; cool completely. In separate bowl, sift flour with soda, salt and baking powder; set aside. In large bowl of electric mixer beat butter, sugar, eggs and vanilla at high speed until light and fluffy about 5 minutes. Reduce speed to low; alternately beat in, one-fourth at a time, cocoa mixture and flour mixture. Grease well and flour three 9-inch cake pans; divide batter evenly among pans. Bake until surface springs back when touched, 25 to 30 minutes. Cool in pans 10 minutes; carefully loosen sides; remove from pans. Cool completely on racks.

While layers cool, make frosting: Place chocolate chips, cream and butter in medium saucepan over medium heat; cook, stirring, until smooth. Remove from heat; using wire whisk, blend in powdered sugar. Place saucepan in large bowl filled with ice; beat frosting until it holds its shape, 7 to 10 minutes.

When layers are cool, assemble cake: Place one layer on cake plate, top side down; spread with half of filling. Place second layer, top side down, on top of first layer; spread with remaining filling. Place third layer on top, top side up. Frost entire cake; refrigerate at least 1 hour before serving.

16 to 20 servings.

Preparation Time: 1 Hour 30 Minutes   *Cooking Time: 30 Minutes*

Treasure Tip: For perfect whipped cream, chill bowl, beaters and cream in refrigerator. To beat with electric mixer, use medium high speed until cream begins to thicken. Lower speed and watch closely. If cream is beaten too long, or is warmer than 45 °, it will turn to butter.

Chocolate Buttermilk Pound Cake

8 (³/₄-ounce) Hershey chocolate bars
1 (5¹/₂-ounce) can chocolate syrup
2 sticks butter or margarine
2 cups sugar
4 eggs
¹/₂ teaspoon baking soda
1 cup buttermilk
2 ¹/₂ cups flour, sifted
2 teaspoons vanilla extract

Preheat oven to 350° F. In top of double boiler, over warm water, melt chocolate bars in syrup; cool. In large bowl of electric mixer cream butter; add sugar; cream until fluffy. Add eggs, one at a time, beating well after each addition. Mix soda and buttermilk; add, alternating with flour, to creamed mixture. Add to cooled chocolate; stir in vanilla; mix well. Place in greased and floured tube or bundt pan; bake 1 hour 20 minutes. Cool in pan 10 minutes; remove from pan; cool completely on rack.   *12 to 16 servings.*

Preparation Time: 25 Minutes   *Cooking Time: 1 Hour 20 Minutes*

Chocolate Walnut Carrot Cake

2 cups light brown sugar, packed
1 cup vegetable oil
4 extra-large eggs
2 rounded teaspoons baking soda
1 tablespoon plus 1 scant teaspoon
   cinnamon
³/₄ teaspoon nutmeg
Pinch salt
¹/₄ cup plus 1 tablespoon
   unsweetened cocoa
1³/₄ cups flour
3 cups carrots, peeled, grated
   (about 1 pound)
2 cups walnuts, chopped
4 ounces white cooking chocolate

Preheat oven to 350° F. Grease and flour 10-inch tube or bundt pan. In large bowl, combine brown sugar, oil and eggs; stir until smooth. In separate bowl sift together soda, cinnamon, nutmeg, salt, cocoa and flour; beat into sugar mixture, mixing well. Fold in carrots and walnuts. Pour batter into prepared pan; bake until toothpick comes out clean, 45 to 50 minutes. Cool in pan on rack 15 minutes. Remove from pan; cool completely on rack. When cake is cool, melt chocolate in top half of double boiler over hot water; pour over top of cooled cake.   *16 servings.*

Preparation Time: 30 Minutes   *Cooking Time: 45 to 50 Minutes*

Treasure Tip: White chocolate isn't really chocolate but a blend of cocoa butter, milk solids, sugar and flavorings.

Chocolate-Strawberry Buttercream Torte

*2 sticks plus 6 tablespoons
   unsalted butter, divided*
2 cups powdered sugar, sifted
½ cup fresh strawberries, puréed
3 tablespoons strawberry preserves
2 (12.9-ounce) boxes brownie mix
3½ cups pecans, finely ground
3 ounces semi-sweet chocolate
3 tablespoons safflower oil
¾ cup unsweetened cocoa powder
¾ cup granulated sugar
Fresh strawberries (garnish)

Up to 1 day ahead, make buttercream: Cream 2 sticks butter and powdered sugar until light and fluffy; mix in strawberries and preserves. Cover; refrigerate until set.

At least 8 hours before serving, make cake: Prepare brownie mix as package directs, adding pecans. Bake in two cake pans as directed for cake-like brownies; cool.

To assemble: Cut each cake in half horizontally. Spread buttercream over all layers except top. Refrigerate 6 hours.

Make glaze: Place chocolate, ½ cup water, remaining butter and oil in top part of double boiler; heat over hot water until melted. Remove from heat; add cocoa powder and granulated sugar; stir until smooth. Cool slightly. Pour glaze over top and sides of cake; arrange fresh strawberries on top. Refrigerate. Remove from refrigerator 1 hour before serving.

10 to 12 servings.

Preparation Time: 35 Minutes   Cooking Time: 30 to 45 Minutes

Mississippi Mud Cake

Cake

2 cups sugar
*2 sticks butter or margarine,
   softened*
4 eggs
1½ cups flour
¼ teaspoon salt
½ cup unsweetened cocoa powder
1 tablespoon vanilla extract
½ cup walnuts or pecans, chopped
3½ cups miniature marshmallows

Chocolate Icing

1 stick butter or margarine
¼ cup (or less) milk
3 cups powdered sugar
½ cup unsweetened cocoa powder
1 teaspoon vanilla extract
½ cup walnuts or pecans, chopped

Make cake: Preheat oven to 350° F. In large bowl of electric mixer, cream sugar and butter until light and fluffy. Add eggs, 1 at a time, beating after each addition. In separate bowl, sift flour, salt and cocoa together; add to butter mixture. Add vanilla and nuts. Pour batter into greased 13 x 9-inch pan; bake 30 minutes.

While cake bakes, make icing: Melt butter and milk together. Sift powdered sugar and cocoa together; add to butter mixture; stir well. Add a little more milk if necessary (frosting needs to be a little runny). Add vanilla and nuts; keep warm. When cake has cooked 30 minutes, cover top of cake with marshmallows. Return cake to oven; bake 3 to 5 minutes more, until marshmallows puff and turn golden brown. Remove from oven. Wait 2 minutes for marshmallows to settle; immediately pour warm icing over marshmallows. Cool before cutting.

12 to 16 servings.

Preparation Time: 20 Minutes   Cooking Time: 35 Minutes

Treasure Tip: Cakes made with unsweetened cocoa powder, which is 100% cocoa, are exceptionally dark and rich. To substitute cocoa powder for one square of unsweetened baking chocolate, use 3 level tablespoons of cocoa and 1 tablespoon vegetable oil or shortening.

Festive Orange Fruit Cake

1½ sticks butter or margarine
1¾ cups sugar, divided
3 eggs
1½ cups dates, chopped
1 cup nuts, chopped
3 cups flour
1½ teaspoons baking soda
1 cup buttermilk
1 teaspoon vanilla extract
1 orange rind, grated
1½ fresh, large Florida oranges, juiced

At least 24 hours before serving, make cake: Preheat oven to 300° F. Cream butter and 1 cup sugar in large bowl of electric mixer. Add eggs, one at a time, beating well after each addition. Add dates and nuts. Sift flour and baking soda together; add to creamed mixture alternately with buttermilk. Add vanilla. Pour batter into well-greased tube pan; bake until done, 1 to 1½ hours. Remove from oven; prick top of cake all over with skewer or fork. Mix orange rind and juice and ¾ cup sugar; pour over hot cake. Allow cake to stand at least 24 hours before serving.   *12 servings.*

Preparation Time: 35 Minutes   *Cooking Time 1 Hour 30 Minutes*

Apple Cake with Buttermilk Glaze

Cake
3 eggs
1¼ cup vegetable oil
1 teaspoon vanilla extract
¼ cup orange juice concentrate, undiluted
2 cups sugar
3 cups flour
1 teaspoon baking soda
1 teaspoon cinnamon
2 cups peeled apples, chopped
1 cup walnuts or pecans, chopped
1 cup flaked coconut

Buttermilk Glaze
1 cup sugar
1 stick butter
½ teaspoon baking soda
½ cup buttermilk

Make cake: Preheat oven to 325° F. In large bowl mix eggs, oil, vanilla and orange juice. Add all other ingredients; mix. Pour into greased and floured tube or bundt pan; bake 1¼ hours.

Toward end of baking time, make glaze: Combine all ingredients in medium saucepan; heat to boiling, stirring constantly. Remove cake from oven; prick top of cake all over with skewer or fork; pour hot glaze over. Let sit in pan 10 to 15 minutes to absorb glaze; remove from pan; cool.

16 to 20 servings.

Preparation Time: 30 Minutes   *Cooking Time: 1 Hour 15 Minutes*

Treasure Tip: To make sure a cake is done, touch the center; if it springs back and the sides have shrunk away from the pan, it is done. Another way is to insert a clean toothpick into the center. The cake is done if the toothpick comes out clean.

Superb Sour Cream Pound Cake

6 eggs, separated, room
 temperature
2 sticks butter, room temperature
3 cups sour cream
3 cups sugar
3 cups cake flour, measured after
 sifting
1/2 teaspoon baking soda
1/2 teaspoon salt
1 tablespoon vanilla extract

Preheat oven to 325° F. Beat egg whites until stiff; set aside. In large bowl of electric mixer cream yolks and butter; add sugar, then sour cream. Set aside for 20 minutes, stirring occasionally to blend. Grease and flour tube pan. Add soda and salt to flour. When sugar mixture is ready, add flour and vanilla; mix about 2 minutes. Fold in egg whites. Pour into prepared pan; bake until cake pulls away from side of pan, about 1 hour 20 minutes. Cool.   *12 servings.*

Preparation Time: 30 Minutes   *Cooking Time: 1 Hour
                                              20 Minutes*

Treasure Tip: If you don't have cake flour, measure 2 tablespoons of cornstarch into a 1-cup dry measure. Fill the cup with all-purpose flour and blend. Never substitute self-rising or plain all-purpose flour for cake flour.

Pumpkin Date Nut Cake

Cake
1 (16-ounce) can pumpkin
3 1/3 cups flour
3 cups sugar
1 cup vegetable oil
4 eggs
1 teaspoon nutmeg
1 teaspoon cinnamon
2 teaspoons baking soda
1 1/2 teaspoons salt
1 cup dates, chopped
1 cup pecans, chopped

Glaze
2 cups powdered sugar
1/2 cup fresh Florida orange juice

Preheat oven to 350° F. Grease and flour tube or bundt pan. Mix 2/3 cup water and all cake ingredients until well blended; pour batter into prepared pan. Bake until knife comes out clean, 1 to 1 1/4 hours. Remove from oven. Make glaze: Mix powdered sugar and orange juice together; pour over warm cake.

12 servings.

Preparation Time: 25 Minutes   *Cooking Time: 1 Hour
                                              15 Minutes*

Treasure Tip: When mixing cake batter, scrape the bowl often with a rubber spatula to blend the ingredients thoroughly. If you use a wooden spoon instead of an electric mixer, mix ingredients 150 strokes per minute of beating time.

Fresh Coconut Cream Cheesecake

2¹/₂ cups grated coconut
1 cup whipping cream, scalded

Crust

²/₃ cup flour
5 tablespoons plus 1 teaspoon well-
    chilled butter, cut into ¹/₂-inch
    pieces
4 teaspoons sugar

Filling

20 ounces cream cheese, softened
1¹/₂ cups sugar
4 eggs, plus 2 egg yolks, room
    temperature
2¹/₂ tablespoons coconut liqueur
1 teaspoon fresh lemon juice
¹/₂ teaspoon vanilla extract
¹/₂ teaspoon almond extract

Topping

1 cup sour cream
¹/₄ cup cream of coconut
¹/₂ teaspoon coconut liqueur or
    coconut-flavored rum
Flaked coconut, lightly toasted
    (garnish)

One to 3 days ahead: In blender or food processor purée coconut and scalded cream until finely shredded; cool while preparing crust.

Prepare crust: Preheat oven to 325° F. Lightly grease bottom of 10-inch springform pan. Blend all ingredients until mixture begins to stick together; press evenly into bottom of prepared pan. Bake until golden brown, about 25 minutes. Cool on rack on counter while making filling. Leave oven on.

Prepare filling: In large bowl of electric mixer, at low speed, beat cream cheese with sugar until blended. Mix in cooled coconut mixture; blend in eggs and yolks, one at a time. Mix in remaining ingredients; pour into prepared crust. Return to oven; bake until sides of cake are dry and center no longer moves when shaken, about 1 hour. Let cake cool on rack until depression forms in center, about 35 minutes.

Leave oven on, or turn off and preheat to 325° F. again. Mix topping ingredients; spread atop cake. Bake 10 minutes to set topping; cool completely on rack. Refrigerate until cake is well chilled, about 4 hours. Cover tightly; refrigerate 1 to 3 days to mellow flavors. When ready to serve, remove from pan; spread toasted coconut flakes in 1-inch band around rim.   *12 servings.*

Preparation Time: 1 Hour   Cooking Time: 1 Hour 10 Minutes

Treasure Tip: To toast coconut, preheat oven to 350° F. Spread coconut on a cookie sheet and bake until golden brown. Watch carefully, because it burns quickly.

Harvest Pumpkin Cheesecake

Crust

¼ cup graham cracker crumbs
½ cup pecans, finely chopped
¼ cup light brown sugar, firmly
   packed
¼ cup granulated sugar
½ stick unsalted butter, melted and
   cooled

Filling

32 ounces cream cheese, softened
1½ cups sugar
5 large eggs
¼ cup flour
¼ teaspoon salt
1 (16-ounce) can pumpkin
2 teaspoons cinnamon
2 teaspoons ginger
2 teaspoons nutmeg
1 tablespoon bourbon or bourbon
   liqueur

Topping

2 cups sour cream
¼ cup sugar
1 tablespoon bourbon or bourbon
   liqueur (or to taste)
16 pecan halves (garnish)

Night before, make crust: In medium bowl combine cracker crumbs, pecans and sugars; stir in butter. Press mixture into bottom and ½ inch up side of lightly greased 9-inch springform pan. Chill crust 1 hour.

Make filling: Place cookie sheet on bottom shelf of oven to catch spills. Preheat oven to 325° F. In large bowl of electric mixer, beat cream cheese until fluffy. Gradually add sugar. Add eggs one at a time, beating after each addition. Beat in remaining ingredients; pour into chilled crust. Bake until cheesecake is firm around edges but still soft in center, about 1 ½ hours. Top of cake will crack. Remove from oven; let sit in pan on rack 5 minutes. Leave oven on.

While cake cools, make topping: In medium bowl whisk together sour cream, sugar and bourbon. Spread mixture on top of cheesecake; bake 5 minutes more. Cool cheesecake in pan on rack; cover and refrigerate overnight.

When ready to serve: Remove side of springform pan; garnish top of cheesecake with pecans. ***12 servings.***

Preparation Time: 30 Minutes   ***Cooking Time: 1 Hour***
30 Minutes

Treasure Tip: *Dark and light brown sugars are not interchangeable. Dark brown sugar has a deeper, more intense flavor than light brown. If the recipe merely says "brown sugar," you may use either dark or light.*

Chocolate Butterscotch Squares

2 sticks butter (no substitute)
16 ounces dark brown sugar
4 eggs, beaten
½ cup, plus 1 tablespoon, flour
1 teaspoon baking powder
1 teaspoon salt
2 teaspoons vanilla extract
1 (12-ounce) package semi-sweet
    chocolate chips
1 cup pecans, chopped
Whipped cream (garnish)

Preheat oven to 350° F. In saucepan over low heat melt butter; add brown sugar. Cook, stirring frequently, until sugar melts; cool. Add eggs; mix well. Add flour, baking powder and salt; mix well. Fold in vanilla, chocolate chips and pecans. Lightly grease 9 x 13-inch metal pan; pour in batter. Bake 40 to 45 minutes. Serve warm, topped with whipped cream; or cool, cut into 1½-inch squares. This is an old family recipe that has been kept secret until now!   **10 to 12 servings.**

Preparation Time: 10 Minutes   **Cooking Time: 40 to 45 Minutes**

Treasure Tip: *Butterscotch is the flavor produced when brown sugar and butter are cooked together. For authentic flavor, butter must be used.*

Chocoholic Cookies

1½ cups semi-sweet chocolate
    chips, divided
½ stick butter, softened
¾ cup sugar
1 egg
1½ teaspoons vanilla extract
½ cup flour
½ teaspoon salt
¼ teaspoon baking powder
½ cup pecans or macadamia nuts,
    chopped

Preheat oven to 350° F. Melt 1 cup chocolate chips in small saucepan over low heat, or in microwave oven 2 to 3 minutes at low power; cool. In medium bowl of electric mixer, cream butter and sugar; add egg and vanilla; beat well; blend in chocolate. In separate bowl, stir together flour, salt and baking powder; add to creamed mixture, mixing well. Stir in nuts and remaining chocolate chips. Drop dough from teaspoon onto lightly greased cookie sheet, spacing 2 inches apart. Bake 8 to 10 minutes.

Makes 36.

Preparation Time: 25 Minutes   **Cooking Time: 8 to 10 Minutes**

Mint Julep Cloud Cookies

2 egg whites
3/4 cup sugar
1/2 teaspoon peppermint extract
2 drops green food coloring
6 ounces semi-sweet chocolate
   chips

Night before, or at least 6½ hours before serving: Preheat oven to 325° F. In small bowl of electric mixer, beat egg whites until stiff; gradually add sugar. Add peppermint and food coloring; beat 30 seconds; stir in chocolate chips. Drop by teaspoon 1 inch apart onto ungreased cookie sheet. Place in oven; immediately turn oven off. Leave cookies in oven overnight or at least 6 hours. Remove from cookie sheet with metal spatula.

Makes 48.

Preparation Time: 10 Minutes   *Cooking Time: 6 Hours or Overnight*

Chocolate Kiss Surprises

1 stick butter, softened
1½ cups powdered sugar, divided
1/2 teaspoon vanilla extract
1/4 teaspoon salt
1¼ cups flour
3/4 cup cashew nuts, finely chopped
24 chocolate kisses, unwrapped

Preheat oven to 375° F. Place rack in center of oven. In medium bowl of electric mixer, cream butter until fluffy; add ½ cup powdered sugar. Using wooden spoon, stir in vanilla and salt. Stir in flour and cashews just until blended. Press scant teaspoonful of dough into your palm. Use thumb of other hand to shape dough into flat disk; place chocolate kiss in center. Bring edges of dough up to cover chocolate kiss completely. Gently roll dough between your palms to form ball; place on ungreased cookie sheet.

Continue making cookies, placing them 1 inch apart on sheet. Bake just until they begin to brown, 10 to 12 minutes. Sift remaining powdered sugar into large bowl; place hot cookies in sugar; roll gently to coat. Cool cookies completely; roll again in powdered sugar. Store in airtight container. *Makes 24.*

Preparation Time: 20 Minutes   Cooking Time: 10 to 12 Minutes

Café con Leche Brownies

Brownies

2 tablespoons instant espresso powder
8 ounces best-quality bittersweet chocolate, chopped
1½ sticks unsalted butter, cut into pieces
1½ cups sugar
2 teaspoons vanilla extract
4 large eggs
1 cup flour
½ teaspoon salt
1 cup walnuts or pecans, chopped

Frosting

8 ounces cream cheese, softened
¾ stick unsalted butter, softened
1½ cups sifted powdered sugar
1 teaspoon vanilla extract
1 teaspoon cinnamon

Glaze

1½ tablespoons instant espresso powder
6 ounces best-quality bittersweet chocolate
2 tablespoons unsalted butter
½ cup heavy cream

Night before, or at least 5 hours before serving, make brownies: Preheat oven to 350° F. Dissolve espresso powder in 1 tablespoon boiling water. In top of double boiler, over barely simmering water, melt chocolate with butter and espresso mixture, stirring until smooth. Remove from heat; cool to lukewarm. Stir in sugar and vanilla. Stir in eggs, one at a time, stirring well after each addition. Add flour and salt; stir just until combined; stir in walnuts. Lightly grease and flour 13 x 9-inch baking pan. Pour brownie mixture into pan; smooth top; bake until toothpick comes out with crumbs stuck to it, 22 to 25 minutes. Cool completely in pan on rack.

Make frosting: Place cream cheese and butter in small bowl of electric mixer; cream until light and fluffy. Add remaining ingredients; beat until well combined. Spread evenly over brownie layer; chill until frosting is firm, about 1 hour.

Make glaze: Dissolve espresso powder in 1 tablespoon boiling water. In top of double boiler, over barely simmering water, melt all ingredients, stirring until smooth. Remove from heat; cool to room temperature. Carefully spread over frosting. Chill brownies, covered, at least 3 hours or overnight. Cut brownies with sharp knife while cold; serve cold or at room temperature. Store, covered, in refrigerator up to 3 days. ***Makes about 24.***

Preparation Time: 40 Minutes   Cooking Time: 22 to 25 Minutes

Treasure Tip: *When melting chocolate in a double boiler, be sure to stir constantly and keep the water in the bottom under the boiling point. If any steam or water mixes with the chocolate, it will become stiff and grainy.*

Wright's Cream Cheese Brownies

Famous brownies from Wright's Gourmet House

Brownies

6 ounces chocolate chips
³/₄ stick butter
4 eggs
1½ cups sugar
1 cup flour
1 teaspoon baking powder
½ teaspoon vanilla extract

Topping

½ stick butter, softened
8 ounces cream cheese, softened
½ cup sugar
2 eggs
1 tablespoon flour
1 cup pecans, chopped

Preheat oven to 350° F. Lightly grease 13 x 9-inch baking pan. In saucepan melt chocolate chips and butter over medium heat, stirring constantly. Set aside; cool. While mixture cools, make topping: Cream butter and cream cheese together; add sugar, eggs and flour; beat until fluffy. Set aside.

When chocolate mixture has cooled to the touch, 10 to 15 minutes, finish brownie base. Beat eggs; add sugar; mix. Add flour, baking powder and vanilla; mix. Add chocolate mixture; mix, but do not overbeat. Pour batter into prepared pan. Pour cream cheese mixture over batter; swirl with knife edge to make marbled effect. Sprinkle pecans over top. Bake 45 to 50 minutes; cool; cut into squares; serve. **Makes 24.**

Preparation Time: 30 Minutes   Cooking Time: 45 to 50 Minutes

Treasure Tip: *For moist brownies, always let melted chocolate cool before adding to other ingredients. If the chocolate is still hot, it will partially cook the eggs. Always use a heavy pan to melt chocolate. Since chocolate scorches easily, keep the heat low, and stir constantly while melting.*

Toffee Diamonds

2 sticks butter
1 cup brown sugar
1 egg yolk
1 cup flour
6 (1.55-ounce) Hershey bars
²/₃ cup pecans, chopped

Preheat oven to 350° F. Line jelly roll pan (15½ x 10½ x 1⅛ inches) with aluminum foil; grease foil very heavily. Cream butter, sugar, egg yolk and flour together. Using spatula, spread mixture over foil (layer will be very thin and will spread as it cooks). Bake until golden brown, 15 to 20 minutes.

While crust bakes, unwrap Hershey bars; lay them on crust as soon as you take it from oven. Quickly spread chocolate layer with spatula; sprinkle nuts on top. While hot, cut into diamond shapes; leave on pan. Refrigerate to cool thoroughly; then remove foil; break cookies into diamonds at cut marks.

15 servings.

Preparation Time: 10 Minutes   Cooking Time: 15 to 20 Minutes

Orange-Laced Chocolate Swirls

2 sticks unsalted butter, softened
1 cup sugar
2 cups flour
2 teaspoons fresh orange rind, grated
1 tablespoon unsweetened cocoa powder

About 1 hour before baking: In large bowl of electric mixer cream butter and sugar until light and fluffy; add flour; beat until dough forms. Transfer half of dough into small bowl. Stir orange rind into half of dough; stir cocoa into other half. Roll out orange dough into 12 x 7-inch rectangle between two sheets of waxed paper; remove top sheet of paper.

Between two more sheets of waxed paper roll out chocolate dough into 11 x 6-inch rectangle; discard top sheet of paper; invert chocolate dough onto orange dough. Discard top sheet of paper. Using bottom sheet as guide, with long side facing you, roll doughs together like a jelly roll, making a 13½-inch long log. Wrap log in waxed paper; chill 45 minutes.

When ready to bake: Preheat oven to 350° F. Cut log crosswise into ¼-inch-thick rounds; arrange rounds 1 inch apart on lightly greased baking sheets. Bake in batches in middle of oven until pale golden, about 10 to 15 minutes. Cool on racks.

Makes about 50.

Preparation Time: 30 Minutes   Cooking Time: 10 to 15 Minutes

Melt-in-Your Mouth Oatmeal Cookies

2 sticks butter or margarine
1 cup brown sugar
1 cup granulated sugar
2 eggs
1 teaspoon salt
1 teaspoon vanilla extract
1 teaspoon baking soda
3 cups oatmeal
1½ cups flour
1 cup raisins
1 cup walnuts or pecans, chopped

Preheat oven to 375° F. In large bowl of electric mixer, cream butter and sugars until fluffy. Add eggs, salt, vanilla and baking soda; mix. Mix oatmeal and flour in separate bowl; add to creamed mixture. Add raisins and nuts; mix with large spoon. Drop by teaspoonfuls onto ungreased cookie sheet. Bake until golden brown, 10 to 15 minutes; cool on racks. *Makes 48 to 54.*

Preparation Time: 20 Minutes   Cooking Time: 10 to 15 Minutes

Treasure Tip: When making cookies, always check them 2 to 3 minutes before the recipe says they'll be done. Ovens vary, and different baking sheets affect results. If you like cookies chewy and slightly soft, keep them in the oven for a shorter time than called for in the recipe. Leave them in longer if you want them to be very crisp.

Pecan Pumpkin Squares

2½ cups flour
1½ teaspoons baking powder
¾ teaspoon cinnamon
½ teaspoon freshly grated nutmeg
½ teaspoon ground cloves
½ teaspoon salt
2 sticks plus 2 tablespoons
    unsalted butter, softened
2 cups light brown sugar, firmly
    packed
2 large eggs
1 cup canned pumpkin
1 teaspoon vanilla extract
8 ounces pitted dried dates, cut
    into thirds (about 1 cup)
1½ cups pecans, chopped

Preheat oven to 350° F. Sift flour, baking powder, cinnamon, nutmeg, cloves and salt into bowl. In large bowl of electric mixer, cream butter and sugar until light and fluffy. Add eggs, one at a time, beating after each addition. Beat in pumpkin, vanilla and ¼ cup water. Place dates in small bowl; toss with ¼ cup flour mixture until well coated.

Gradually add remaining flour mixture to pumpkin mixture, beating slowly. Stir in date mixture and pecans, stirring until well combined. Pour into greased 13 x 9 x 2-inch baking pan; bake until toothpick comes out clean, 45 to 60 minutes. Cool on rack; cut into 12 squares. *Makes 12.*

Preparation Time: 30 Minutes   Cooking Time: 45 to 60 Minutes

Treasure Tip: Double-acting baking powder is the most common type in today's supermarkets. It acts twice—when it is first mixed and again when the oven's heat releases the full force of the leavening gases.

French Sugar Cookies

2 sticks butter, softened
2 cups sugar
2 eggs
1 teaspoon vanilla extract
3½ cups flour
1 teaspoon baking soda
½ teaspoon salt

1 to 2 hours before baking: Cream butter in large bowl of electric mixer until light and fluffy; gradually add sugar, then eggs, mixing well. Add vanilla. Mix flour, baking soda and salt; add to creamed mixture 1 cup at a time. Batter will be stiff. Chill 1 to 2 hours.

When ready to bake: Preheat oven to 350 ° F. On well-floured surface, roll part of dough to ¼-inch thickness. Cut with cookie cutters into desired shapes; bake until edges just begin to brown, 5 to 10 minutes. Repeat until all dough is used. (Note: If desired, brush with beaten egg and sprinkle with colored sugar before baking.) *Makes 72.*

Preparation Time: 15 Minutes   Cooking Time: 5 to 10 Minutes

Deep South Praline Cookies

1 cup sugar
1½ cups pecan halves
2 sticks unsalted butter, softened
⅔ cup dark brown sugar, firmly
    packed
1 large egg
¼ teaspoon almond extract
2¼ cups flour
1 teaspoon baking soda
1 teaspoon salt

To make Praline: In heavy saucepan combine sugar and ⅓ cup water; place over moderately high heat; stir to dissolve sugar. Bring to boil, stirring. Boil, without stirring, until mixture begins to turn golden. Swirl pan and boil syrup until syrup turns deep caramel in color. Stir in pecans; pour immediately onto lightly greased foil, spreading pecans in single layer. Let praline cool completely; peel off foil. Grind praline coarsely in food processor.

Make cookies: Preheat oven to 350° F. In large bowl of electric mixer cream together butter and brown sugar. Add egg and almond extract; beat until smooth. Sift remaining ingredients into butter mixture; add praline; stir until thoroughly combined. Drop rounded teaspoons of batter 2 inches apart onto well-greased baking sheets. Bake cookies in middle of oven until golden, 12 to 15 minutes. Cool on baking sheets until easily removed, about 5 minutes; transfer to racks; cool completely. Store cookies in airtight container up to 1 week.

Makes about 50.

Preparation Time: 40 Minutes   Cooking Time: 12 to 15 Minutes

Guava Butter Cookies

1 stick butter or margarine,
    softened
¼ cup light brown sugar, firmly
    packed
1 egg, separated
1 teaspoon vanilla extract
1 cup sifted flour
1 cup walnuts or pecans, finely
    chopped
Guava jelly

About 45 minutes before baking: In small bowl of electric mixer beat butter, sugar, egg yolk and vanilla until smooth; stir in flour until combined. Refrigerate 30 minutes. Preheat oven to 375° F. Roll dough into balls 1 inch in diameter. Beat egg white slightly. Dip balls in egg white; roll in walnuts. Place 1 inch apart on ungreased cookie sheet. With thumb make indentation in center of each cookie. Bake until delicate golden brown, 10 to 12 minutes. Remove from oven; cool on rack. When cool, place a little jelly in indentation of each cookie.   *Makes 24.*

Preparation Time: 20 Minutes   Cooking Time: 10 to 12 Minutes

Creamy Grapefruit Pie

10 (2½-inch) oatmeal cookies,
  finely crushed (1 ⅔ cups)
½ cup plus 3 tablespoons sugar,
  divided
½ stick butter or margarine, melted
½ cup milk
½ cup grapefruit juice concentrate,
  undiluted
1 pint vanilla ice cream, softened
1 fresh grapefruit, sectioned
  (garnish)

At least 4½ hours before serving: Combine cookie crumbs and 3 tablespoons sugar; stir in melted butter. Press into bottom and up sides of 9-inch pie plate; place in freezer to chill. In small bowl of electric mixer beat milk and ½ cup sugar at medium to low speed to dissolve sugar, about 2 minutes. Add juice; mix well; add ice cream by spoonfuls; beat on low speed until blended. Pour into prepared crust. Freeze until firm, at least 4 hours.

Before serving: Peel, section and seed grapefruit; garnish pie with grapefruit sections. ***8 servings.***

Preparation Time: 15 Minutes

Chocolate Angel Pie

Meringue Shell

2 egg whites
⅛ teaspoon salt
⅛ teaspoon cream of tartar
½ cup sugar
½ cup pecans, chopped
½ teaspoon vanilla extract

Chocolate Filling

8 ounces semi-sweet chocolate, or 8
  ounces chocolate chips
1 cup whipping cream
1 teaspoon vanilla extract

At least 4 hours before serving, make meringue shell: Preheat oven to 300° F. In small bowl of electric mixer, beat egg whites until foamy. Add salt and cream of tartar; beat until soft peaks form. Gradually add sugar; continue beating until stiff. Fold in nuts and vanilla. Turn into lightly greased 8- or 9-inch pie pan. Make nest-like shell, building sides up ½ inch above top of pan. Bake until light brown, 50 to 55 minutes; cool.

Make filling: Melt chocolate with 3 tablespoons water in saucepan over low heat; cool until thickened. Whip cream until stiff. Add vanilla to cooled chocolate mixture; fold in whipped cream. Turn into cooled meringue shell; chill until firm, about 2 hours. ***8 to 10 servings.***

Preparation Time: 30 Minutes   Cooking Time: 50 to 55 Minutes

Chocolate Coconut Pie

Crust

1 stick butter, softened
1 (7-ounce) bag flaked coconut

Filling

2 sticks butter, softened
1 cup sugar
3 ounces unsweetened chocolate
3 eggs, room temperature
1 teaspoon vanilla extract
2 tablespoons (or less) brandy or
    bourbon
1 cup lightly toasted walnuts,
    chopped

Topping

1 cup whipping cream
2 tablespoons powdered sugar
1 tablespoon brandy or bourbon
    (optional)

Night before, or at least 5½ hours before serving, make crust: Preheat oven to 350 ° F. Combine butter and coconut. Press into pie pan to form "crust" about ¼ inch thick. Bake until evenly brown, 5 to 10 minutes; set aside.

Make filling: In food processor or electric mixer, blend butter and sugar. Melt chocolate in saucepan over low heat; remove from heat. When chocolate is still quite warm (150° F. on candy thermometer), add eggs, one at a time, blending well after each addition. Add vanilla and brandy to chocolate mixture. Pour chocolate mixture into butter mixture; blend; add nuts. Pour filling into crust; chill 5 hours or overnight.

Before serving, make topping: Whip cream with powdered sugar until stiff peaks form. Add brandy, if desired. Spread over pie just before serving.   *10 servings.*

Preparation Time: 20 Minutes   Cooking Time: 10 to 15 Minutes

Key West Brandy Alexander Pie

1 envelope unflavored gelatin
⅔ cup sugar, divided
⅛ teaspoon salt
3 eggs, separated
¼ cup Cognac
¼ cup Crème de Cacao
2 cups whipping cream, divided
1 (9-inch) graham cracker crust
Freshly grated nutmeg

Night before, or several hours before serving: In saucepan sprinkle gelatin over ½ cup cold water; stir to dissolve. Add ⅓ cup sugar, salt and egg yolks; stir to blend. Heat over low heat; stir in Cognac and Crème de Cacao; cool. Refrigerate until partially set. Beat egg whites until stiff; gradually beat in remaining sugar. Fold into gelatin mixture. In separate bowl whip 1 cup cream until stiff; fold into gelatin mixture; turn into crust. Refrigerate several hours or overnight.

Just before serving: Whip remaining cream until stiff; spread over pie. Sprinkle with nutmeg; serve.   *8 servings.*

Preparation Time: 10 Minutes   Cooking Time: 5 Minutes

Treasure Tip: When separating eggs, make sure that none of the yolk enters the bowl with the white. If there is only a small amount of yolk, you may be able to retrieve it by capturing it with the eggshell. If you cannot remove all traces of yolk, start over. The slightest fat from the yolk will lessen the volume of the beaten whites.

Chocolate Pecan Toffee Mousse

From rg's restaurants

Crust

1 pound pecan pieces
½ cup sugar
1 stick unsalted butter, melted

Mousse

28 ounces semi-sweet chocolate
¼ cup vegetable oil
1 quart heavy whipping cream

Toffee Sauce

4 sticks unsalted butter
3½ cups sugar
1 quart heavy cream

Night before, or early in day, make crust: Preheat oven to 325° F. Grind pecans in food processor about 45 seconds; place in medium bowl. Add sugar to melted butter; heat and stir until thick, smooth paste forms. Remove from heat; add ½ cup water, stirring constantly to create syrup. Pour over pecans; mix thoroughly. Butter and flour two 12-inch tart pans. Press pecan mixture into pans; bake until golden brown, about 10 minutes. Remove from oven; cool at room temperature.

Make mousse: Melt chocolate in top of double boiler over hot water; add vegetable oil; stir until mixture is smooth and almost liquid. Whip cream to form soft peaks; add chocolate, stirring constantly (slow speed of hand mixer works fine). When combined, refrigerate 2 hours. Remove from refrigerator; stir by hand to make sure mousse is smooth and without lumps. Spoon into pastry bag; pipe mousse into pecan crusts. Refrigerate.

Make sauce: Melt butter in saucepan over medium to high heat; add sugar. Cook, stirring frequently, until mixture reaches deep caramel color. Don't worry if butter and sugar separate at this point. Remove from heat; add heavy cream, stirring constantly.

Caution: When adding cream, mixture will bubble up and release very hot steam. The chef suggests using a long-handled whisk or wearing an oven mitt while stirring in cream. After cream is added, pour sauce into container; cool; refrigerate. Reheat before serving.

To serve : Cut each pie into 12 to 16 pieces. Place on individual serving plates; top with 2 tablespoons warm Toffee Sauce.

2 (12-inch) pies, 24 to 32 servings.

Total Preparation and Cooking Time: 1 Hour

Treasure Tip: Chef Michael Bortz of rg's recommends using the very best chocolate to make this dessert, it is well worth the cost! The menu at rg's says this recipe "pays the rent!"

Fresh Peach Pecan Pie

1 cup sugar
3 tablespoons flour
2 tablespoons cornstarch
2 tablespoons butter
3 tablespoons fresh orange juice
1 tablespoon freshly grated orange peel
¼ cup pecans, chopped
2 cups fresh peaches, sliced
1 (9-inch) unbaked pie shell (not deep-dish)

Preheat oven to 450° F. Mix sugar, flour and cornstarch in saucepan; add butter and orange juice. Cook over low heat until thick. Add orange peel, pecans and peaches; place in pie shell. Bake 10 minutes; reduce heat to 325° F.; bake 30 minutes more.

6 to 8 servings.

Preparation Time: 30 Minutes   *Cooking Time: 40 Minutes*

Treasure Tip: A good topping for this pie is whipped cream flavored with a little Grand Marnier.

Rich Butterscotch Pie

¾ cup dark brown sugar, firmly packed
⅓ cup flour
½ teaspoon salt
3 eggs, separated
3 tablespoons butter, softened
1 teaspoon vanilla extract
1 (9-inch) pie shell, baked and cooled
6 tablespoons granulated sugar

Preheat oven to 325° F. Combine brown sugar, flour and salt in top of double boiler. Blend in 2 cups water; cook over simmering water, stirring constantly, until thick and smooth. In small bowl of electric mixer beat egg yolks until thick and lemon-colored. Add small amount of hot mixture to egg yolks; mix well. Add yolks to hot mixture. Cook, stirring constantly, 3 minutes. Remove from heat; add butter and vanilla. Cool slightly; spoon into pie shell.

Make meringue: Wash and dry mixer beaters and small bowl. Place egg whites in bowl; beat until soft peaks form. Continue beating while adding sugar, 1 tablespoon at a time; beat until stiff peaks form. Spread meringue over warm filling, sealing to edge. Bake until meringue is lightly browned, about 15 minutes. Cool before serving.

8 servings.

Preparation Time: 30 Minutes   *Cooking Time: 15 Minutes*

Key Lime White Chocolate Pie

Crust

1¼ cups flour

½ cup graham cracker crumbs, divided

½ cup macadamia nuts, finely chopped, divided

6 tablespoons butter, chilled

2 tablespoons fresh key lime juice, chilled

4 ounces white chocolate

Filling

8 ounces cream cheese, softened

1 cup sweetened condensed milk

3 egg yolks

¾ cup low-fat lime-flavored yogurt, drained

⅓ cup fresh key lime juice

Meringue

½ cup fresh key lime juice

1 cup sugar

3 egg whites, room temperature

About 2 hours before serving, make crust: Combine flour, ¼ cup graham cracker crumbs and ¼ cup nuts in mixing bowl. Cut in butter with pastry blender or two knives until mixture is uniform. In separate bowl combine lime juice and ¼ cup cold water; sprinkle over flour mixture, 1 tablespoon at a time, until dough forms a ball.

Sprinkle remaining graham cracker crumbs onto waxed paper or breadboard. Roll crust into circle ⅛-inch thick and 1½ inches larger than inverted pie plate. Gently ease dough into pie plate, being careful not to stretch dough. Trim edge even with pie plate; flute. Prick entire shell with fork or toothpick. Sprinkle remaining nuts into shell. Chill 1 hour.

Preheat oven to 375 ° F.; bake crust 15 to 20 minutes; cool completely. When crust is cool, melt chocolate in small saucepan over low heat; drizzle chocolate over bottom of cooled crust.

Make filling: Beat cream cheese and condensed milk together until smooth. Add egg yolks, one at a time, mixing well after each addition. Slowly stir in yogurt and lime juice. Spoon mixture into crust; chill while making meringue.

Make meringue: Preheat oven to 375° F. Combine lime juice and sugar in 2-quart saucepan. Cook to soft ball stage over medium heat, stirring often. (Use candy thermometer to determine soft ball stage, or drop a little syrup into cold water to see if soft ball forms.)

In small bowl of electric mixer, beat egg whites until soft peaks form. Continue beating; pour hot syrup over egg whites; beat at medium speed until glossy, stiff peaks form. Spread meringue on top of pie, sealing to edges. Bake until meringue is lightly browned, about 10 minutes. **6 to 8 servings.**

Preparation Time: 45 Minutes   *Cooking Time: 30 Minutes*

Palma Ceia Margarita Pie

Crust

1 cup pretzel crumbs
⅓ cup butter, melted
3 tablespoons sugar

Filling

1 envelope unflavored gelatin
½ cup fresh lime or lemon juice
4 eggs, separated
1 cup sugar, divided
¼ teaspoon salt
1 teaspoon freshly grated lime or
*   lemon peel*
⅓ cup tequila
3 tablespoons Triple Sec
Fresh lime slices (garnish)

Early in day: Thoroughly combine all crust ingredients; press into greased 9-inch pie pan; chill thoroughly. Soften gelatin in lime juice. Beat egg yolks in top of double boiler; blend in ½ cup sugar, salt and lime peel. Add softened gelatin; cook over boiling water, stirring constantly, until slightly thickened and gelatin is completely dissolved. Pour into mixing bowl; stir in tequila and Triple Sec. Cool thoroughly, but do not let mixture thicken.

In small bowl of electric mixer, beat egg whites until foamy. Gradually add remaining sugar; continue beating until soft peaks form. Gently fold egg whites into cooked mixture. Let mixture set slightly; swirl into chilled pie shell. Garnish, if desired, with fresh lime slices. Chill until set; serve.   *8 servings.*

Preparation and Cooking Time: 40 Minutes

Treasure Tip: When making pies with crumb crusts, you can vary the flavor by adding finely ground walnuts, pecans or almonds to the crumbs. As an alternative, add a teaspoon or two of brandy, rum or fruit liqueur.

Grand Marnier Strawberry Pie

3 pints strawberries, washed, dried
*   and hulled*
1 10-inch pie shell, baked
½ cup sugar
2½ tablespoons cornstarch
¼ cup Grand Marnier
Whipped cream, flavored to taste
*   with sugar or Grand Marnier*

At least 3 hours before serving: Select nicest looking strawberries; stand up one-half to two-thirds of berries in pie shell, fitting in as many as possible. Place remaining berries in saucepan. If berries are very large, cut them up first. Mash strawberries. Bring to boil over medium to high heat. Mix sugar and cornstarch; add to berries with Grand Marnier.

Cook, stirring constantly, until clear and thick, lowering heat, if necessary, to prevent sticking. Pour syrup over berries in pie shell, coating all berries and filling in spaces in between. Refrigerate at least 2 hours. Top with flavored whipped cream before serving.   *10 servings.*

Preparation Time: 30 Minutes   *Cooking Time: 5 to 10 Minutes*

Florida Mango Pie

2 (9-inch) pie shells
1 cup brown sugar
3 tablespoons cornstarch
3 large, firm, ripe mangoes, peeled
  and sliced
1 tablespoon butter or margarine
1 teaspoon cinnamon

Preheat oven to 450° F. Place bottom crust in pie pan. Mix brown sugar and cornstarch. Place layer of mango slices in pie shell; sprinkle with brown sugar mixture. Continue layering to top of pan, 3 to 5 layers. Dot with butter; sprinkle with cinnamon. Cover with top crust; cut 3 to 4 slits in crust to vent. Bake 10 minutes; reduce heat to 350° F. Bake until crust starts to turn golden brown, about 40 minutes. This tastes similar to peach pie.   *8 servings.*

Preparation Time: 10 Minutes   *Cooking Time: 40 Minutes*

Chocolate Peanut Butter Pie

1 cup graham cracker crumbs
³/₄ cup lightly salted peanuts,
  coarsely chopped
³/₄ stick butter, melted
¹/₄ cup sugar
6 ounces semi-sweet chocolate
3 ounces sour cream, room
  temperature
4 ounces cream cheese, softened
1 cup sifted powdered sugar
1³/₄ cups heavy cream, divided
1 cup smooth peanut butter
2 tablespoons vanilla extract

Night before: Preheat oven to 450° F. Combine crumbs, peanuts, sugar and butter; press into 9-inch pie pan or springform pan. Bake 7 minutes; cool. Melt chocolate in top of double boiler over warm water; thoroughly beat in sour cream. Pour chocolate mixture into crust; smooth; chill. Beat cream cheese and powdered sugar until light and fluffy. Add ¹/₄ cup cream, peanut butter and vanilla, combining well.

In chilled bowl with clean beaters, beat remaining cream until soft peaks form. Stir one-third of cream into peanut butter mixture; gently, but thoroughly, fold in remaining cream. Fill pie shell; refrigerate overnight. Serve chilled.   *6 to 8 servings.*

Preparation Time: 45 Minutes   *Cooking Time: 7 Minutes*

Peerless Pumpkin Chiffon Pie

1 cup brown sugar
3 egg yolks
1½ cups canned pumpkin
½ cup milk
½ teaspoon salt
2 teaspoons cinnamon
½ teaspoon ground ginger
¼ teaspoon allspice
1 tablespoon gelatin
3 egg whites
3 tablespoons sugar
1 (9-inch) pie shell, baked and
    cooled

In saucepan combine brown sugar, egg yolks, pumpkin, milk, salt, cinnamon, ginger and allspice; cook over medium heat until thickened. Soften gelatin in ¼ cup cold water; add to pumpkin mixture; combine well. Place in refrigerator to cool. Beat egg whites and sugar until stiff peaks form. When pumpkin mixture begins to set, fold in egg whites. Pour into pie shell; chill until firm.   *8 servings.*

Preparation and Cooking Time: 20 Minutes

Treasure Tip: One tablespoon of gelatin can turn about 2 cups of liquid into a solid. To soften gelatin, sprinkle it over the liquid and let it soak for about 3 minutes until it absorbs the moisture and becomes translucent.

Southern Maple Sweet Potato Pie

3 extra-large eggs, plus 1 egg yolk,
    plus 2 egg whites
½ cup light brown sugar, firmly
    packed
2 tablespoons unsalted butter,
    melted
1 teaspoon vanilla extract
4½ teaspoons pure maple syrup
1½ cups pecan pieces
1 (10-inch) pie shell, unbaked
2½ cups fresh sweet potatoes,
    peeled, cubed
¼ teaspoon ground ginger
¼ teaspoon cinnamon
Pinch ground cloves
⅓ cup sugar
1 cup unsweetened whipped cream

Place sweet potatoes in large saucepan; cover with water; bring to boil over medium heat. Cook until tender, about 15 minutes; drain. Add ginger, cinnamon and cloves; whip until almost smooth. Mashed sweet potatoes should measure about 1½ cups. Refrigerate 20 minutes. Preheat oven to 350° F. In medium bowl combine whole eggs, egg yolk and brown sugar; stir until sugar dissolves and mixture is smooth. Add butter, vanilla and syrup; blend well. Sprinkle pecans evenly over pie shell; pour filling into shell. Bake until golden brown, about 30 minutes; cool to room temperature.

In large bowl, beat egg whites until frothy; gradually add sugar; continue beating until stiff peaks form. Fold into cooled sweet potato mixture. Gently spoon sweet potatoes on top of mixture in pie shell; smooth surface with spatula. Bake at 350° F. until filling is firm, about 20 minutes. Cool. Serve cold, garnished with whipped cream.

8 to 10 servings.

Preparation Time: 45 Minutes   *Cooking Time: 1 Hour*
                                              10 Minutes

Treasure Tip: For tender sweet potatoes, buy small to medium ones. Make sure that the skin is firm, with no bruises. For easy peeling, choose potatoes that are rounded, not curved and twisted.

Shaum Torte

Torte

4 egg whites, room temperature
¼ teaspoon cream of tartar
¼ teaspoon salt
1 ¼ cups sugar
1 teaspoon white or cider vinegar
1 teaspoon vanilla extract

Topping

Vanilla ice cream
Fresh strawberries, raspberries or
　peaches (optional)
Chocolate sauce (optional)

Preheat oven to 250° F. In small bowl of electric mixer beat egg whites, cream of tartar and salt until very stiff. Add sugar, 1 tablespoon at a time, beating constantly. Add vinegar and vanilla, a drop at a time; beat until mixture mounds well.

Lightly grease cookie sheet or line with parchment paper or good-quality brown paper. Mound meringue mixture onto cookie sheet in serving-size circles, or make one large, pie-shaped circle. Shape so that there is a rim and a center well. Bake 1 hour. Cool on cookie sheet; carefully remove with metal spatula.

Fill centers with ice cream; top with fresh fruit or chocolate sauce. To serve, cut large torte into wedges. Store meringues in an airtight container. **8 servings.**

Preparation Time: 20 Minutes　　　　**Cooking Time: 1 Hour**

Creamy White Chocolate Mousse

6 ounces white chocolate, finely
    chopped
1 envelope unflavored gelatin
2 egg yolks
1/2 cup plus 1 tablespoon sugar,
    divided
2 1/4 cups heavy cream, cold, divided
1 1/2 tablespoons unsalted butter
12 ounces semi-sweet chocolate,
    finely chopped
2 teaspoons Grand Marnier, or
    other orange-flavored liqueur
Raspberry or caramel sauce
    (optional)
Chocolate curls or thin chocolate
    squares (garnish)

Early in day: Melt white chocolate, stirring constantly, in top of double boiler over simmering water. Remove from heat; cool to tepid. In small saucepan sprinkle gelatin over 2 tablespoons water; let stand until softened, about 5 minutes. Heat over very low heat, stirring constantly, until gelatin is dissolved. Cool to lukewarm; do not let it congeal.

With electric mixer at medium speed, beat egg yolks and 6 tablespoons sugar until pale yellow and tripled in bulk, about 5 minutes. Stir large spoonful of yolk mixture into gelatin until blended; drizzle gelatin mixture back into remaining yolk mixture, beating constantly. Add white chocolate, one-third at a time, to egg mixture, beating at low speed.

In separate bowl, whip 1½ cups heavy cream until stiff peaks form; fold one-fourth of cream into chocolate mixture to lighten; gently fold in remaining cream. Pour mixture into 6-cup dome-shaped mold; refrigerate until firm, about 2 hours.

Make dark chocolate layer: Heat remaining heavy cream, remaining sugar and butter over low heat to simmering. Remove from heat; add semi-sweet chocolate; stir. Cool in refrigerator until tepid and rather firm, about 1 hour. Remove from refrigerator; beat in Grand Marnier until soft and smooth. Spread over mixture in mold; refrigerate until set, 30 to 45 minutes.

To serve: Unmold by dipping into lukewarm water 5 seconds, repeating if necessary; loosen sides with knife. If desired, spread raspberry or caramel sauce on serving platter; unmold mousse on top of sauce. Decorate mousse with chocolate curls or thin chocolate squares. ***8 servings.***

Preparation and Cooking Time: 1 Hour

Dark Chocolate Mousse

2 cups half-and-half
1 (12-ounce) bag chocolate chips
3 egg yolks
Splash of rum, brandy or vanilla
    extract
Whipped cream and grated
    chocolate (optional)

2½ hours before serving: Scald half-and-half. Place chocolate chips, egg yolks and rum in blender or food processor; add half-and-half; blend until smooth. Pour into dessert glasses; chill until firm, about 2 hours. Garnish, if desired, with whipped cream and grated chocolate. ***6 servings.***

Preparation and Cooking Time: 10 Minutes

Chocolate Toffee Trifle

1 (18.25-ounce) box devil's food
    cake mix
1 (3.9-ounce) package instant
    chocolate pudding mix
½ cup Kahlua (optional)
1½ cups milk
6 (1⅛-ounce) Heath bars, frozen,
    wrapped
1 (16-ounce) container whipped
    topping or whipped cream

Night before: Bake cake in 13 x 9-inch baking pan according to package directions. Cool; cut into 1-inch cubes. Pour pudding mix into bowl; add milk and Kahlua; mix well. Leave Heath bars in wrappers; pound with hammer to crush. In very large glass bowl layer, in order: half of cake cubes, half of pudding mixture, half of whipped topping and half of Heath bars; repeat layers. Cover with plastic wrap; refrigerate overnight.

12 to 14 servings.

Preparation and Cooking Time: 45 to 50 Minutes

Flan de Leche (Spanish Custard)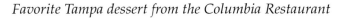

Favorite Tampa dessert from the Columbia Restaurant

3 cups sugar, divided
6 eggs
1 teaspoon vanilla extract
¼ scant teaspoon anisette
Pinch salt
2 cups boiling milk

Early in day: Preheat oven to 350° F. Boil 1 cup sugar and ½ cup water until brown; pour into six custard cups. Beat eggs; add 2 cups sugar, vanilla, anisette and salt; beat again. Gradually add boiling milk, mixing well. Strain through cloth or china colander. Divide mixture among custard cups; put cups in pan filled with water; bake 30 minutes. Do not let water boil, or custard will be filled with holes. Cool in refrigerator.

When ready to serve: Press edges of custard with spoon to break away from mold; turn upside down on individual serving plate.

6 servings.

Preparation Time: 20 Minutes   *Cooking Time: 30 Minutes*

Flan de Leche Nuevo

*½ to 1 cup plus 2 tablespoons
   sugar, divided
1 (14 ½-ounce) can sweetened
   condensed milk
5 eggs
Dash salt
1 cup plain milk
1 cup evaporated milk
¼ cup sherry
1 tablespoon vanilla extract*

Day before, or up to 2 hours before serving: Preheat oven to 350° F. Caramelize 1 cup sugar by placing in 10-inch flan pan or 1½-quart casserole dish. Sprinkle with water; place in oven until sugar starts to turn dark brown. (Or use microwave: Place ½ cup sugar and ½ cup water in 1-pint glass measuring cup; stir well. Microwave on high 10 to 12 minutes, until a light but rich brown. Syrup continues to cook after microwaving, so don't let it get too dark before taking from oven.) Pour syrup into 1½-quart casserole; quickly rotate casserole to coat bottom and about halfway up sides with caramel. Let cool to harden before adding custard.

Combine condensed milk, eggs, 2 tablespoons sugar and salt in blender or food processor; blend. Add plain and evaporated milks, sherry and vanilla. Pour over caramelized sugar; place in larger pan of water. Bake 1 to 1¼ hours, removing when toothpick inserted in center comes out clean. Turn out on plate; cover; store in refrigerator. Serve warm or chilled.   *8 servings.*

Preparation Time: 20 Minutes Cooking Time: 1 Hour 15 Minutes

Southern Strawberry Shortcake

*4 cups strawberries, sliced
Sugar to taste
2 cups flour, sifted
2 teaspoons baking powder
1 teaspoon salt
5 tablespoons butter
½ cup milk
1 cup whipping cream*

Early in day, or 4 hours before serving: Wash, hull and slice strawberries; place in bowl. Sprinkle with sugar; set aside at room temperature to let juice form.

When ready to make biscuits: Sift flour, baking powder and salt into mixing bowl. With pastry blender, cut in butter until coarse and grainy; stir in milk. Form dough into ball; roll out ½-inch thick on lightly floured board. Cut into six 3-inch rounds; place on ungreased baking sheet; bake 15 minutes. Split warm biscuits. Whip cream until stiff. Place some of berries and juice on bottom half of each biscuit; cover with top half of biscuit, more berries and whipped cream; serve.   *6 servings.*

Preparation Time: 20 Minutes   Cooking Time: 15 Minutes

Classic Banana Pudding

3 eggs, separated
1 cup plus 3 tablespoons sugar,
   divided
3 tablespoons flour
Dash vanilla extract
1 cup milk
4 ripe bananas, peeled and sliced
40 vanilla wafers

In small bowl of electric mixer beat egg yolks until thick and lemon-colored. Mix 1 cup sugar and flour; slowly add to yolks; add vanilla. In skillet, over medium heat, warm milk until almost boiling; stir in yolk mixture. Cook, stirring, until thickened. Remove from heat; cool. In 1½-quart casserole layer, in order, some of pudding, bananas and vanilla wafers; repeat layers until all are used. In small bowl of electric mixer, beat egg whites with 3 tablespoons sugar until stiff peaks form. Spread meringue on top of pudding; broil or bake in 450° F. oven briefly to brown meringue. Serve.   **6 servings.**

Preparation Time: 15 Minutes   *Cooking Time: 5 to 10 Minutes*

Ginger Soufflé à L' Orange

Soufflé

½ stick butter or margarine
¼ cup flour
¼ teaspoon salt
¼ teaspoon ground ginger
1 cup milk
4 eggs, separated
1 teaspoon vanilla extract
2 tablespoons candied ginger,
   finely diced
¼ teaspoon cream of tartar
⅓ cup sugar

Orange Sauce

½ cup sugar
4 teaspoons cornstarch
Dash salt
½ teaspoon orange peel, freshly
   grated
½ teaspoon lemon peel, freshly
   grated
¼ cup fresh orange juice
1 tablespoon fresh lemon juice

About 2 hours before serving: Preheat oven to 325° F. Prepare soufflé dish: Measure waxed paper or foil to go around top of 1-quart soufflé dish with 1-inch overlap. Fold in thirds lengthwise, accordion-style. Extend collar 2 inches above top of dish; fasten with tape or pins. In small saucepan melt butter; blend in flour, salt and ground ginger; add milk. Cook over medium heat, stirring, until mixture thickens and bubbles; remove from heat. Beat egg yolks until thick and lemon-colored; gradually stir hot mixture into yolks, mixing well. Stir in vanilla and candied ginger. Beat egg whites with cream of tartar until soft peaks form; gradually add sugar, beating to stiff peaks. Fold yolk mixture into egg whites; pour into ungreased soufflé dish. Set in shallow pan; pour hot water into pan to 1-inch depth. Place in oven.

Make Orange Sauce: In small saucepan, thoroughly combine sugar, cornstarch and salt. Stir in 1 cup water; bring to boil. Reduce heat to medium; cook, stirring constantly, until thickened. Cool slightly; stir in remaining ingredients; keep warm. Bake soufflé until knife inserted halfway between center and edge comes out clean, about 1¼ hours. Peel off collar; serve immediately with Orange Sauce.   **6 to 8 servings.**

Preparation Time: 30 Minutes   *Cooking Time: 1 Hour*
15 Minutes

Treasure Tip: *The purpose of a collar around a soufflé dish is to hold the soufflé as it rises. Individual soufflés are prepared in ramekins. Since soufflés are served straight from their baking dishes, the dishes are made of attractive materials that withstand high temperatures.*

Pecan Praline Brie with Fruit

From Selena's Restaurant in Hyde Park

1 pound red or green seedless
  grapes, or any seasonal fresh
  fruit
³/₄ cup dark brown sugar
4 teaspoons butter
2 teaspoons light corn syrup
2 ounces pecans, chopped
1 mini Brie cheese wheel (about 1
  pound)

Rinse, drain and divide grapes or fruit into small clusters or pieces; refrigerate. Make praline: Place sugar, butter, corn syrup and 1 tablespoon water in small saucepan; simmer 3 minutes; stir in pecans. Cut Brie into 2-ounce wedges; arrange on round serving platter. Spoon 1 teaspoon praline mixture over each wedge. Garnish each portion with grapes or fruit. Wonderful addition to a buffet table! ***8 servings.***

Preparation Time: 15 Minutes   ***Cooking Time: 3 Minutes***

Strawberry Trifle with Crème Pâtisserie

5 egg yolks
1 cup powdered sugar
1 ¹/₂ tablespoons flour
1 cup milk
¹/₂ teaspoon vanilla extract
1²/₃ cup heavy cream, whipped,
  divided
1 (3-ounce) package soft
  ladyfingers
¹/₄ cup sherry
Raspberry jam
2 cups fresh strawberries, sliced

Make Crème Pâtisserie: In deep saucepan beat egg yolks and powdered sugar until thick and lemon-colored; add flour; blend well. Stir in milk; cook over medium heat until thick and smooth. Cool; add vanilla; fold in ²/₃ cup whipped cream.

Make trifle: Lay ladyfingers flat on work surface; sprinkle with sherry; spread with jam. Arrange one-third of ladyfingers in bottom of glass serving dish; top with one-third of strawberries and one-third of Crème Pâtisserie; repeat layers twice. Top with 1 cup whipped cream. ***Serves 6.***

Preparation and Cooking Time: 30 Minutes

Treasure Tip: *Extra egg whites can be frozen in a jar or an ice cube tray for later use in meringues or angel food cakes.*

Summertime Deep-Dish Peach Cobbler

Pastry

2 cups flour
2 teaspoons sugar
¾ teaspoon salt
1½ sticks butter, chilled
1 small egg
2 teaspoons fresh lemon juice

Filling

1 heaping tablespoon cornstarch
1 cup granulated sugar
¼ cup brown sugar
1 tablespoon fresh lemon juice
8 cups fresh peaches, peeled, sliced
(about 1 dozen medium to large
peaches)

Make crust: In large bowl blend flour, sugar and salt. With pastry blender cut in butter until particles are the size of peas. Beat egg; blend in lemon juice and ¼ cup cold water. Sprinkle over flour mixture, 1 tablespoon at a time, tossing with fork to mix. Form into ball; wrap in plastic wrap or waxed paper; refrigerate.

Make filling: Mix cornstarch and ¾ cup water in medium saucepan; add sugars and lemon juice. Cook over medium heat until thickened. Place peaches in large bowl; pour hot mixture over peaches; stir; set aside. Remove dough from refrigerator. Roll out about two-thirds of dough to ⅛-inch thickness on lightly floured surface. Line deep casserole dish with dough; weight bottom with pie weights or dried beans. Place in cold oven; turn to 375° F. Roll remaining dough to ⅛-inch thickness; with knife, gently cut into ½-inch-wide strips.

Remove dish from oven after 10 minutes; leave oven on. Remove pie weights or beans. Fill pie dish with one-third of peach mixture. Cut 6 to 8 strips of dough the correct length to form a layer of dough over peaches; repeat layers once. Pour remaining peaches and juice into dish; place remaining dough strips on top of cobbler, using warm water to pinch to bottom and side crusts. (There should be enough dough to make lattice design.) Bake at 375° F. 40 minutes; reduce temperature to 300° F. Bake 30 minutes more. If edges start to over-brown, cover with foil strips. Serve warm. ***8 servings.***

Preparation Time: 1 Hour   Cooking Time: 1 Hour 10 Minutes

Refreshing Strawberry Sherbet

3 pints ripe strawberries
2 cups sugar
Juice of 3 oranges
Juice of 3 lemons
⅓ cup Grand Marnier or orange-
flavored liqueur

Night before, or early in day: Wash, drain and hull strawberries. Place in large bowl; add sugar, orange and lemon juices; mix well. Let stand 3 hours. Place mixture in food processor or blender; blend until smooth. Stir in Grand Marnier; place in freezer until edges are about 1-inch thick. Pour into large bowl; beat until smooth. Freeze until firm. ***12 servings.***

Preparation Time: 15 Minutes

Florida Tangerine Ice Cream

½ cup milk
2½ cups heavy cream, divided
⅔ cup sugar
Peel of 4 tangerines, freshly grated,
    divided
4 egg yolks
½ cup fresh tangerine juice
2 teaspoons fresh lemon juice

Early in day: Place milk, ½ cup cream, sugar and half of peel in small saucepan; heat over low heat until sugar dissolves, about 5 minutes. Do not let mixture boil. Cool. In bowl beat egg yolks with cooled milk mixture until combined. Pour into saucepan with remaining cream.

Cook over low heat, stirring constantly with wooden spoon, until thickened to consistency of custard. Eggs will cook if mixture becomes too hot. Strain; add remaining peel. Add tangerine juice and 2 teaspoons lemon juice; whisk together; chill. Pour into ice-cream maker; freeze according to manufacturer's directions.   ***Makes 3 pints.***

Preparation Time: 40 Minutes

Lime Ice Cream

4 eggs
1 cup sugar
1 cup light corn syrup
⅔ cup fresh lime juice
2 teaspoons lime rind, freshly
    grated
2 cups light cream, lightly
    whipped
3 cups heavy cream, lightly
    whipped

Early in day: Place eggs and sugar in large bowl of electric mixer; beat until lemon-colored. Add corn syrup, lime juice and rind and cream. Mix well. Pour into ice-cream maker; freeze according to manufacturer's instructions.   ***Makes ½ gallon.***

Preparation Time: 10 Minutes

Mango Ice Cream

Mango Purée
2 large ripe mangoes, peeled and
   cubed (about 1½ cups)
3 tablespoons fresh lemon juice
2 tablespoons sugar

Ice Cream
1 egg, plus 2 egg yolks
⅓ cup sugar
½ cup milk
1 cup heavy cream

Make mango purée: Combine all ingredients in glass or china bowl; let sit 2 hours. Purée in food processor or blender; strain to remove any fibers. Use at once or freeze. Frozen mango purée can be used to make drinks, pies and ice cream all year long.

When ready to make ice cream: In large bowl of electric mixer, beat eggs and egg yolks at high speed until light and fluffy. Gradually add sugar; lower speed; add milk, cream and mango purée; mix well; chill. Pour chilled mixture into ice-cream maker; freeze according to manufacturer's instructions.
Makes about 1 quart.

Preparation Time: 30 Minutes

Chocolate-Coconut Orange Shells

4 Florida navel oranges, or other
   seedless oranges
2 tablespoons miniature semi-
   sweet chocolate chips
4 teaspoons Crème de Cacao
⅛ teaspoon cinnamon
¼ cup pecans, chopped, toasted
¼ cup flaked coconut, toasted

Several hours before serving: Rinse oranges; pat dry with paper towels. Slice 2 oranges in half crosswise; cut off bottoms of each half to make flat surface. With grapefruit spoon scoop out orange sections into colander, reserving juice. Remove membrane from shells; discard. Cover orange shells with plastic wrap; refrigerate.

Peel and section remaining 2 oranges. In bowl combine orange sections, chocolate chips, Crème de Cacao, cinnamon and some of orange juice. Cover; chill thoroughly.

Just before serving: Stir in nuts and coconut; add a little more orange juice if necessary. Spoon mixture into orange shells; serve.
4 servings.

Preparation Time: 30 Minutes

Sweet Oranges with Sugar Brickle

¹/₄ cup sugar
2 Florida Navel oranges, or other seedless oranges
3 tablespoons Grand Marnier, or other orange-flavored liqueur
³/₄ teaspoon candied ginger, minced
¹/₃ cup whipping cream
1 teaspoon powdered sugar

About 2 hours before serving: Combine sugar and 1½ teaspoons water in small, heavy saucepan; cook over medium heat until sugar dissolves and mixture caramelizes and turns golden brown. Pour onto foil-lined baking sheet; tilt to spread to ¼-inch thickness. Cool completely; chop coarsely in food processor.

Peel oranges, removing outer membrane. Cut crosswise into slices; place in shallow dish. Sprinkle with Grand Marnier and ginger; chill 1 hour. In medium bowl of electric mixer, beat cream and powdered sugar until stiff peaks form.

To serve: Spoon oranges and Grand Marnier into serving dishes; top with whipped cream. Sprinkle with caramelized sugar pieces. *2 servings.*

Preparation and Cooking Time: 30 Minutes

ACKNOWLEDGEMENTS

The Junior League of Tampa, Inc. would like to recognize the generous contributions of time, energy and resources from countless individuals. Our gratitude goes to all those listed here and anyone we may have inadvertently failed to mention.

CONTRIBUTORS
Mr. and Mrs. Alfred S. Austin
Continental Airlines
The Greater Tampa Chamber of
   Commerce
Florida Hospitality Group
Body By Design, Inc.
Even Keel Farm, Inc.
International Travel
MacDill Air Force Base
Moberg Studios
The Mack Company
University of Tampa

ADVISORY PANEL
Cindy Coney
Marlyn Cook
Hilary Davis
Robin DeLaVergne
Celia Ferman
Sandra Gardner
DeeDee Gray
Martha Craig Hardman
Jo Beth Harrison
Jane Hewit
Gloria Howell
Wynnette Howell
Mary Merryday
Kay Mullen
Beth Reid
Heidi Robson
Kathy Stephens
Jean Suringa
Ashley Thomas
Mary Audrey Wilson

EDITORIAL CONSULTANT
Rose M. Grant

SPECIAL EVENTS
Melissa Ackles
JoEllen Archerd
Julie Aufderheide
Maria Beaugrand
Susan Cheatwood
Cheryl Conner
Mary Beth Dickinson
Kristan Evans
Angela Giovenco
Florence Harmon
Donna Kieffer
Susan Lang
Janni Lifsey
Lea Orchard
Karen Palori
Cynthia Ruff
Pamela Wilkerson
June Williams

PHOTO PROPS
Alvin Magnon Jewelers
Antique Pine Imports
Patti Ayala
Jeanne Lee Blackmar
Dottie and Phil Buckingham
Anne Comer
Chris Cordell
Danny DeLaRosa
Floral Impressions
Patty Goldfinger of
   Longaberger Baskets
Margaret Gore
Jill Gruber

Carole Guyton
Terilee Hebert
Henry B. Plant Museum
Bonnie and J.B. Hickey
Jacobson's
Lesley Lee
Kathy Nolen
Pirate's Toy Chest
Pottery Barn
The Garden Party
Kim Reed
John Sutton
Ashley Thomas
Topiary, Inc.
Ann and Jim VonThron
Williams Sonoma
Ye Mystic Krewe of Gasparilla

PHOTO ASSISTANCE
Busch Gardens
Hal Colbert
Jim Comer
Julianne Coney
Tom Daley
Bill Dunlop
Hall of Fame Bowl
Bonnie and J.B. Hickey
Gene Langford
Jim Lee
William Lee
Lt. Mike Paoli
Helen Richards
Barbara and Les Ryals
Mike Schulze
University of Tampa Crew Team
Ybor Square

RECIPE TESTERS
Testing Captains
Carole Anderson
Deborah Anderson
Nancy Bayless
Hedy Bever
Susan DePaoli
Mary Sue Frank
Mary Anne Ingram
Susan Isbell
Gaye Jones
Carol Kingston
Mildred Loomis
Joan McKay
Margaret Parker
Lynn Pearce
Camille Thomas
Lynn Townsend
Betty Wood

Testers
Cathey Alexander
Martha Allen
Janet Alter
Rae Ann Alton
Bretta Arthur
Janice Banks
Karen Bauman
Susan Beaugrand
Kimberly Brannan
Susan Bridgers
Heddy Brown
Barbara Buchanan
Betty Calfee
Susan Carter

Lisa Cave
Adele Clarke
Theresa Compton
Karen Crawford
Byron Crowder
Pamela Davis
Robin DeLaVergne
Libby Dickinson
Mary Beth Dickinson
Mary Margaret Dolcimascolo
Elizabeth Drake
Debra Eger
Saffie Ellerman
Katherine Essrig
Kristan Evans
Celia Ferman
Frances Fernandez
Lisa Fields
Lisa Fogarty
Nancy Fogarty
Cherie Ford
Mary Sue Frank
Joanne Frazier
Susan Gage
Ann Giles
Deborah Goldblatt
Malinda Gray
Kathleen Greene
Robin Greiwe
Nancy Gruendel
Janis Guzzle
Lola Hanley
Brett Harrison
Vicki Hayes
Sarah Heithaus
Nonita Henson
Laura Herndon
Gloria Howell
Barbara Hunt
Elizabeth Jessee
Julianne Johnson
Virginia Jones
Mike Kanter
Peggy Kanter
Nell Lee Keen
Carole King
Pam LaPan
Ellie Lastra
Layne Lenfestey
Mary Alice Lopez
Margaret Lovenbury
Verna Lee Lupo
Cynthia Martin
Marsha Martin
Timmi Macfarlane
Nedra McCraw
Lauren McLamore
Ruthanne McLean
Lyn Meyerson
Anne Morris
Marejane Moses
Cynthia Mullen
Rhoda Murray
Mary Nelson
Stephanie Nelson
Kathy Nolen
Laura Oak
Jackie O'Connor
Dali Ogden

Brenda Orcutt
Kathy Owen
Jenifer Ownby
Ellen Palmer
Sarah Pariseau
Maria Pearson
Anne Person
Karen Pesce
Anne Quinlan
Denise Rasmussen
Eryn Ratchford
Becky Rauenhorst
Margaret Rials
Carla Rosequist

Mary Kay Ross
Phyllis Russell
Adajean Samson
Shirley Savage
Suzanne Savarese
Gwyn Schabacker
Kathleen Schaffnit
Ann Cooper Schell
Susan Sharp
Nancy Shivers
Lauren Stallings
Susan Steele
Jean Suringa
Ashley Thomas

Laura Tillman
Ann Turner
Patricia Van Dyke
Ann VonThron
Susan Waddell
Janna Walker
Deborah Warner
Susan Watterworth
Leigh Ann Weinbren
Ellen Westerfield
Rhonda Whitehead
Lee Williams
Mary Audrey Wilson

RECIPE CONTRIBUTORS

The *Tampa Treasures* Committee wishes to thank the family of the late Beverly Hall Farrior for their generous contribution of her extensive recipe collection for use in the development of this cookbook.

Deborah Wehle Anderson
Janet Johnston Anderson
Katharine Gray Anderson
Peggy White Anderson
Stephanie Hill Andrews
Leslie Heusel Angell
Linda McNeer Annis
Joan Welsh Astell
Rebecca Devitt Aylward
Cherie K. Backer
Marcia Radke Ballard
Lesley Shackelford Bateman
Bunny Foster Bauernfeind
Rosalie A. Baya
Nancy Gibbons Bayless
Susan Schwartz Beaugrand
Cynthia Cloud Bedell
Regina Hudson Birrenkott
Virginia Bever
Margaret Biddy
Lynn Ginsburg Billingsley
Elizabeth Zemp Black
Carroll Neal Boden
Patricia Power Bohannan
Jane Murphy Bone
Anna Thompson Boswell
Elizabeth Barlow Brandes
Mrs. E.B. Bradford
D.J. Brandon
Jane Montgomery Brannan
Kimberly Harvey Brannan
Anne Blake Brewer
Susan Molthrop Bridgers
Elizabeth A. Bronson
Carolyn Eick Brown
Anamaria Bruno
Lynn Weber Bruskivage
Nancy Bond Bryant
Caroline Nation Burt
Scottie Burton
Elizabeth Jessee Byrd
Rebecca McMullen Caldwell
Patricia Mayes Campbell
Leigh E. Carlson
Patricia Delany Carte
Gael Gallwey Carter
Susan Vasiloff Carter
Lisa J. Cave
Rebecca Black Charles
Abigail Beazley Chilldon
Susan McKell Clark
Ralphael M. Clarke

Dana Proctor Clayton
Carol Ann Smith Colbert
Anne Nickell Comer
Theresa Loy Compton
Cynthia Daley Coney
Christine Weatherly Cordell
Martha Kaye Covington
Eleanor Calvert Crowder
Christine Collins Curry
Susan Norton Curtis
Della Cury
Pat Turner Daley
Elizabeth Hall Darr
Marsha Daskevich
Hilary Howell Davis
Pamela Kearney Davis
Linda J. Dawkins
Jennifer deAlejo
Robin Wright DeLaVergne
Susan K. DePaoli
Diana Devoe
Penelope Creighton Dewell
Mary Beth Baldy Dickinson
Ann Dodson
Mary Margaret Smith Dolcimascolo
Elizabeth Bregler Drake
Linda Edge
Debra Aubrey Eger
Vicki Mixon Elsberry
Norma Emery
Suzanne Adams Ennis
Lisa Murphy Erdman
Marilynn York Evert
Beverly Hall Farrior
Christie Farrior
Cecelia Davis Ferman
Martha Sale Ferman
Frances Garcia Fernandez
Margaret Burke Fernandez
Mary Claire Fitzgibbons
Sandra Davis Fleischman
Patricia Usher Fleischmann
Lynn Loomis Fluharty
Deborah Foley
Harriet Protiva Foster
LeeAnn Goldsmith Foster
Nancy Lee Foster
Mary Sue Gray Frank
Joanne Hecker Frazier
Melissa Murrane Frey
Susan Lytle Gage
Elizabeth A. Gerwe

Joyce Saul Gerwe
Martha Hanley Gibbons
Ann Sowell Giles
Mary P. Glasgow
Linden Murphy Glickman
Deborah Hunter Goldblatt
Carla J. Grandoff
Sherilynn McElvy Graves
Beverly Bacon Gray
Kathleen Sexton Greene
Jennifer Brock Gregory
Cynthia Ervin Hadlow
Gretchen Gray Hall
Anne Salem Hampton
Ed Hardman
Martha Craig Hedrick Hardman
Lanier Harper
Pamela Griffiths Harris
Brett Harrison
Elizabeth Drake Harvey
Doris Cannon Harvey
Lou Parmelee Hatton
Nancy Heilman
Sarah Connor Heithaus
Nonita Cuesta Henson
Jane Hughey Hewit
Bonnie Hickey
Elizabeth Whidden Hill
Sally Door Hill
Mrs. Harry Hobbs
Holly Brown Hodges
Lisa S. Holmes
Chris Holt
Gloria Roberts Howell
Terri Thomson Huerta
Beth Huff
Mary Matthews Hulse
Marilyn Husler
Sharon Ingham
Tricia Irwin
Susan Steele Isbell
Barbara Jacobs
Jan R. Johnson
Julianne Woods Johnson
Sandra Johnston
Cheryl A. Jones
Mrs. Garrett W. Judy
Michael E. Kanter
Deborah Reineman King
Karla Dann Kirkwood
Karen Hackett Koestner
Leah P. Koulouris

Nancy Nelson Kouwe
Frances Protiva Kruse
Beth Kuly
Mary Ellen Douglas LaCrosse
Susan E. Lang
Sarah Beth Snead Lankford
Ellie Jernigan Lastra
Kristine Tjernstrom Lay
Lee Leavengood
Lesley Murphy Lee
Layne Boyet Lenfestey
Ann Weber Lester
Deborah Moore Lester
Mary Lou Moss Lester
Norma Elam Lester
Laura Lindeman
Elizabeth Martin Linebaugh
Carole Dalton Lins
Charlotte Jordan Logan
Lelia C. Logan
Mildred Mook Loomis
Margaret Ferguson Lovenbury
Marilyn Poe Lunskis
Timmi Kearney Macfarlane
Judith Moore Marks
Marie Marsicano
Cynthia Hulse Martin
Lela L. McClure
Judy McElvy
Martha McGinnis
Dede Andrews McKay
Joan Hedrick McKay
Terrin Few McKay
Julianne Cone McKeel
Debra Lozier McKell
Lauren Bryant McLamore
Ellen Harmon McLean
Ruthanne Padgett McLean
Martha Brown McMichael
Rhoda McMullen
Grace Gilliam McPherson
Linda Porter Meloy
Janet Yadley Mendez
Mary McKeever Merryday
Lyn Hodes Meyerson
Kim Braisted Miller
Lorraine Brayden Miller
Kim Sears Millisor
Marjorie Woodbery Millsap
Nice Minor
Janice Poe Mitchell
Cindy Moline
Lorene Pollard Moore
Anne Cullen Morris
Marejane Moses
Melinda Hughey Moshell
Cynthia Bollinger Mullen
Katharine Hoag Mullen
Trisha Muniz
Mary Kathryn Murphy
Ann Murray
Rhoda Grandoff Murray
Linda Green Myers
Nancy Harvey Mynard
Martha Lester Nelson
Stephanie Smith Nelson
Suzanne W. Nelson
Elaine Weiner Newman

Marjorie Knapp Nickell
Kathleen Gaffney Nolen
Jacqueline Holdstock O'Connor
Sally Burrows Olsson
Lea Snow Orchard
Brenda Kinley Orcutt
Nancy Oswald
Marsha Swann Otte
Jenifer Cullis Ownby
Mimi Paine
Nickoletta O. Pappas
Sarah Izard Pariseau
Barbara Parker
Margaret Eskridge Parker
Patricia Daniel Pead
Lynn Stichter Pearce
Maria Enriquez Pearson
Ann C. Peck
Robin Cozart Pendino
Anne Joughin Person
Karen LaCrosse Pesce
Ann Parks Petersen
Nancy Hill Peterson
Peggy Phillips
Harriet Lenfestey Plyler
Carol C. Pooley
Susan Spainhour Preston
Helen Coles Price
Harriet Bunn Warren Protiva
Helen Protiva
Denise Hillman Rasmussen
Eryn Thomas Ratchford
Rebecca Hewit Rauenhorst
Isabel Byrd Rawlinson
Allison Williams Reddick
Kim Bever Reed
Marion Reed
Beth Quigley Reid
Tami Reina
Frances Hyer Reynolds
Anne Horsley Riegle
Lauraine Martin Roddy
Sue Bachaus Rohrlack
Carla Cozart Rosequist
Franci Golman Rudolph
Cynthia Hill Ruff
Pamela Turbow Rush
Leabeth Russell
Barbara Harvey Ryals
Karen E. Ryals
Marilyn Samaha
Lauren Moore Sasser
Shirley McKay Savage
Suzanne Harris Savarese
Carroll Cone Saxton
Gwyn Fogarty Schabacker
Kathleen Maloney Schaffnit
Ann Cooper Knight Schell
Mary Wharton Schroeder
Brenda Schwarzkopf
Rebecca James Scott
Mary Scourtes
Ginger Tarr Shea
Mary Jo Merrill Shenk
Nancy Mackenzie Shivers
Nancy Curlee Silverfield
Nancy Newbern Skemp
Leslie Ann Curry Smith

Margaret Vance Smith
Nell Glenn Smith
Virginia A. Smith
Thelma Snyder
Diane Somers
Linnore Olsen Stallings
Susan Jones Steele
Carol Stanley Stefany
Kathryn Malesky Stephens
Sue Stiner
Wendy Stone
Marianne E. Strauss
Debbie Sulzer
Jean Samson Suringa
Cheryl Brown Sykes
Ashley Thomas
Laura J. Tillman
Lynn Rice Townsend
Deborah Kun Tozier
Ann Sasser Turner
Jean Forbes Turner
Patricia Sanders Van Dyke
Ann D'Albora VonThron
Susan C. Waddell
Dottie Walters
Deborah Fleming Watson
Susan Webb
Vivian Webb
Hillary Frank Weber
Teresa Templin Weibley
Leigh Ann Abraham Weinbren
Susan Welch-Kelley
Joyce O'Neal Wellman
Mary Fran Madden Whitaker
Judith Gilmore Whittlesey
Suzanne Wightman
Helen Roberson Williams
Joan Hurn Williams
Mary Win Wilson
Nan Kelly Wilson
Patricia Jinx Wilson
Henry Winkler
Betty Hall Wood
Barbara Anderson Woods
Nancy Cooper Wulbern
Motsy Wynn
Janice Massari Wynne
Barbara M. Yadley
Victoria Cozart Yarnal
Mary Jo Eggner Yates
Laura Case York
Elizabeth Bergen Zabak

Restaurants
Chavez at the Royal
Columbia Restaurant
Louis Pappas Restaurant
Mise en Place
Mott & Hester Deli
Outback Steakhouse
rg's Restaurants
Saltwaters Grill at Hyatt Regency
Selena's Restaurant
Shells
Silver Ring Cafe
Tony's Restaurant
Valencia Garden Restaurant
Wrights Gourmet House
Yesterday's Restaurant

INDEX

Recipes with this symbol () appear in our menus and photographs